D0816719

The Female as Subject

Michigan Monograph Series in Japanese Studies
Number 70
Center for Japanese Studies
The University of Michigan

The Female as Subject:
Reading and Writing in Early Modern Japan

edited by

P. F. Kornicki, Mara Patessio, and G. G. Rowley

This book was financed in part
through a generous grant
from the Department of East Asian Studies
at the University of Cambridge.

Center for Japanese Studies
The University of Michigan
Ann Arbor   2010

Copyright © 2010 by The Regents of the University of Michigan

All rights reserved.

Published by the Center for Japanese Studies,
The University of Michigan
1007 E. Huron St.
Ann Arbor, MI 48104-1690

Library of Congress Cataloging-in-Publication Data

The female as subject : reading and writing in early modern Japan / edited by
P. F. Kornicki, Mara Patessio, and G. G. Rowley.
    p. cm. — (Michigan monograph series in Japanese studies ; no. 70)
    Includes bibliographical references and index.
    ISBN 978-1-929280-64-3 (hardback : alk. paper) — ISBN 978-1-929280-65-0
(pbk. : alk. paper)
    1. Japanese literature—History and criticism.   2. Women and literature—
Japan.   3. Books and reading—Japan.   4. Women in literature.   I. Kornicki,
Peter F. (Peter Francis)   II. Patessio, Mara, 1975–   III. Rowley, G. G., 1960–

PL722.W64F46 2010
895.6'093522—dc22

                                                                  2010032006

This book was set in Palatino Macron.
Kanji set in Hiragino Mincho Pro.

This publication meets the ANSI/NISO Standards for Permanence of Paper
for Publications and Documents in Libraries and Archives (Z39.48—1992).

Printed in the United States of America

Library
University of Texas
at San Antonio

Contents

❀

Illustrations

❀

Tables

❀

Introduction

P. F. Kornicki, Mara Patessio, and G. G. Rowley

❀

Over the last twenty years the spotlights have turned on literate women of the past in many societies, on books written for women such as conduct books, on books written by women, on women's reading, and on the participation of literate women in cultural, intellectual, and political movements. Many are the questions that have been posed and are now being addressed. What, for example, does the widespread appearance of reading women in painting and other forms of artistic representation mean? How much does it reflect women's autonomy as readers and what is the significance of the male gaze of the artist? Do crude equations of the private-public distinction with gendered spheres retain any credibility in light of feminist challenges to Jürgen Habermas's notion of the "public sphere" and in light of recent empirical studies of women in the public eye?[1]

The case for examining these issues more closely has been persuasively argued by Tiziana Plebani in her study of the "gender of the book." She has drawn attention to the perception in Europe, even in the age of manuscripts, that some books were intended for women to read, to the

---

1. Bollmann 2006; Smith and Taylor 1996; Eger et al. 2001.

1

growing consciousness of women as part of the market for printed books, to the slanted representation of women's reading as leisure rather than study, to rising anxieties about what women were reading, and to the publication of technical manuals for women in such fields as embroidery, lace, medicine, and cosmetics.[2] Many others have considered representations of women readers in pictorial art and the cultural and political significance of women as readers in the early modern world both in the West and in China, and their work provides an essential comparative context in which to consider women and the book in Japan.[3]

It goes without saying that in Japan, as elsewhere, there had been individual elite women readers from antiquity, but it is only after the rapid development of commercial publishing in the early seventeenth century that images of women readers proliferate, for example, in the ukiyo-e prints of Sugiura Jihei and Hishikawa Moronobu. Is it true, then, that women readers had become a recognizable phenomenon by the 1670s, and if so how had they acquired their literacy, what did they use it for, and what were they reading? Were any of them writing as well as reading, and if so for what audiences? And who were these women?

The history of books, of reading, of authorship, and even of education in Japan has overwhelmingly privileged the male experience, but, as will be clear from the chapters that follow, it is undeniable that women were a recognized segment of the commercial market for books before the seventeenth century was over. The essays in this volume, therefore, seek to bring the particularities of the Japanese experience to the fore and to answer some of the questions mentioned above. But there is much we do not know, and much we will probably never know, so it is as well to recognize from the outset the limitations imposed by, among other things, the male domination not only of record keeping in the past but also, until recently, of historiography in Japan. And in other areas where cross-cultural comparisons seem desirable, we lack at this stage sufficient information or documentation to be able to contribute with data from Japan. An obvious example of this is the role of women in the book trade, which is well attested, for example, in China and Italy.[4] It is not difficult to suppose that the wives and daughters of booksellers in Japan not only had a hand in running the business, as was the case with other family businesses, but also perhaps did some block carving or printing as well, but so far no concrete evidence has come to light.

---

2. Plebani 2001, pp. 37–45, 48–54, 58–59, and elsewhere.
3. Hull 1982; Rieger and Tonard 1999; Flint 1993; Pearson 1999; Snook 2005; Idema and Grant 2004; Ko 1994.
4. Brokaw 2007, pp. 14–24, 101–5, 545–46; Parker 1996.

Since the pioneering work of Sharon Sievers and Gail Lee Bernstein, among others, there has been growing interest in the West in the women of the Edo and Meiji periods. A turning point was the publication in 1998 of Anne Walthall's biography of Matsuo Taseko. This traces the involvement of a remarkable woman in the literary, intellectual, and political worlds of her time, which have hitherto been overwhelmingly understood as men's worlds. Just how far, though, does that "understanding" need to be corrected?

At the time this volume was envisioned, each of its three editors had already for some years, in different ways, been working on some of these questions. Rowley completed a PhD at Cambridge University in 1994 on Yosano Akiko's involvement with *The Tale of Genji* and had since been working on earlier women readers of *Genji*; Patessio completed a PhD at Cambridge in 2005 on women and the public sphere in early Meiji Japan; and Kornicki was working on women readers of *The Tale of Genji* and Chinese conduct books in the seventeenth century. It was, however, the publication of Tiziana Plebani's *Il "genere" dei libri* (2001) that suggested a more comprehensive approach to the issues and encouraged us to invite a small group of scholars from Canada, Germany, Japan, the Netherlands, and the United States to Cambridge for a workshop in September 2006. These essays are the result.

This volume, then, places women as readers, writers, and activists at center stage and aims to show through a variety of approaches that the standard narratives of literate life in Japan in the Edo and Meiji periods are incomplete. For example, ever since Fukuzawa Yukichi fulminated against *Onna daigaku*, a primer for women first published in the early eighteenth century, as a textbook for women's repression, it has enjoyed an unenviable reputation. Is this deserved, though? True enough, it enjoins women to be obedient to men at all stages of their lives. What has been lost sight of, however, is the fact that *Onna daigaku* takes women's literacy for granted; women readers were even encouraged to make a copy by hand for later reference. Rising female literacy obviously suited commercial publishers, who had long recognized that women constituted a distinct market for books, but the crucial point, surely, is that, far from frowning upon literate women, moralists accepted female literacy as a fait accompli. When we recall that later editions of *Onna daigaku* contained any amount of illustrations, practical information, and even amusement, we might conclude that Fukuzawa was attacking a straw man and that this notorious text may have been appreciated by female readers for reasons other than its moral message.

In the opening chapter, P. F. Kornicki sets the scene with an examination of the evidence for women's literacy and its uses. Educational opportunities for girls were limited, but in the right circumstances and with supportive parents some did attain even sinological literacy and many became poets. By global standards, then, it can be argued that Japanese women enjoyed a comparatively favorable educational environment for the time. Next, G. G. Rowley's chapter concentrates the focus on the early decades of the Edo period and the tradition of women's reading of *The Tale of Genji*. For noblewomen especially, knowledge of *Genji* was an essential part of the cultural capital necessary to their success as ladies-in-waiting, wives, or concubines. Joshua S. Mostow's essay focuses on *One Hundred Poets One Poem Each* (*Hyakunin isshu*) and *Tales of Ise*, and he contrasts the centrality of *Hyakunin isshu* to women's education throughout the Edo period with the different didactic trajectories of *Ise* and *Genji*. Itasaka Noriko, on the other hand, traces the transition in depictions of reading women from noblewomen of the past to contemporary courtesans to urban commoner women.

Anna Beerens's essay uncovers the presence of women artists and poets in networks of late Edo period male intellectuals. She uses a prosopographical analysis in order to demonstrate how information regarding the levels of literacy and education of women from different backgrounds can be obtained. This information, though limited because of the nature of the material available, can be used to advance our understanding of women's participation in literate society during the Edo period and provides a valuable methodological tool for doing so.

Bettina Gramlich-Oka examines the Confucian curriculum designed by Inooka Gisai for his daughter Shizu, who is best known as the mother of historian Rai San'yō. Far from the blind obedience recommended by *Onna daigaku*, Gisai allowed Shizu—and by implication other women, too—full agency over her own intellectual abilities. Within a properly feminine sphere, a woman could pursue the Confucian Way and practice self-cultivation as well as a man. In the next chapter Yabuta Yutaka uses a cache of letters and other documents relating to a young woman named Nishitani Saku living in the vicinity of Osaka in the closing years of the Edo period to explore the literacy and education of rural women. Many of the documents are in Saku's own hand and demonstrate the practical benefits of literacy, particularly for the purpose of keeping in contact with family members absent from home. This is literacy at a lower level than that demonstrated by other studies of commoner women living in the countryside, as Yabuta points out, and the documentary record is all the more valuable for that.

Atsuko Sakaki analyzes a collection of stories by the prolific writer Arakida Rei. Despite various twentieth-century attempts to resurrect Arakida from obscurity, she has remained an "inconvenient figure" for historians of Japanese literature, Sakaki argues, at least in part because she wrote of people and places far distant from her own time. In the collection of stories considered here, Sakaki shows how Arakida's reconfiguration of the original Chinese sources reveals complex relations between the foreign and the domestic, the supernatural and the ordinary, the female and the male, and the imaginative and the realistic, and also offers insight into this writer's negotiation with literary history and formation of subjectivity in it.

Sugano Noriko's essay brings the story into the Meiji period. It analyzes the public speeches Kishida Toshiko made during the years 1882 and 1883, how these were received by her audiences and the media, and the ways in which her message changed during those years from one arguing for women's rights to one focusing on women's education. In particular, Sugano argues that Kishida used an old ideology, that of women's "three obediences" to father, husband, and son, to espouse a new message regarding women's education. Mara Patessio looks at women's participation in the print media during the late nineteenth and early twentieth centuries, especially in *Jogaku zasshi* and *Fujo shinbun*, and at circulating discourses over what were suitable and unsuitable readings for young women. She analyzes the reasons for the appearance, in 1889 and 1890, of discussions over so-called dangerous novels for girls and how these were intertwined with criticism of girl students and their presence in public society. The study of those magazines sheds light on how, by 1900, women had empowered themselves and were able to respond to such criticism.

Anne Walthall concludes our volume by analyzing the common characteristics of Edo period male and female education and literacies, comparing them to the changes brought forward during the Meiji period. She notes the role of happenstance in women's access to education in the Edo period and the haphazard nature of much of their learning. She also argues that it is important to discuss not only what women gained from the new education system of 1872 and the other venues that had opened up for women but also what women lost in the process in terms of education and employment opportunities.

Owing to the high cost of color illustration, and because what is important in the illustrations used is their content, we have opted for black and white or halftone illustrations, depending on the originals. Those who wish to see full color versions will find a library of illustrations on the project website: http://jwomen.ames.cam.ac.uk/index.html.

Finally, we are grateful to the contributors and participants, whose commitment and enthusiastic participation made the workshop such a stimulating experience. Kate Wildman Nakai of Sophia University kindly attended the workshop to draw the threads together at the end and to help us take the debates forward. All the contributors to this volume participated in the workshop; Laura Nenzi also participated, but her contribution, on women's travel diaries, was already bespoke and has been published as part of her recent monograph on the subject (2008).

We are deeply indebted to the Leverhulme Trust, which gave its unstinting support to the "Women and Books in Japan" project, making it possible in particular for Patessio to work on the project full time from 2005 to 2007. The workshop, which was held over four days in Cambridge on 5–9 September 2006, benefited from generous grants given by the Toshiba International Foundation and the Great Britain Sasakawa Foundation; we would like to express our indebtedness to both foundations for their generosity. One day of the workshop was spent in the pleasant surroundings of the Cathedral Close in Norwich where we were the guests of the Sainsbury Institute for the Study of Japanese Art and Culture. The hospitality shown us by the institute's staff and the chance to change the setting for a day were much appreciated. At the editing stage the assistance of Thomas Harper and Rebekah Clements was invaluable, and Anne Walthall kindly allowed us to use the title of her presentation at the conference as the title for the volume. Finally, we extend our thanks to Bruce Willoughby for his enthusiastic acceptance of this book and the anonymous reader whose comments helped us to make it more coherent.

1

Women, Education, and Literacy

P. F. Kornicki

In 1638 the *shōya* (headman) of a fishing village on the Inland Sea suddenly died. What followed was remarkable: twenty household heads put their names to a petition asking his widow, O-Sen, to take over as head of the village. She eventually consented and served in this capacity for two years. This was not the only case in the Edo period of a woman assuming such a position, but very few other cases are known.[1]

In this case neither the circumstances nor the consequences are known, but the very existence of this document demonstrates that already village administration had assumed a bureaucratic character that required somewhat more than basic literacy.[2] Of course, this did not mean that more than a handful of villagers needed to be literate, but since this document was addressed specifically to O-Sen, and since in her role as *shōya* she would have

---

1. The village was on the island of Manabe in what is now southwestern Okayama Prefecture. For the text, see Kasaoka 2001, pp. 229–30. See also Sadakane 1986, pp. 20–23; and, for another example of a woman assuming such a position in 1600 in a coastal village near modern Fukuoka, *Fukuma chōshi*, pp. 3, 32.
2. See Ooms 1996, chap. 1, esp. pp. 66–70, on an illiterate woman's use of scribes and helpers in the eighteenth century to produce the complex documents needed in village disputes.

had to deal with correspondence from the *daikan*, the local representative of the daimyo in Okayama, she must have been equipped with the requisite level of literacy. How did she acquire this? In all likelihood she acquired it at home, for commoner schools lay far off in the future. Having acquired it, how did she use it? Like other women, she can have had no expectation of becoming *shōya*, so her literacy was surely not acquired for that end. Did she, then, read books? We do not know, but the evidence of later women suggests that those who had acquired this degree of literacy usually did so. Is this isolated case, so far removed from centers of cultural, economic, and political power and so early in the Edo period, of any significance? Readers will be best placed to judge when they have finished this book.

In the pages that follow, I attempt to sketch the outlines of what we do know about women's education and literacy in the Edo period, to suggest fruitful approaches, and to raise questions that will need to be answered in the future. First, I focus on the question of education: what educational opportunities were there for women in the Edo period and how much allowance do we have to make for chronological, regional, or social variation? Second, I turn to books for women and women's reading: the publication of books for women signified recognition, at least for commercial purposes, of the woman reader, but why were they reading and what else were they reading? Finally, I survey the range of women's writing in all genres and ask why poetry was so dominant. The emphasis throughout will be on the seventeenth and nineteenth centuries, with consequential neglect of the eighteenth, in order to highlight the trends and changes.

Education and Literacies

Neither for boys nor for girls did education in the Edo period constitute a "system." As Dore and now Rubinger have shown, to say nothing of the huge Japanese literature on the history of education, there was enormous variation in educational provision both diachronically and synchronically from area to area; differences between urban and rural provision in, for example, the area around Osaka were unlikely to be the same as those for areas such as southern Kyushu or northern Japan.[3] For this reason attempts to arrive at a national picture are likely to be more misleading than helpful. When it comes to education for girls, it is even more difficult to gather reliable data; this is because of the lack of provision made for commoners, let alone women, at the domain schools (*hankō*) because of the widespread

---

3. Dore 1992; Rubinger 2007.

assumption, which is difficult to confirm, that girls were more likely to be educated at home and because some at least were hesitant about displaying their learning.[4] Given the lack of a "system," it will be necessary, therefore, in the pages that follow to trace women's education according to separate criteria such as status, locality, and language.

Only in one domain did the daimyo's government take any interest in the education of women: in 1841 Tsuyama domain (Okayama Prefecture) set aside a room for commoner women with a female teacher to provide instruction both in needlework and in morality by means of such texts as *Onna daigaku* (Greater Learning for Women) and *Onna imagawa* (Imagawa Letter for Women).[5] What is significant about this is, first, that samurai girls were excluded, presumably because it was expected that they would be provided for in other ways, and, second, that this move came so late in the day, when commoners' schools were already widespread. It can safely be asserted, therefore, that the education of commoner women was a subject that for the most part did not concern samurai officialdom in the Edo period, whatever may have been the case in the early Meiji period to follow.

The earliest record of women's education in the Edo period so far brought to light dates from 1616 and relates to aristocratic girls in Kyoto. Their education, undertaken by their fathers or hired (female?) tutors, began with the hiragana syllabary and copying out *waka* poetry. They learned Chinese characters from the *Thousand Character Essay* (*Qianzi wen*, J. *Senjimon*) and by doing *sodoku* (a form of rote learning that involved reciting the received Japanese reading of the text aloud in unison) of canonical Chinese texts, and their education was not considered complete until they had studied *waka* composition, Japanese and Chinese texts, and Japanese history.[6] Needless to say, such an education and at such an early date can only have been for the privileged few and in all likelihood represented what had been the case for court women for centuries, as shown in Rowley's account of aristocratic women's reading in this volume. The difficulty lies in assessing how quickly and in what forms educational practices for women spread geographically and socially.

By the middle of the seventeenth century the education of girls had become a matter for serious reflection. For example, the influential sinologist Yamaga Sokō (1622–85), lectured his followers about it, citing Zhu Xi's advice that girls should be instructed at home in such texts as the *Analects*,

---

4. Tocco 2003 provides a well-considered examination of education for women in the Edo period and the problems it poses.
5. Umihara 1988, p. 260.
6. Shiga 1977, p. 231.

the *Classic of Filial Piety, Biographies of Women* (*Lienü zhuan*, J. *Retsujoden*) and *Commandments for Women* (*Nü jie*, J. *Jokai*). He argued that the education of girls should not differ from that of boys except in that compliance and obedience should be the goal and that their eyes and ears not be sullied by anything inappropriate. Further remarks he made, deploring the contemporary habit of employing female teachers in the home to instruct girls in the reading of texts such as *The Tale of Genji* and *Tales of Ise*, indicate that the profession of home teacher was by then open to women.[7] At around the same time, Nakamura Ekisai argued that women ought to be literate so as to be able to educate their children if widowed. Therefore, girls had to be taught the rudiments of writing and arithmetic like boys and then, from the age of eight or so, be taught by their mother or a home teacher and made to read Chinese texts such as those mentioned by Yamaga Sokō so as to acquire womanly virtues.[8]

Other sinologists of the seventeenth century, including leading figures such as Fujiwara Seika, Hayashi Razan, Kumazawa Banzan, and Kaibara Ekiken, also addressed the subject of the education of girls and took it for granted that it was desirable.[9] But what girls were they talking about? Although none of them made it clear, it seems a priori probable that they were referring to girls born to their own class, the middle and upper ranks of the samurai. The conclusions we can tentatively draw from these writings, then, are that girls of this background in the seventeenth century were expected to be educated and were commonly educated at home by parents or tutors, that moral inculcation was the perceived goal, and that girls were expected to be able to read Chinese texts. It might be added that since most samurai of this status resided in castle towns the samurai daughters in question were likely to be urban residents.

There is a parallel here with sixteenth-century Europe, where Juan Luis Vives (1492–1540) considered knowledge to be indispensable to virtue and therefore saw education of girls as desirable. His *Instruction of a Christian Woman* was first published in Latin in 1524, suggesting some confidence that women readers of Latin could be found, although it later appeared in innumerable vernacular translations; in it he warned against access to secular literature and saw women's reading in terms of moral improvement, like sinologists in seventeenth-century Japan.[10]

7. *Yamaga Sokō zenshū shisōhen*, vol. 6, pp. 299–301; Kornicki 2005, pp. 147–93.
8. Nakaizumi 1966, pp. 322–24.
9. Ibid., chap. 9. See also Tocco 2003, pp. 194–97.
10. See Erdmann 1999, pp. 19–20; and Bornstein et al. 1978, p. 535, among others. For East Asian parallels, see Carlitz 1991, pp. 117–48; and Kornicki and Nguyen 2009.

What, then, of girls of lower status and in rural areas? For the seventeenth century we have very little evidence, but in 1662 an edict issued throughout the province of Tosa in Shikoku noted that while *shōya* and better-off peasants were teaching their children, including girls, writing and arithmetic, the children of poorer peasants were not being taught; although differences in wealth and talent were inevitable, all should be taught the basics in the evenings or in their spare time, it was urged.[11] The Tosa domain was not, of course, proposing to provide any facilities for this purpose, nor does it seem that any effort was made to enforce this recommendation. And it is perhaps worth noting that the name at the bottom of this edict was that of Nonaka Kenzan, the father of Nonaka En (1660–1725), perhaps the first woman doctor in Japan.[12] Nevertheless, the suggestion that *shōya* daughters in Tosa were being taught the basics calls to mind the case of O-Sen mentioned at the outset. Whether this sort of provision was ever extended in rural Tosa to the children of poorer peasants, however, particularly in the seventeenth century, must remain extremely doubtful.

There were indeed some who were doubtful of the value of education for women. Kōchiya Kasei (1636–1713), a highly educated man who owed his prominence in a village in the vicinity of Osaka to his sake-brewing business and extensive landholdings, considered that boys should not be illiterate and if they had time should apply themselves to books but that "anything outside the work of the household is strictly unnecessary for girls." He went on to discuss the connections between poetry and licentiousness and to cite the case of a young girl who had learned to write well but could not find a husband because writing well was not a skill she needed in a farming household.[13] He does not seem to be ruling literacy out for girls altogether, and the doubts about the morality of writing poetry suggest that he was well aware that by the end of the seventeenth century *haikai* poetry composition had spread far and wide. His concerns about marriageability were later to be echoed in the Meiji period in debates on higher education for women, and the notion that peasants, and particularly their women, should not aspire beyond their station in life is common to later writers of farming manuals.

Much later Matsudaira Sadanobu (1758–1829) famously wrote:

> I consider it best for women to be illiterate. Intellectually talented
> women cause great harm. Scholarship is absolutely unnecessary

---

11. *Nonaka Kenzan kankei monjo*, p. 170. This seems to be the same document as that cited by Rubinger (2007, pp. 40–41), albeit from a different source.
12. Since her father was imprisoned and later executed, a professional career may have been her only means of survival.
13. Nomura and Yui 1955, pp. 231–33.

> for them and it should be quite enough for them if they can get to
> the point that they can read books in *kana*.[14]

Again, in spite of the unpromising start, it seems that Sadanobu was not opposed to the education of women per se. And it is clear from his other writings that, far from opposing women's education, he considered it more desirable that they read the Four Books of the Confucian tradition as a source of moral instruction than that they turn to classical Japanese literature.[15]

Even though neither of these writers was implacably opposed to education for women, from what little concrete evidence there is it seems that for rural commoners, unlike samurai daughters, education and the acquisition of literacy were very much a matter of the chance of favorable circumstances. Circumstances were decidedly not favorable for a woman in what is now rural Niigata Prefecture who in 1800 was forced to write an abject letter of apology to her husband and parents-in-law for her selfishness in having used her spare time to learn to write.[16] The likelihood is that in more remote rural communities female literacy was far from being taken for granted and remained a matter of controversy if not of disapprobation.

For the daughters of urban merchants, however, it might be thought that the expectations would have been greater for pragmatic reasons. Enomoto Yazaemon (1625–86), a merchant in Kawagoe, records that toward the end of the seventeenth century, when his fourteen-year-old daughter was getting married, he provided her with a number of books to take to her new home, adding that he expected her husband to explain them to her. These books included the primer *Imagawa-jō* (The Imagawa Letter), conduct books such as *Nijū shikō* (Twenty-four Examples of Filial Piety), and *Chōjakyō* (Millionaire's Bible), and a guide to achieving wealth.[17] She had obviously, therefore, already acquired some degree of literacy, and the matter-of-fact way in which her father records this gift suggests that it was not out of the ordinary. More evidence is to be found in a picture book produced by Nishikawa Sukenobu in the early eighteenth century; this contains a number of illustrations showing women engaged in literate professions, including a *haikai* poet and a doctor. There had indeed already been examples of both in the seventeenth century, so the probability is that this scene is a recognition of a social reality rather than a figment of the imagination. But there are also several scenes showing women in urban mercantile settings making use of their literacy to pore over account books or the like. How widespread this was we

14. Matsudaira 1893, vol. 1, p. 37.
15. Tocco 2003, p. 196.
16. Yoshikawa 1996, p. 853.
17. Ōno Mizuo 2001, p. 74.

have no way of knowing, but the most explicit testimony to the education of women for commercial purposes is the *Onna shōbai ōrai* (Commercial Primer for Women), which seems to have been published for the first time in 1806 in Kyoto in a compendium volume that included two other texts for women. The illustrations show women engaged in bookkeeping and administration in commercial enterprises, and the text includes commercial expressions, technical terms for different types of goods, shop names of various kinds (*yagō*), and so on.[18] It seems undeniable that this represents the visible side of the provision of commercial education for women in the Edo period. The activities of female entrepreneurs in Osaka such as Tatsuuma Kiyo (1809–1900) were dependent on some form of commercial education, as was the wife of the owner of a rapeseed oil business just outside Kyoto in the early nineteenth century, who, as the diary of a clerk reveals, was involved in scrutinizing the accounts of the business.[19]

A related question is that of the literacy of courtesans.[20] Numerous paintings and prints by Hishikawa Moronobu and other artists in the seventeenth and eighteenth centuries depict courtesans in the act of reading, as shown in Itasaka's contribution to this volume, and the biographies of leading courtesans suggest that an education in *waka* composition was a sine qua non.[21] Fujimoto Kizan (1624–1704), in his exhaustive study of the pleasure quarters, *Shikidō ōkagami* (Great Mirror of the Way of Love), completed in 1678, stated unequivocally that courtesans needed to study poetics so as to be able to please their less boorish clients and ought to be able to write beautifully so as to be able to keep up a correspondence.[22] How far these ideals were lived up to remains, of course, a matter of speculation. Some of the many prints and illustrations showing courtesans with books may represent an idealization, but the connection is so widespread in visual representation even in the seventeenth century that it is difficult to dismiss it out of hand. How the necessary literacy and literary skills were acquired is unclear, but since some courtesans were indentured as young girls it is likely that some education was provided in the pleasure quarters. There is some visual evidence that appears to support this supposition, but there is also a passage in

---

18. Ishikawa 1973, pp. 585–89, original 1806 text available at http://ir.u-gakugei.ac.jp/handle/2309/7884 (accessed 21 March 2009). For other examples, see Umihara 1988, pp. 258–59.
19. Lebra 1991; Rubinger 2007, pp. 122–24.
20. On the earlier history of courtesan culture in Japan, see Goodwin 2007.
21. See, for example, Link 1980, pp. 100, 127; and Clark 1992, pp. 51, 76. According to the biography of Yachio (b. 1635), she had a good calligraphic hand, her *haikai* verses were anthologized, and she had someone recite classical texts such as *The Tale of Genji, Tsurezuregusa,* and *Kokinshū* to her (Noma 1961, p. 564).
22. Noma 1961, pp. 144–45, 243.

Yoshiwara suzume (Sparrow of the Yoshiwara, 1667) advising that "managers should make sure that when girls are being raised as apprentices (*kaburo*) they take trouble over their writing" and going on to mention familiarity with poetry and works such as the *Tales of Ise*.[23] And Engelbert Kaempfer recorded that apprentice courtesans received instruction in letter writing and were generally well educated.[24]

The archetype of the literate courtesan is of course Sempronia, one of the participants in Catiline's conspiracy in 63 BCE: "[W]ell educated in Greek and Latin literature, she had greater skill in lyre-playing and dancing than there is any need for a respectable woman to acquire."[25] Closer to Japan and doubtless more influential was the courtesan culture of the late Ming. As Ropp has observed, "[T]he courtesan culture of the late Ming was very important in helping to make literacy and skill in poetry, painting, calligraphy, and music all desirable qualities for a woman to have." Their literary skills were brought to the attention of the public through the publication of poetry written by courtesans, and some became famous for their literary skills.[26] In seventeenth- and eighteenth-century Japan there seem to have been courtesans of similar talents and fame. Suzuki Harunobu's album *Seirō bijin awase* (Beauties of the Brothels, 1770) contains a number of poems by courtesans, as does Kitao Masanobu's *Seirō meikun jihitsushū* (Collected poems of Famous Courtesans in Their Own Hands) of 1783.[27] Did they, too, make poetic and calligraphic skills desirable attributes in nonaristocratic women as in Ming China?

By the early nineteenth century there were large numbers of institutions in most parts of Japan, rural and urban, offering some kind of basic education. These are conventionally referred to as *terakoya* but actually went under a variety of names such as *tenaraisho* (place for learning to write); their distribution density varied chronologically and synchronically from area to area, and what they taught varied also. Thanks to the efforts of local historians who have documented the existence of obscure elementary schools through memorial stones put up by pupils to their teachers (*fudezuka*, "brush mounds") and through documentary evidence, we now know of the

---

23. See, for example, *Yūjo hyōbankishū*, vol. 1, p. 11; and Ono Susumu 1965, vol. 1, p. 339. Takame of Shinmachi in Osaka was said in 1656 to quote from the *Tales of Ise*, *Tsurezuregusa*, and *Kokinshū* (Ono Susumu 1965, vol. 1, p. 207).
24. Bodart-Bailey 1999, p. 143.
25. Handford 1963, p. 192.
26. Ropp 1993, p. 113. See also Ropp 1997, p. 25. On the "Four talented courtesans of Qinhuai" in the sixteenth century, see Chang and Saussy 1999, p. 230.
27. Seigle 1993, pp. 148–50.

existence of many more schools than previously. Some of them took only boys, some took boys and girls (educated separately in some cases, together in others), and a few took only girls.[28] As we get closer to the end of the Edo period, we find an increasing number of extant records that tell us of the gender composition of these schools thanks to the distinction between boys' and girls' given names, often accentuated by the use of only hiragana for the girls' names. Although we cannot extrapolate from this data to make assumptions about earlier periods, we can learn much from it of the extent to which girls were participating in education outside the home by the early nineteenth century, and there is some corroborative evidence in the form of accounts by Europeans and Americans who visited Japan in the mid–nineteenth century.[29] Nevertheless, it must be remembered that school attendance was often seasonal (it declined during the busy times in the farming year) and that some pupils attended for only a year or two.[30] Furthermore, the education of girls should not necessarily be seen as a sign of an intrinsic belief in the value of giving girls a good education; questions of family, status, marriageability, and employability all doubtless had a part to play.

An early example of a school with good records surviving is that established in 1792 by a samurai of the Kii domain. It was called the Jukendō, and it operated in a rural area that has now been subsumed into Matsuzaka city; the records of the school survive up to 1822, the year before his death. During those thirty-one years a total of 478 boys and 165 girls attended from villages near and far and not merely from the upper echelons of rural communities. Pupils learned reading, writing, arithmetic and *sodoku*, and roughly 10 percent of the girls, compared to 30 percent of the boys, subsequently went into service in mercantile enterprises.[31] Girls thus formed 25 percent of the total number of pupils and fewer than 20 of them entered commercial service, for which a basic education would surely have been essential. Other examples include a school operating in 1803 in Takasaki (Gunma Prefecture) where 39 girls were enrolled out of a total of 181 (21 percent), and another in

---

28. An example of a school for girls only is that founded by the married daughter of a Tosa domain samurai in 1847 in what is now rural Kōchi Prefecture in Shikoku. The school continued until 1872 and was attended by fifty girls, who were taught basic literacy and then how to read conduct books for women such as *Onna daigaku* and *Onna imagawa*, as well as *waka* anthologies such as *Hyakunin isshu* and *Kokinshū*. See the results of a survey carried out in 1871 in Kōchi-han 1986, pp. 180–81.

29. Smith 1861, p. 96; Bousquet 1877, pp. 554–55. Smith, the bishop of Victoria, Hong Kong, spent ten weeks in Japan before 1861, while Bousquet resided in Japan for four years beginning in 1872. See also Carrothers 1879, pp. 103–9.

30. See the work by Aoki Michio and others cited in Rubinger 2007, p. 156.

31. Mie 1994, pp. 62–63, 928–95.

1855 in Ōmama (also in Gunma), where 19 girls were enrolled out of a total of 78 (24 percent).[32]

It would, however, be a serious mistake to extrapolate from these cases to other commoners' schools throughout Japan. Take, for example, the records of a school improbably named the Hall of Fun (Kiraku Dōjō) in what is now inland Yamaguchi Prefecture. The record of entrants runs from 1855 to 1873, and 145 names are listed, 22 of them girls (15 percent of the total); however, all but 5 of the girls were enrolled between 1869 and 1873, so out of a total enrollment of 81 up to 1868, girls represented merely 6 percent.[33] Low percentages of female attendance in other rural areas have already been well documented, and it is as well to recall the heavy burden of agricultural and domestic work that fell on the shoulders of many women in farming villages.[34] However, once attention is paid to the economy of individual villages there is considerable variation to be seen, with notably higher rates ranging from 25 to 30 percent found in villages where agriculture was complemented by other economic activities such as silk or cotton production, provision of transportation facilities, or integration into the food economy of a nearby town or city. What is more, it has been shown that in such cases even poorer households were more likely to send their daughters to be educated. This explains the higher rate at the Jukendō, which took in pupils from villages around Matsuzaka, and at schools in post villages on transportation routes or in villages supplying a city with food and vegetables.[35] A further sign of the impact of geography upon education is the fact that, by the 1850s if not before, girls from rural areas in the vicinity of Osaka were going to Osaka to board and attend schools there in the 1850s, as Yabuta's contribution to this volume shows.[36]

Thus we have to recognize huge social and geographical differences in the educational chances for women. While Ishikawa Ken has found that in the late Edo period girls were almost as likely to go to school as boys, in the southern part of Kyushu or the northern part of Honshu it was a very different story even as late as the 1880s. What is more, within rural communities, if not towns, education tended to be distributed according to family status.[37] A further consideration is that what girls learned at school was not neces-

---

32. Takasaki Shishi Hensan Iinkai 2002; Ōmama 1995. In 2006, Ōmama became part of the new city of Midori.

33. Iwakuni 2001, pp. 1730–36.

34. Tone 1989, p. 229.

35. Ibid.

36. Tondabayashi 1998, pp. 887–93.

37. Tone 1989, p. 232, summarizing the work of Ishikawa Ken; Walthall 1990; Rubinger 2007, pp. 134–35.

sarily the same as what boys learned, even assuming that they attended for the same number of years. A girl called Doi Taki, attending a school in the vicinity of Osaka, kept a record of what she studied at school, and it was apparently the same syllabus as that followed by the boys, consisting of hiragana writing skills, numbers, seasonal greetings, how to write documents for loans, local place-names and the sights of Kyoto.[38] At this basic level, doubtless the syllabus was indeed the same, but how many boys went on to study *Onna daigaku* and how many girls ever did any *sodoku* of the Four Books? Some certainly did, as we shall see below, but the records of a school in rural Tosa from the 1820s indicate that the syllabi for boys and girls diverged once both had learned hiragana, the words for colors, and calendrical signs, and common names, with girls going on to use *Onna imagawa* and *Onna shōbai ōrai* as writing texts, and when it came to texts for reading there was no overlap at all.[39] This is also apparent from Yamakawa Kikue's account of her mother's education in the 1860s in Mito: here, too, it was considered that women who were highly educated would find it difficult to marry.[40]

The question of literacies in the Edo period has been exhaustively considered by Rubinger, and he has much to say on the subject of female literacies, as has Walthall in this volume. Particularly striking is the illiteracy rate of 96 percent recorded by the Ministry of Education in Kagoshima in 1884.[41] But, as with access to schooling, there is such variation regionally and socially throughout Japan that generalization is largely meaningless. Although there is a close correlation between educational provision and literacy, it is important not to overlook other avenues to literacy through home tutoring, apprenticeship training, and so on.

A word should be added here about specialized literacy in sinological texts, which has long been thought to have been the preserve of men. As we have seen, Yamaga Sokō and others in the seventeenth century were recommending that women read Chinese conduct books for women, and this was even before some of them were translated into Japanese. It is hard to escape the conclusion that at least some of the elite women at whom their remarks were aimed were indeed able to read Chinese, at least in Japanese editions with glosses, and indeed this is clear from Gramlich-Oka's contribution to this volume. In the same way, Stevenson has been able to show that the

---

38. Tondabayashi 1998, p. 866.
39. Kagami 1985, p. 1066.
40. Yamakawa 1992, pp. 24–38.
41. Rubinger 2007, p. 168. Given that by this time there was already a Women's Normal College in Kagoshima and the prefecture was the second in Japan to develop kindergartens, there must be some doubt about the accuracy of this figure.

assumption that women in Europe did not use Latin is false by document-ing those who knew enough to be able to compose in Latin.[42]

In the seventeenth century and later, there were indeed some women who were able to put their sinological reading to use as poets or in other ways (see below), so it should not be supposed that women were necessar-ily cut off from Chinese. It is true that most of the private sinological acad-emies, to say nothing of the domain academies, did not admit women to their courses, but there were exceptions. One example is the private acad-emy called Suisaien run by Murakami Butsuzan (1810–79) in a village on the Nakatsu Highway in Kyushu (now Yukuhashi city in Fukuoka Prefecture), which was in operation from 1834 to the early Meiji period. The syllabus cov-ered sinology and some Japanese writings in Chinese, such as Rai San'yō's *Nihon gaishi* (Unofficial History of Japan), and many of the students were Buddhist clergy. There was only one woman ever admitted to the school, Setsu in 1838, and she may have been a nun, but Butsuzan did give occa-sional lectures for women as well.[43]

In a few cases diaries, autobiographies, and other documentary sources show that some women were receiving a sinological education. Atomi Kakei (1840–1926), for example, who in 1875 founded the forerunner of what is now the Atomi Gakuen in Tokyo, was born in the village of Kizu, between Kyoto and Nara, where her father ran a school, but in her late teens she went to Kyoto and studied both sinology and Japanese literature for two years.[44] And Hatoyama Haruko (1861–1938), who was the daughter of a Matsumoto domain samurai and later became an educator, recalled that she was taught to read sinological texts in the *sodoku* fashion by her father and neighbor-ing sinological teachers so well that by 1873 she was teaching other pupils, although, she added, she did not understand the texts at that stage.[45] Other examples include several women who ran *shijuku* (private academies) in Edo in the mid–nineteenth century and taught sinology among other subjects. In 1859 one of them took over the academy her father had founded, and she taught, in addition to ancient Japanese texts, the Four Books, the Five Clas-sics, and various historical works; it must be supposed that she acquired this learning under the supervision of her father.[46] Etsu Inagaki Sugimoto (1873–

---

42. Stevenson 2005. See also Ferrante 1980, pp. 9–42.
43. Tomoishi 1955, pp. 32–34, 41, 246.
44. Umihara 1988, p. 285; Takahashi 1989; Mehl 2001, pp. 579–602; http://www.atomi.ac.jp/enkaku/shozo.html (accessed 20 July 2007).
45. Hatoyama 1981, pp. 329–31, 353. Hatoyama's autobiography was serialized in *Shinkatei* in 1916–19 and published as a book in 1929. She is discussed by Tocco, who also raises the case of Aoyama Chise (1857–1947), who studied sinology in Mito with a woman teacher (2003, pp. 203–5). See also Hastings 2002.
46. Sugano 1998, pp. 153–54.

1950), who in the 1920s taught Japanese at Columbia University in New York, recorded that in the early Meiji period she studied the Four Books, although "it was very unusual for a girl to study Chinese classics."[47] It is clear, however, that it was not completely unknown. Fewer women still seem to have had training in medicine, although here, too, there are exceptions such as Nonaka En and Ine (1827–1903), the daughter of Philipp Franz von Siebold.[48]

At the top end of the scale of female literacy in the Edo period were those women who were writers and poets and those who participated in various intellectual movements. The former will be mentioned briefly below, but of the latter so far only a sketchy account can be given. Perhaps the most famous case, in the West at least, is that of Matsuo Taseko (1811–94), whose intellectual formation in Kokugaku (National Studies) circles and political activities have been explored by Walthall.[49] Kokugaku, indeed, seems to have been particularly welcoming to women participants, although the relative lack of information on women's involvement in sinology or Rangaku (Western Studies) may be partly due to the unevenness of the documentary record. On the other hand, it has been argued that the appeal of Kokugaku for women was its focus on Japanese rather than Chinese literary classics and the possibility of learning by correspondence or from peripatetic teachers, which rendered travel unnecessary.[50]

At any rate, it was common in Kokugaku circles to keep records of acknowledged followers. For example, Motoori Ōhira (1756–1833), who in 1799 became the adopted son and intellectual heir of Motoori Norinaga, had a record made of all his followers from 1798 to 1833. This lists 1,034 men but also 71 women from near and far, in some cases the mothers, wives, or daughters of male followers and in other cases without any male connection mentioned.[51] Seldom do we have much more information about the intellectual pursuits of women interested in Kokugaku, but the diaries and writings of Iseki Takako (1785–1844), the daughter of a Bakufu retainer, are a welcome exception. It is clear that she read widely in Kokugaku writings and in her intellectual engagement with Kokugaku sided with Norinaga against his critics.[52] She divorced her first husband and married again but remained childless. How much of her intellectual life would have been possible had

47. Sugimoto 1990, p. 34.
48. Hirao 1973, pp. 45–49; Umihara 1988, pp. 279–80. On Ine, see Walthall's contribution to this volume.
49. Walthall 1998. See also Sekiguchi 2008.
50. Umihara 1988, p. 278.
51. Mie 1994, pp. 65–67, 998–1031. For the female followers of other Kokugaku scholars and the details of the fifty-eight female followers of Kamo Mabuchi (1697–1769), an earlier Kokugaku scholar, see Umihara 1988, pp. 277, 282–83.
52. Fukazawa 2004, pp. 65, 72–87. For Iseki Takako's diary, see Fukazawa 1978–81.

she lived a more conventional life? This seems to be a case of "happen-stance," as discussed in Walthall's contribution to this volume.

The other movement in which women seem to have been active in documented quantities was Shingaku (Learning of the Heart), which was founded by Ishida Baigan (1685–1744) in the early eighteenth century. His chief follower, Tejima Toan (1718–86), went out of his way to address women both in his writings and in his public lectures, and an illustration of a Shingaku lecture in progress published in Kyoto in 1781 shows a crowd of women listening at the margins; what is more, it was Shingaku women who were responsible for spreading the teachings to Edo and Hiroshima.[53] Much documentation on the role of Shingaku women has come to light from the province of Shinano (now Nagano Prefecture), where Shingaku was introduced by Nakamura Shūsuke (1732–1816). In 1777 Nakamura opened a Shingaku school in Kashio village (now part of Kōshoku city), and he named it the Kyōansha. A list of those who became "friends" of the Kyōansha and where they came from survives and is summarized in table 1. From this is it clear that women formed just over 20 percent of the total, and although they were overwhelmingly in Shinano some lived in distant parts of the province.[54] Although it is not clear what one had to do to become a "friend," it appears that the Kyōansha brought together men and women from a large geographical area and, together with at least six other Shingaku schools established in Shinano by 1800, perhaps provided the only opportunity for some kind of what we would call further educa-

TABLE 1

Female and Male Friends of the Kyōansha in Shinano

	Shinano F	Shinano M	Elsewhere F	Elsewhere M	Totals
1777–87	48	147	0	0	195
1788–93	470	1,790	26	109	2395
1794–1805	331	1,182	16	129	1,793
Totals	849	3,119	42	238	4,383

Source: Data from Kōshoku 1988, p. 704.
Note: F = female; M = male.

53. *Kōkyō dōjikun* 1781, opening; Robertson 1991. Sawada deals with the values of Shingaku but has little to say on the role of women; on Shingaku education for girls, however, see Sawada 1993, pp. 114–16.
54. Kōshoku 1988, pp. 696–707. For the record itself, see Nagano 1984, pp. 879–932.

tion for the rural population, with the moral emphasis that was customary in Shingaku.[55]

The other area in which literate women were active, and in increasing numbers in the nineteenth century, was teaching. It is clear from evidence cited above that women were serving as home teachers by the middle of the seventeenth century, but information on the eighteenth century is scarce. However, among the abundant data relating to pre-Meiji education collected by the Ministry of Education in the 1880s there is a great deal of detail pertaining to women teachers. Although this information needs to be supplemented with data gathered by local historians over the last fifty years, it does at least show us that a minimum of 176 women were running *terakoya* in the first half of the nineteenth century and a further six were running *shijuku*. Of these *terakoya* run by women, 53 were in Edo, constituting one-tenth of all teachers there; 16 of the proprietors were of samurai status while the remainder were not. The oldest school listed was founded in 1781, but most of the rest were founded after 1830.[56] As Sugano has shown, in some of these cases the women teachers were taking over schools founded by older male relatives, but in others the schools appear to be the result of initiatives taken by women either to support their families or for charity; not surprisingly, the ratio of girls to boys was consistently high in schools run by women, and in a few cases they even seem to have had male employees working under them. Nevertheless, it should be remembered that almost a third of women proprietors of *terakoya* were in Edo, demonstrating the greater opportunities that cities, and particularly the largest of them all, offered to women.

The prosperous silk-weaving town of Kiryū (Gunma Prefecture) had at least five schools run by women, although the Ministry of Education data record only two for the whole of Gunma. The first of which much is known was run by Tamura Kajiko (1785–1862), who was the wife of a silk merchant and a follower of the Kokugaku scholar Tachibana Moribe. She was a good calligrapher who seems to have spent some time as a confidential secretary (*yūhitsu*) in the women's quarters (*ōoku*) of the shogun's castle in Edo; she ran her school, the Shōseidō, in Kiryū from circa 1829 to 1861. One of her pupils was Mochizuki Fuku (1839–1909), the wife of a calligrapher, who herself ran a school from 1861 to 1872. Fuku's school was attended by 35 boys and 120

---

55. For the distribution of the "friends" and the locations and dates of the other Shingaku schools, see Kōshoku 1988, p. 705.

56. Sugano (1998) presents a detailed analysis of the 1880s data. As she points out, the distinction between *terakoya* and *shijuku* in the Ministry of Education's survey is not entirely clear, but it appears to be based on the curricula, with *shijuku* offering more advanced courses in sinology, Japanese literature, medicine, and so on.

girls, and the curriculum went from the basics to the Four Books and Five Classics. On the recommendation of her teacher, she had gone up to Edo to work as a confidential secretary at the Sonobe domain residence, where she had studied sinology, and she returned to impart her knowledge to children in Kiryū.[57]

When more details like these come to light, it may become possible to correlate the emergence of women teachers and the provision of educational opportunities for girls with particular kinds of social and geographical contexts. The work of local historians scattered in local journals needs to be assembled to add flesh and blood to the statistics. The data already available have convinced some that the presence of women teachers in the Edo period, foreshadowing what was to become normal in the Meiji period, is a sign of "modernity" in the making.[58]

In the Meiji period, the passing of the education act of 1872, which provided for compulsory education for both boys and girls, was the first stage in the systematization of education under state control, but at the same time specialized girls' schools of various kinds came into being. The need for these had been anticipated in the Edo period. In 1837 a Bakufu retainer, Okumura Kisaburō (Jōzan), published a proposal for the establishment of girls' schools to inculcate desirable qualities in the women of Edo.[59] And some years later Yoshida Shōin (1830–59), in one of his prison writings, referred to the writings of Yamaga Sokō on women's education and described it as a pressing need in a time of crisis. He proposed that official funds be used to establish girls' schools run by scholarly widows of good moral character and at least forty-five years of age.[60]

After the Meiji Restoration some domains did in fact do so, mostly with access restricted to samurai girls and with limited curricula (but including pistol practice in one case). The syllabus of the Matsue Domain School, founded in 1871, required girls to tackle *Onna daigaku* and two Chinese texts, the *Analects* and *Biographies of Women*.[61] In the same year the authorities in Iwakuni (Yamaguchi Prefecture) proposed founding a school that would be open to all girls irrespective of social status, including the children of farmers and merchants; the inspiration came from news of the development

---

57. Kiryū 1988, pp. 40–41; *Kiryū hataya no ichihime nitarō*, 1998. See also Tocco 2003, pp. 207–8; and Takai 1991.
58. Suzuki Yoshitaka 1981, p. 35.
59. Okazaki-Ward 1993, pp. 84–91; Sugano 1997, p. 234. The full text can be seen and downloaded at http://archive.wul.waseda.ac.jp/kosho/to02/to02_02287/ (accessed 23 March 2009).
60. Shiga 1977, pp. 249–54.
61. Umihara 1988, pp. 261–65.

of education for women in Kyoto, and the proposal was explicitly linked to national goals.[62] Indeed, as Rubinger points out, the provision of uniform education had also been anticipated by a Bakufu proclamation.

> Teachers who run schools both within the city of Edo and without should instruct children enthusiastically and treat them equally. Everyone—boys and girls, high and low—should be able to read and write appropriate to their station.[63]

However much the content of education in the Meiji period may have registered a break with the past, there is a growing awareness now that in terms of commitment to provision and of the institutions themselves there was not a little continuity.[64]

Books for Women

In the first decades of the Edo period, when movable-type printing was challenging the dominance of wood-block printing, three conduct books for women appeared, each in at least two typographic editions: *Menoto no sōshi*, *Jokunshō* and *Jokunshū*.[65] These may have differed little from what had been available in the sixteenth century, but the point was that they were in print and their appearance marks the beginning of a perceived female audience for commercial publications.

The first books for women to circulate and be read in Japan, as in Vietnam and Korea, had been of Chinese origin. This is not to say that there were no Japanese writings for women before the Edo period, for there had been books such as *Menoto no sōshi* and *Mi no katami*, but few of these were printed in the Edo period whereas the much older Chinese books for women were printed both in the original and in translation.[66]

The principal Chinese books for women were *Biographies of Women* (*Lienü zhuan*, J. *Retsujoden*) and *Admonitions for women* (*Nü jie*, J. *Jokai*), both of which were produced in the Han dynasty. In Korea *Biographies of Women* in particular had been printed both in Chinese-text editions and in translation, and it had inspired and influenced conduct books for women for centuries; in China in the late Ming it had been updated and transformed in a variety

---

62. Iwakuni 2001, pp. 1762–65.
63. Rubinger 2007, p. 117; for the dating of this proclamation, see note 15 on page 210.
64. See Sugano 1998, p. 140.
65. Kawase 1967, vol. 1, p. 481–83; Asakura 2006, pp. 10–16.
66. Shiga 1977, p. 144–47.

of illustrated editions.[67] In Japan *Biographies of Women* was first printed in a Chinese-text edition in 1653–54.

The first attempt to adapt some of these biographies for Japanese women without knowledge of Chinese seems to have been made by Hayashi Razan (1583–1657) in a manuscript entitled *Kejoshū*, probably meaning "Collection to Educate Women."[68] This was a translation of some biographies from the original Chinese text of *Samgang haengsildo* (J. *Sankō kōjitsuzu*, Illustrated Guide to the Three Bonds), a Korean collection that included retellings of some of the biographies published in a Japanese edition circa 1637.[69] It may seem surprising that Razan should have resorted to a Korean collection, but at this stage of the Edo period Korean scholarly works written in Chinese enjoyed considerable esteem and were being reprinted, and in some cases translated, in Japan.[70] However, Razan's *Kejoshū* has never been published, and the first printed adaptation of *Biographies of Women* was *Kana retsujoden* (1655), a partial rendering into Japanese by Kitamura Kigin (1624–1705); this was followed by a Japanese translation of *Samgang haengsildo* published in the 1660s. Somewhat later a Japanese version of *Biographies of Women* containing biographies of Japanese women was published under the title *Honchō retsujoden* (1668). The pattern remained popular, for yet another Japanese version was published as late as 1913, which included biographies of more recent figures, including Inoue Tsū (1660–1738), the poet Kaga no Chiyo (1703–75), and Matsuo Taseko, while Elizabeth Starling's *Noble Deeds of Woman* (1835) had been presented to Japanese readers as a Western version of *Biographies of Women* when it was published in Japanese translation in 1879.[71]

It is perhaps significant that *Biographies of Women* was not reprinted after the seventeenth century either as Chinese texts or in translation, and the implication must be that the demand for it fell off, although it was still being recommended to women in 1787, alongside *The Tale of Genji*, the *Tales of Ise*, and *Tsurezuregusa*.[72] *Admonitions for Women*, however, appeared in a new translation in 1812 with a preface by Matsudaira Sadanobu, thus demonstrat-

---

67. Deuchler 2003, pp. 142–69; Carlitz 1991; Mou 2002; Kakehi 1982, pp. 289–324.
68. Nakamura Yukihiko 1982, pp. 7–29.
69. *Sankō kōjitsuzu*, pp. 255–72. On the Korean editions, see Shibu 1992, pp. 85–132.
70. Abe 1965.
71. Kumagaya 1913; Miyazaki 1879 (facsimile at http://www.lib.nara-wu.ac.jp/nwugdb/j008/, accessed 23 March 2009). *Noble Deeds of Woman* appeared in its ninth edition in 1883 and was evidently a popular book in England. On Inoue Tsū's activities as a poet and sinological scholar, see Chikaishi 1973, pp. 371–91. On Kaga no Chiyo, see Hla-Dorge 1936; and Szentiványi 2008.
72. See *Onna kuku no koe* (1787) in Emori 1993–94, vol. 4, pp. 26–27.

ing that he, at least, did see a moral purpose to women's reading.[73] The one Chinese text that seems to have remained especially popular in translation was the *Four Books for Women* (*Nü sishu*, J. *Onna shisho*), which was first published in Japan in 1656 in a translation by Tsujihara Genpo (1622–ca. 1691), a scholar in the employ of the Kuwana domain; this was reprinted in 1772 and then in 1835 repackaged in an illustrated edition with pictures showing Japanese (not Chinese) women engaged in various literate activities.[74] In 1883 a new translation of the *Onna shisho* was published; this was prepared by Wakae Nioko (1835–81), whose reputation as a sinologist had earned her a position as governess in an aristocratic household in Kyoto in the 1860s and who had remained a fervent antiforeigner even in the Meiji period.[75]

As mentioned at the beginning of this section, books in Japanese aimed at women were already being published by 1650, and these were followed by some translations of Chinese texts. By 1670 booksellers had woken up to the existence of a market for such books, and nothing is more eloquent of this than the appearance in the classified *Shojaku mokuroku*, catalogs produced by the publishers, of a new category, *nyosho*, "books for women." Such books had appeared in earlier catalogs, but it was in the 1670 catalog that they were gathered together for the first time and given their own classification.[76] The books included in that year are listed in table 2. None of the items listed is in Chinese, although Chinese books for women are listed elsewhere in the catalog, but several of the items (nos. 1 and 5) are Japanese translations of Chinese books for women.[77] As notes in the catalog make clear, several of the books were considered to provide "teaching" for women; in other words, this is a list of books written exclusively for women and mostly with a covert or explicit didactic content.

These nineteen titles, however, by no means represent an exhaustive list even of all the books for women that had been published and were available in the 1670s. Why, for example, were Kitamura Kigin's Japanese version of

73. *Sō Daiko jokai wage* (1812), translated by Hotta Masazane, daimyo of Ōmi Miyakawa domain, facsimile at http://www.lib.nara-wu.ac.jp/nwugdb/edo-j02/html/j044/ (accessed 23 March 2009).

74. For the text of *Onna shisho*, see *Tōyō jokun sōsho*, vol. 3. The 1835 edition bears the title *Onna shisho geibun zue*; judging by the copy in Ōsaka Furitsu Nakanoshima Toshokan, the text of the translation is identical to that of the 1656 edition except for some slight orthographic changes.

75. Tsuji 2003, pp. 227–41. Tsuji is reliant on Kajiwara 1917, which I have not been able to consult. Wakae's *Wage onna shisho* was published in Osaka in 1883. In 1914 yet another translation, by Ōta Hideo, was published, *Shin'yaku onna shisho* (Eibundō).

76. For all the references to *nyosho* in the catalogs, see Shidō Bunko 1962–64, vol. 1, pp. 51, 100, 145, 200–201, 214; vol. 2, p. 40; vol. 3, pp. 139, 178, 216.

77. *Onna shisho* is not a faithful translation of *Nü sishu*; see Aoyama 1982, p. 14.

TABLE 2

Nyosho (Books for Women) in the 1670 Booksellers' Catalog

	Title	Dates of Publication (wood-block editions unless stated otherwise) and Contents
1	*Jokai*	1656; Japanese version of *Nü jie*, a Han dynasty text for women
2	*Menoto no sōshi* with *Jokunsho*	1646; two conduct books (the first is a pre-Edo text)
3	*Jokunshō*	1639 (movable type), 1642, 1658; conduct book
4	*Kagamigusa*	1647, 1669; conduct book by Nakae Tōju
5	*Onna shisho*	1656; Tsujihara Genpo's translation of Chinese texts for women
6	*Honchō jokan*	1661; biographies of Japanese women
7	*Honchō retsujoden*	1668; biographies of Japanese women
8	*Kenjo monogatari*	1669; biographies of Chinese and Japanese women
9	*Onna shorei [shū]*	1660; etiquette guide
10	*Onna kagami [hidensho]*	1650, 1652, 1655; practical manual
11	*Onna shikimoku*	1660 plus older undated editions; etiquette and guide to letter writing
12	*Onna teikin*	Ca. 1658; calligraphy primer and guide to letter writing
13	*Onna shogaku bunshō*	1660; calligraphy primer and guide to letter writing
14	*Kaoyogusa*	Seems not to be extant; contents unknown
15	*Nyohitsu tehon*	Seems not to be extant; calligraphy primer for women
16	*Nyohitsu ōrai*	Ca. 1661; calligraphy primer for women
17	*Nishikigi*	1661; guide to letter writing
18	*Nyohitsu bunshō*	Seems not to be extant; calligraphy primer and guide to letter writing[a]
19	*Onnayō bunshō*	Oldest extant edition 1682; calligraphy primer and guide to letter writing

[a]An undated manuscript copy is in the Mochizuki Bunko, Tōkyō Gakugei Daigaku.

Biographies of Women, and *Hime kagami* (1661) not listed?[78] Another important work omitted is *Kuyamigusa*, which was first published in 1647 and evidently found favor with the reading public, for it was reprinted in 1649, 1659, 1669, and 1680; this, however, is listed in a different section of the catalog.[79]

It is important, of course, not to fall into the trap of supposing that these books were all that women were reading. In fact, at this time male scholars were much concerned about the popularity with women readers of classical literature such as *The Tale of Genji* and *Tales of Ise*. Indeed, the list of other books thought appropriate for women to read continued to expand in the late seventeenth and early eighteenth centuries to include those very works.[80]

Several of the items listed were guides to letter writing for women, and from the middle of the seventeenth century onward these were a staple part of the stock of booksellers; similar books were also published for men. The versions for women, most of which were written by women, were unsurprisingly in literary Japanese (*wabun*) whereas those for men tended to be in a style that was much closer to *kanbun*. Furthermore, the sample letters for women not only touched on such matters as gifts, greetings, and celebrations but included units of measurement and counting systems, suggestive of the needs of a mercantile audience.[81] Many of these, like other conduct books and primers for women, reinforced the message with illustrations of women reading books, and the books are often identified as literary works such as *The Tale of Genji*.[82]

By the late seventeenth century, books were also being published that at least ostensibly were aimed at a courtesan market. One of the earliest was *Hidensho*, which was published sometime before 1655 and carries the subtitle "Way of Educating in the Shimabara [Pleasure Quarter in Kyoto]." It carries information about the manners and behavior of courtesans and may have been a guide for brothel keepers as much as a conduct book for courtesans; however, it also includes instructions on how to write letters to new clients, pointing out that only by writing the letters in their own hands can they convey sincerity.[83] *Yoshiwara-yō bunshō* (Sample Letters for Use in the Yoshiwara, 1660s) contains a collection of sample letters, mostly from courtesan to client, and there seems little doubt that by this time the practice

78. For details and a discussion of these and other seventeenth-century books for women, see ibid.
79. *Edo jidai josei bunko*, vol. 8.
80. Kornicki 2005.
81. Amano 1998.
82. Koizumi 1998, plates; Emori 1993–94, vol. 1, pp. 26, 205, vol. 4, p. 28 and elsewhere.
83. Ono 1965, vol. 1, pp. 61–62, 79; vol. 2, p. 51.

of letter writing had become much more widely diffused, at least to sustain amours. It was only a few years later, in 1674, that a collection appeared that purported to contain the love letters of twenty identifiable Shimabara courtesans; authentic or not, they served as a set of sample letters, with the added cachet of a glamorous pedigree.[84]

By the end of the seventeenth century conduct literature for women was becoming an important part of the market, and it has attracted growing interest; as in Britain and elsewhere, much of this literature is now being reprinted and reconsidered.[85] The most famous, or perhaps infamous, work of this kind is of course *Onna daigaku* (Greater Learning for Women), which was first published at the beginning of the eighteenth century and is a work of Japanese authorship in spite of the implied connection with one of the Four Books in the title; the text is no longer thought to have been written by Kaibara Ekiken, although it is obviously indebted to some of his writings.[86] It is true enough that the bare text is discouragingly full of prescriptions and prohibitions for women, but that is not all there is to *Onna daigaku*. As Yokota and others have shown, the prescriptions fit very uncomfortably with the reality of working women, divorce, and the influence of courtesan culture, and most editions include not only the text of *Onna daigaku* but also a host of informative material, as well as numerous illustrations, which bracket the text in ways that might militate against a sense of its oppressiveness.[87] After all, there is very little to tell us precisely how women in the Edo period read and interpreted *Onna daigaku*; as Handlin and others have observed, there is in Chinese conduct books for women as well a disjunction between prescriptions and realities, and the prescriptions need to be understood in the context of a society in which men as much as women were expected to behave in conformity with behavioral norms.[88] The question posed by Carlitz with respect to China ("[D]id the packaging of women's virtue as a commodity result in ethics as entertainment?") is equally applicable to Japan, as

---

84. Ibid., vol. 2, pp. 123–35, 136–44.
85. The thirty volumes of *Conduct Literature for Women* (St. Clair et al. 2000–2006) contain a vast collection of works published in Great Britain from the sixteenth to the nineteenth centuries. For Japan there is *Edo jidai josei bunko* in one hundred volumes. In addition, many other texts are included in the microfilm series *Ōraimono bunrui shūsei* on Koizumi Yoshinaga's *Ōraimono* database (http://www.bekkoame.ne.jp/ha/a_r/indexB.htm, accessed 23 March 2009) and on the Hiroshima University Textbook Web site, which includes downloadable facsimiles of original texts (http://cross.lib.hiroshima-u.ac.jp/, accessed 23 March 2009). On other such sites, see Sakaguchi 2003, pp. 4–6 (www.fas .harvard.edu/~rijs/pdfs/tsushin/etsushin9_2.pdf, accessed 23 March 2009).
86. On the question of authorship, see Tocco 2003, pp. 199–200.
87. Yokota 1999, pp. 153–67; 1995, pp. 363–87. Koizumi 2003–6 contains a large number of later reprints and rewritings of *Onna daigaku*.
88. Handlin 1975.

lavish editions packed with entertainment and information reduced the ethical content to a fraction of the whole.[89] Furthermore, in spite of Fukuzawa Yukichi's famous criticisms of *Onna daigaku*, as Sugano shows in her contribution to this volume, it is not the case that even an activist for women's rights such as Kishida Toshiko dismissed *Onna daigaku* out of hand, and throughout the 1870s and 1880s innumerable new versions were published, testifying to the success of *Onna daigaku* as a brand.[90] There seems, therefore, to be ample room for a reconsideration of the ways in which *Onna daigaku* was read and understood.

The Osaka publisher Kashiwaraya Seiemon specialized in producing books for the female market and printed several lists of books for women that were attached to the end of conduct books for women he had published. One attached to the 1769 edition of *Joyō chie kagami* (Mirror of Knowledge for Women) lists other conduct books, as well as picture books and books of designs. A much longer one, entitled "Catalog of Books It Is Profitable for Women to Read," includes a large range of picture books and editions of *Hyakunin isshu* (One Hundred Poems by One Hundred Poets).[91] Although copies of his books and other conduct books can be shown to have reached rural households, there is little evidence to show how they did so. However, Suzuki's discovery of a stock list maintained by a Matsumoto bookseller that includes an 1808 list of *"onnamono"* (items for women) and of a Matsumoto edition of *Onna imagawa* suggests that local book trades were in all probability fully aware of the female market.[92] By that time, however, there was a huge variety of books published with an audience of women in mind; they are often collectively referred to as *jokunmono*, but the term is not necessarily reflective of reading practices, particularly in the case of items containing information related to leisure pursuits.[93]

To what extent did women individually own these or other books? In the Tondabayashi area southeast of Osaka, some inventories of women's possessions brought with them on marriage include books, mostly *Onna daigaku* and *Hyakunin isshu*, and in what is now Nagano Prefecture a woman brought a copy of an edition of the *Classic of Filial Piety* (Chinese

---

89. Carlitz 1991, p. 118.
90. On Fukuzawa's criticisms, see Sugano 2006, pp. 78–95. For the Meiji versions, see Koizumi 2003–6, vols. 5–9.
91. Matsudaira Bunko 2–1, Shimabara Toshokan, Shimabara; "Jochū no mitamai eki aru shomotsu mokuroku," appended to the copy of *Onna daigaku takarabako* (1772 edition) in the Mikami-ke archives (box 1, B-IV/2), Kyōto Furitsu Tango Kyōdo Shiryōkan, Amanohashidate, and to the 1814 edition of *Onna daigaku takarabako*; Saji monjo F19, Fukuoka Kenritsu Toshokan, Fukuoka.
92. Suzuki Toshiyuki 2007, pp. 102, 112.
93. On later conduct books for women, see Rühl 1997, pp. 287–312.

text annotated and glossed) with her on marriage, but documentary evidence of this sort is rare.[94] Few if any women seem to have used their own ownership stamps (*zōshoin*), but, for example, several women in the Yasuoka family, merchants at Enoshima near Kamakura, wrote their names on the covers of printed copies of conduct books for women published in the 1850s and 1860s; these included three separate copies of *Onna shōsoku ōrai*, suggesting that each woman had her own copy.[95] On the other hand, the books belonging to the wives and concubines of the daimyo of the Owari domain were recorded in the catalogs of the domain library, and these included not only bridal copies of the classic anthologies of court poetry, naturally manuscripts in the hands of fine calligraphers, but also printed copies, for example, of *Kogetsushō* (1673), Kitamura Kigin's extensive commentary on *The Tale of Genji*; Terajima Ryōan's encyclopedia *Wakan sansai zue* (1713); and Akisato Ritō's illustrated guidebook, *Tōkaidō meisho zue* (1797). Shinkun (1654–92), the wife of the third daimyo, owned forty-two books, including printed copies of historical works such as *Azuma kagami* and *Genpei jōsuiki*.[96]

Manuscripts remained an important part of book culture in the Edo period, and this particularly applied to books owned by women. After all, they were explicitly advised in *Onna daigaku* to make their own copies for future reference.[97] Sometimes manuscripts bear the names of their female owners with dates of copying or reading, as in the case of Abe Otame in the 1820s and Kaneko O-Yufu in 1860, both in Yamaguchi.[98] Noro Kinu, daughter of a doctor in a village 10 kilometers from Yokkaichi in the early nineteenth century, had a collection that included *Shōbai ōrai* and *Hyakunin isshu*, all manuscripts.[99] In 1781 the daughter of a Fukuoka domain samurai made her own copies of several manuscript accounts of the history of the domain, and Kaibara Ekiken's account of the Kashiimiya shrine in Fukuoka was copied by a woman in the early nineteenth century.[100] Some conduct books, too, survive only in the form of manuscripts such as the one Nonaka En wrote in

---

94. Tondabayashi 1998, p. 867. For the copy of *(Keiten yoshi) Kōkyō*, see Suzuki Toshiyuki 2007, p. 181.
95. Yasuoka Tadao archives, Fujisawa-shi Monjokan, Fujisawa. See Fujisawa 1995, p. 106. For what seems to be a much earlier example, see Kornicki 2005, p. 171.
96. Hōsa Bunko, 1988.
97. Kornicki 2006, pp. 23–52. Manuscript copies of *Onna daigaku* are many. Examples include Kurosawa Taeko-ke monjo 6309 and Kanbe Kanetaka-ke monjo 11375 and 11539, in Gunma Kenritsu Monjokan, Maebashi.
98. Kyōkasho Bunko Bunsei 2 and 3, Ansei 11 and 14, in Yamaguchi-ken Monjokan, Yamaguchi.
99. Komono 1987, pp. 606–7. Note that some of the manuscripts listed here date from the 1850s and must have been intended for her daughters or nieces.
100. Yasumi monjo 56–9, 64, in Fukuoka Kenritsu Toshokan, Fukuoka; Kashiimiya monjo 20, in Fukuoka Kenritsu Toshokan (microfilm).

the seventeenth century for a girl about to marry and one transmitted from generation to generation by a family of Shinto priests.[101] Manuscripts made by women are legion, and, as we shall see, many of the compositions of women, such as travel diaries, remained in manuscript form until recently.

What books did women read apart from the conduct books, how and where did they read them, and what impact did their reading have on their lives? These are, alas, questions that it is difficult still even to attempt to answer. In the seventeenth century *The Tale of Genji* and *Tales of Ise* were at the center of a debate about what women should not be reading, and the inference is that they were indeed being read by women, as both Rowley and Mostow's contributions to this volume demonstrate. Meanwhile, visual representations of women reading in relaxed poses are increasingly suggestive of leisure reading rather than study.[102] In later centuries how much of the audience for popular literature women formed is unclear, although the comic novelist Jippensha Ikku was thought at the time to have a large following among rural women, while the romantic novels of Tamenaga Shunsui abound with scenes in which the female characters are reading his books, sometimes in bed, sometimes standing up, sometimes aloud.[103] There is confirmation of the practice of reading standing up, a familiar enough practice now in rush hour trains, from Kinahan Cornwallis (1839–1917), a Londoner who worked as a journalist in New York and arrived in Shimoda in 1856. He recounts having seen "a young girl standing fan in hand at an open door reading. . . . Observing my curiosity to see the book which she held, she handed it to me. It was thin, and . . . intermixed with numerous wood-cuts." He concluded that it was a book on natural history, surely mistakenly.[104]

As for the final question, very few indeed are the men who have left us accounts of their reading and their impressions of what they read, whether in the form of commonplace books, marginalia, or autobiographies.[105] The same holds true for women, although Walthall has documented Matsuo Taseko's fund-raising activities for Kokugaku publications, her recourse to cousins to borrow books she wanted to read, and the impact her reading had on her.[106] Tadano Makuzu (1763–1825) did make some mention of her reading in *Solitary Thoughts* (*Hitori kangae*). In what is clearly a reference to conduct

101. Nonaka En 1891, pp. 699–701; *Onna no chikamichi*, manuscript Uchida-ke (Bōfu-shi) Wa-30, Yamaguchi-ken Monjokan.
102. Kornicki 2005. See also Bryson 2003, pp. 89–118.
103. Suzuki Toshiyuki 2007, p. 37; Tamenaga Shunsui 1971, pp. 392, 403, 421, 500, 520, 591, and elsewhere.
104. Cornwallis 1859, pp. 41–45.
105. Hackel (2003, p. 110) points out that in early modern England the lack of women's marginalia is due to the fact that they rarely read at a desk.
106. Walthall 1998, pp. 35–37, 115–16.

books, she wrote that "traditional teachings for women are wrong in trying to suppress young women's preference for the up-to-date." She attributes the quality of her written Japanese to the fact that she had read the *Tales of Ise* as a child and says that she had been invigorated by the Kokugaku writings she had read, difficult though they were; she says that she was unable to read Chinese texts, although she does from time to time quote from the *Analects* and other texts. Her conclusion that "It is better for a woman who will become a wife not to study things too deeply" can perhaps be taken as a reflection both of orthodox thinking on learned women and of the practical difficulties that faced married women who aspired to learning.[107]

Writing Women

Although some of the women writers of the Heian period are household names, and women writers of the modern period from the early Meiji onward need no introduction, women writers of the Edo period are almost entirely missing from such standard collections as *Nihon koten bungaku taikei*, not to mention Western histories of Japanese literature. As a result of recent work, however, few would now agree with Aston's claim in 1899 that when it comes to the Edo period, "Women disappear completely from the world of literature."[108] It is nevertheless true that the profile of women's writing in the Edo period differs substantially from that of men principally because so much of it was unpublished and so little of it was prose. The poetry/prose imbalance will be clear from table 3, but the relationship between published and unpublished writings is less amenable to quantification. Although many works written by men in the Edo period circulated only in manuscript, this was most commonly because there were either problems of censorship or a desire to keep the contents from becoming public knowledge.[109] While it is clear that reasons of censorship did not prevent the publication of the women's writing that has survived, most women, with the exception of poets, appear to have written without expectation of (or desire for?) wide circulation through print.

One thing leaps out from table 3, and that is the preponderance of women engaged in Japanese poetry, not just *waka*, the genre hallowed by

---

107. Goodwin et al. 2001, pp. 174–75, 179–82, 185. See also Kado 2006; and Gramlich-Oka 2006b.
108. Aston 1899, p. 232. See also Kado 1998. Two key collections are *Edo jidai joryū bungaku zenshū*; and Ono Sachiku 1898.
109. Kornicki 2006.

TABLE 3

Women Writers Listed in *Joryū chosaku kaidai*

	Edo Period, 1600–1867 (% and number)		Meiji and Taishō Periods, 1868–1926 (% and number)	
Poets and diarists of the imperial family	9.76	(223)	2.90	(7)
Other *waka* poets	32.90	(753)	64.60	(155)
Haikai poets	53.80	(1230)	13.80	(33)
Writers of prose and Chinese verse	3.60	(82)	18.80	(45)
Total number	2,288.00		240.00	

Source: Joshi Gakushūin 1939. Figures in parentheses in table 3 are the raw numbers calculated from entries in Joshi Gakushūin, *Joryū chosaku kaidai* (1939). Since that pathbreaking work was published in 1939, many other writers have come to light, but they do not seem appreciably to alter the statistical distribution. Many women, of course, composed in several genres, but here they have been assigned to one category on the basis of the preponderance of their output.

courtly associations, but to an even greater extent the more demotic form *haikai*.[110] What the table obscures, however, is the significance of the final category. Broken down, it reveals the following writers: *kanshi* (Chinese poetry), 25; diarists, 15; Shingaku and other scholarly writings, 14; prose writings, including conduct books, 10; *monogatari*, 7; guides to letter writing, 5; and mathematical writings, calligraphy books, and *kibyōshi*, 1 each. Much of the prose written by women in the Edo period circulated in manuscript, but one exception to this generalization is the category of conduct books written by women and calligraphy manuals for women, which necessarily had to be written by women. Such books were already being published by 1649, and in most cases the women calligraphers (authors) are named. For example, Isome Tsuna, whose dates are unknown, wrote and published a number of works in both categories in the late seventeenth century.[111] While the 45 women listed for the Meiji and Taishō periods were overwhelmingly writers of fiction and other prose that was published, Patessio's contribution to this

---

110. On this point, see Szentiványi 2008.
111. Koizumi 1997, pp. 48–74; 1998. For a useful guide to the script used in these books, see Yoshida Yutaka 2004. For biographies of women calligraphers, see Ichikawa 1991, which includes Den Sute, Inoue Tsū, Ōtakazaka Isako, the mother of the scholar Keichū, and a number of Kyoto courtesans.

volume reveals how many more women were active in the world of public print through the newly emerging media of newspapers and magazines.

Most numerous among the prose writings seem to have been travel diaries, most of which were written without thought of publication and many of which have only recently been brought to light. These have now begun to attract attention for the evidence they provide of gendered perspectives on travel and space, as well as of the possibilities for exercising literary imagination.[112] The most prominent writer of fictional narratives is Arakida Rei, who is the subject of Sakaki's contribution to this volume; her works circulated in manuscript until they were rescued by Yosano Akiko in the Meiji period. Iseki Takako, who has already been mentioned in connection with her reading of Kokugaku writings, not only made her own copy of a study of *Utsuho monogatari* by Kuwabara Yayoko, of whom little is known, but also wrote a number of prose narratives based on early *monogatari* literature in style and subject matter, including a parodic version of *Taketori monogatari*. Another example is Ōgimachi Machiko's *Matsukage nikki*. None of these prose works was printed, although several narratives by women telling of their escapes from besieged castles at the beginning of the Edo period were written down by others and printed much later.[113]

The existence of a number of prominent women writers of *kanshi* (Chinese verse), some of whom are discussed by Walthall in her contribution, is further evidence of the access of some women to a sinological education. Ema Saikō (1789–1863) is perhaps the most famous, but there were many others, including Tachibana Gyokuran (ca. 1733–94), who was related to the daimyo of Yanagawa domain and in 1764 published a collection of Chinese verse, *Chūzan shikō*, with a preface by the eminent sinologist Hattori Nankaku.[114]

As table 3 shows, however, the number of women who are known to have practiced as poets in Japanese and have left at least some verses to posterity is infinitely greater than the number of prose writers or poets who practiced in Chinese. One of the first to make her mark as a published poet was Den Sute (1634–98), daughter of the local representative (*daikan*) of the

---

112. For some little-known examples, see Tottori Kenritsu Hakubutsukan 2006, pp. 33, 41, 43, 86, 105, for travel diaries, and p. 50 for a composition by a member of the daimyo's family. See also Nenzi 2008; Fukai 1995; Shiba 1997; and Shiba 2005. Shiba 2004, pp. 153–60, contains a useful table showing women's travel diaries from the Edo period. Maeda 2001 contains a number of diaries from the Fukuoka area.

113. Fukazawa 2004, pp. 219–302. These are *Oan monogatari* and *Okiku monogatari*, printed together in 1837 (Kado 1998, pp. 34–41). For a translation of the former by T. J. Harper, see Shirane 2002, pp. 39–41.

114. Fister 1991, pp. 108–30; Maeda 1999, pp. 223–53; Fukushima Riko 1995.

daimyo of the Kaibara domain in Tanba. She married young in 1648 and had six children but moved with her husband to Kyoto where they both studied *waka* and *haikai* poetry under Kitamura Kigin and others. In 1664 she was widowed, and in 1681 she took the tonsure, but well before that, in the 1660s, she had already had a number of her verses included in various published *haikai* collections.[115] Tagami Kikusha (1753–1812), the daughter of a Chōfu domain samurai, was another who married young, in 1768; she was widowed in 1776, took the tonsure in 1781, and began a series of trips, in the course of which she walked around eight thousand kilometers. These two cases are reminiscent of the Heian period practice in which women, on reaching middle age, took the tonsure as a metaphor for the move from a sexually active life to a more contemplative, literary or scholarly one.[116] What is remarkable about Kikusha is that she not only had a number of her verses published in various collections, but she also is one of the few women to have authored printed books in her lifetime. In 1794 Tachibanaya Jihei, a Kyoto publisher who specialized in work by Bashō's followers, published a collection she edited in memory of her teacher, and in 1812 he published *Taorigiku* (Hand-Plucked Chrysanthemum), a collection edited by Kikusha herself consisting mostly of her own verse.[117]

These two cases suggest different patterns identifiable from the biographies. The first is that of something akin to a companionate marriage in which husband and wife share the same literary interests and practice them together. Other examples resembling Den Sute are Hatori Ikkō in Takasaki, who married a well-known poet and published a *haikai* collection in 1758; Shiba (Watarai) Sonome (1664–1726), who was married to a *haikai* poet, achieved renown as a follower of Bashō while working as an ophthalmologist, and published several collections; and Ōtakazaka Isako (1660–99), who married a Confucian scholar employed by the Tosa domain and in 1694, at the request of a daimyo, wrote *Karanishiki* (Chinese Brocade), a conduct book that testifies to her sinological learning.[118]

The second pattern is that of women like Tagami Kikusha or Iseki Takako, who were freed of domestic ties by widowhood, the tonsure, or even divorce. Nagamatsu Nami (1714–81), better known as the nun Shokyū (Moroku), was the daughter of a *shōya* in Karashima (Fukuoka Prefecture)

---

115. Mori Shigeo 1928. Attached to Kaibara Rekishi Minzoku Shiryōkan is a new exhibition center devoted to Den Sute, http://edu.city.tamba.hyogo.jp/bunka/rekisi01.htm (accessed 23 March 2009).
116. Groner 2002, pp. 245–88.
117. Ueno Sachiko 2000, vol. 2, pp. 835–88, 915–20, 1009–31.
118. Takasaki Shishi Hensan Iinkai 2004, p. 687; Haga et al. 1993, p. 198. *Karanishiki* was published posthumously in 1800. On Sonome, see Kado 1998, pp. 307–8.

and married the *shōya* of a neighboring village. She escaped from this un-congenial marriage by eloping with a doctor of poetic tastes and went on to publish three collections of verse while her collected poems were published posthumously in 1786–87. Other examples are Yabe Masako (1745–73), who left her husband on account of his adultery and, returning to her parents' home, devoted herself to *waka* poetry; and Miwada Masako (1843–1927), who was widowed in 1878 and promptly opened a private academy for sinology in Matsuyama in 1880.[119]

The inclusion of verses by women in many published collections and the publication of books of poetry edited by, or containing the verses of, women leave no room for doubt that as poets, and in favorable circumstances, ca-pable women had no insuperable difficulty gaining recognition or much hesitation about venturing before the public (on women in a Kyushu poetry circle, see Beerens's contribution to this volume). This impression is rein-forced by the existence of a number of anthologies devoted to the works of women poets. The first was *Onna hyakunin isshu* (1688), which seems to have been put together by Isome Tsuna, but this includes women poets up to the end of the Muromachi period and they are mostly drawn from the official court anthologies. Other works of the this kind with an increasing focus on poets of the Edo period were *Nyōbō hyakunin isshu* (1780), *Retsujo hyakunin isshu* (1847), and *Onna hyakunin isshu* (1851). *Retsujo hyakunin isshu*, for example, was illustrated by Hokusai and includes many poets from the Edo period, each with a biography, an image, and a poem; among them are several famous courtesans, Inoue Tsū, and Yabe Masako.[120] The association in some of these anthologies with female poets from earlier periods suggests that, as a literary field occupied by women from the Heian period onward, *waka* poetry written by women was already much too hallowed by tradition to be denied their epigones in the Edo period.

When in 1939 the Joshi Gakushūin, an elite educational institution for women in Tokyo, completed a pathbreaking survey of women's writing from 1600 to 1912, Nagaya Junji, the president, wrote in his preface, "Although the number of works written by women in recent times [1600 to 1912] is not inconsiderable, owing to the womanly virtue of modesty, these works have mostly been kept secret and are not widely known."[121] For the most part they are still not widely known, even in Japan, and recovery work is continuing;

119. Ōuchi et al. 1986, pp. 406–75; Haga et al. 1993, pp. 1056–57. On Shokyū see Sato 2000, pp. 1–44, which contains a translation of a travel diary by her. On Miwada, see Mehl 2001.
120. *Edo jidai josei bunko*, vol. 90. A digital version of *Retsujo hyakunin isshu* can be found at http://ir.u-gakugei.ac.jp/images/EP22000008/kmview.html (accessed 23 March 2009).
121. Joshi Gakushūin 1939, preface.

letters and local archives are revealing much more of the lives and circum-stances of women who wrote. It would not have been possible to write an essay of this length without the pioneering work of the Joshi Gakushūin and many scholars over the last few decades. The essays in this volume likewise stand on their shoulders and thus enjoy the luxury of being able to explore key issues in depth. They demonstrate that the bleak view of the cultural life of women in the Edo period needs to be tempered somewhat without forgetting for a moment the constraints that prevented many women from obtaining an education or opportunities to read and write and from reach-ing the wide audience that male writers could take for granted.

As Kado Reiko, one of the pioneers in the study of women's writing, has argued, it has been supposed for too long that women had no part to play in the cultural life of the Edo period.[122] It has now become evident, on the contrary, that over the two and a half centuries of the Edo period it became more common for girls to be educated outside the home, for women to be their teachers, for books to be written and published with a female read-ership in mind, and for women to engage in literary and intellectual pur-suits. Yet much remains unknown. We know very little about the reading of women beyond the horizons of conduct books, calligraphy manuals, and classical literature. Were women just as likely as men to read popular litera-ture? If so, why are there no expressions of male anxiety about this and why are there so few traces of women seeking to write it as well as read it? And why were their prose writings only published posthumously while many women saw their poetry in print in their lifetimes and some even produced books of poetry? Given how much there is still to learn, it is appropriate to finish this essay with unanswered questions.

---

122. Kado 1998, p. 10.

2

The Tale of Genji: Required Reading for Aristocratic Women

G. G. Rowley

❀

For a thousand years, *The Tale of Genji* (*Genji monogatari*) has been required reading for aristocratic women in Japan. Murasaki Shikibu (973?–1014?) herself tells us that during the winter of Kankō 5 (1008) the first edition of her *Tale* was compiled for the empress to present to her emperor. She also laments the theft of further chapters: no less than the empress's noble father had taken them for another, younger daughter who was being prepared for entry to the court of the crown prince and would one day be empress herself.[1] From its very inception, then, *Genji* was an aristocratic text, produced and consumed by women at the highest echelon of Japanese society. Until the early seventeenth century, when a complete text was printed, first in movable type and then in a succession of wood-block editions, *Genji* remained an aristocratic text, its manuscripts the property of aristocrats and aristocrats its principal interpreters.

---

1. Murasaki Shikibu describes in her diary the preparation of a presentation copy of *The Tale of Genji* and the theft of further chapters. See Bowring 1996. Murasaki was in the service of Shōshi (988–1074), empress of the Ichijō Emperor (980–1011; r. 986–1011); the thief was Shōshi's father, Fujiwara no Michinaga (966–1027); and his younger daughter was Kenshi (994–1027), later empress of the Sanjō Emperor (976–1017; r. 1011–16).

Once it was available to anyone with sufficient means to buy it, however, *Genji* sparked considerable debate as to whether it was a suitable book for women. P. F. Kornicki discussed this subject in an essay published in 2005, and in the present volume Joshua S. Mostow expands the debate by comparing early modern editions of *Tales of Ise* (*Ise monogatari*), *One Hundred Poets, One Poem Each* (*Hyakunin isshu*), and *Genji*, focusing on their different target audiences. Needless to say, in the new world of commercial publishing noblewomen did not constitute a market for books, and the available evidence suggests that they continued to read classical texts in manuscript. Nor was there a debate as to whether they should or should not read *Genji*. On the contrary, aristocratic women were expected to know *Genji* well, and evidence of this expectation can be found in numerous texts throughout the post-*Genji* history of Japanese literature. There were Buddhist objections to fiction, to be sure, but such objections were not directed specifically at women.[2] And in 1193, when Fujiwara Shunzei (1114-1204) declared in his judgment on a round of the *Poetry Contest in Six Hundred Rounds* (*Roppyakuban uta-awase*) that "to compose poetry without having read *Genji* is deplorable," he did not exclude noblewomen who wrote poetry from the force of his dictum.[3]

This essay is about the place of *The Tale of Genji* in the lives of aristocratic women. Three representative texts from three disparate periods are discussed; each of them illustrates a different facet of these women's engagement with *Genji*. The first represents the recognition that *Genji* was part of a noblewoman's requisite knowledge, the second a reaffirmation of that knowledge for a later generation of noblewomen, and the third the way in which such knowledge continued to be rewarded even as the debate about the suitability of *Genji* as reading for nonaristocratic women gathered pace in the early modern period.

Recognition

One of the oldest known *Genji*-related texts is the *Genji no mokuroku* (Catalog of *Genji* Chapters), in which a total of fifty-six chapter titles are listed.[4] The catalog forms part of a variant text (*ihon*) of a larger work called the

---

2. Even *The Three Jewels* (*Sanbōe*, 984), in which fiction is memorably disparaged ("Their words flow forth unchecked, as flotsam upon the sea; unlike reeds at the river's edge, they have no root in truth" [Rowley 2000, p. 18]), was compiled by Minamoto Tamenori (941?–1011) as a spiritual guide for just one woman, the troubled Princess Sonshi (966–85), when she became a nun.
3. "*Genji mizaru uta yomi wa ikon no koto nari*," in *Roppyakuban uta-awase*, p. 187.
4. The text is transcribed in Hashimoto Shinkichi 1972, pp. 336–37. For a translation and discussion in English, see Gatten 1977, pp. 11–15.

Renchūshō (Notes for Those within the Blinds, 1151–56).[5] The *Renchūshō* was originally compiled by Fujiwara Suketaka (fl. mid- to late twelfth century) for Hachijō-in (1137–1211), "favorite daughter" of the retired Toba Emperor (1103–56; r. 1107–23).[6] The work is described in modern secondary sources as an encyclopedia of essential knowledge for "those within the blinds," that is, aristocratic women. Such knowledge included lists of annual observances at the palace, emperors, empresses, Kamo and Ise vestals, government offices (*seifu hyakkan*) and the like, as well as more discursive entries on subjects such as the preservation of health (*yōjō*), music, and Japanese poetry. Although the standard text (*rufubon*) of the *Renchūshō* does not include the *Genji no mokuroku*, by the end of the twelfth century the list of *Genji* chapter titles had been added to it. The resulting variant text is known as the *Hakuzōshi* (Book for Complete Beginners, 1199–1201); until it was destroyed in the conflagration that followed upon the Great Kantō Earthquake of 1 September 1923, the *Hakuzōshi* was the oldest extant text of the *Renchūshō*.

Why would the compiler of an encyclopedia of essential lore for noblewomen decide to include a list of *Genji* chapter titles? In an age when *Genji* circulated only in manuscript, its chapters were bound individually, stored in boxes, and thus could easily get out of order. As Inaga Keiji explains, such lists provided the information needed to read the tale in the correct order, and one probably accompanied every set of chapters. They also told which chapters went together to form sets (*narabi*), such as the ten "Uji Prince chapters" noted in the *Genji no mokuroku*, for example, and were thus useful keys to recalling from memory the plotline of *Genji*.[7] The inclusion of the *Genji no mokuroku* setting forth this summary knowledge in a work designed for women "within the blinds" is evidence that they were expected to read those chapters. After all, Shunzei's dictum that "to compose poetry without having read *Genji* is deplorable" clearly demands a detailed knowledge of *Genji*. We also note that, like Shunzei, the compiler of the *Hakuzōshi* still seems to assume that any noblewoman can read *Genji* and acquire this knowledge without the aid of commentary.

Reaffirmation: Keifukuin Kaoku Gyokuei

Aristocratic women who knew *Genji* well and made use of that knowledge in their own writing abound in the literature of the late Heian and Kamakura

---

5. The dates are from Atsuta 2000, p. 13, based on a study of the recently discovered Reizei-ke Shiguretei Bunko manuscript, which dates from 1265–75.
6. "Favorite daughter" is from Wheeler 2008, pp. xii, 231, 260.
7. Inaga 1967, pp. 20–26.

periods. Once we reach the war-torn sixteenth century, however, writers of any sort are thin on the ground. Keifukuin Kaoku Gyokuei, born in 1526 and still alive in 1602, possessed what it seems reasonable to assume was the maximum knowledge a noblewoman in this century might have had of *The Tale of Genji*.[8] More than three hundred years had passed since the *Hakuzōshi* was compiled; many readers now required not only a catalog of chapters but also some degree of help from commentary to make their way through *Genji*. Gyokuei believes it is important that aristocratic women continue to read the tale, and she has strong views on the sort of help that will serve them best.

Gyokuei was the daughter of one of the highest of ranking courtiers (*kugyō*), Konoe Taneie (1503–66), who had already been appointed chancellor (*kanpaku*) the year before her birth, and would in 1537 be made grand minister of state (*daijō daijin*).[9] The Konoe survived *sengoku*, the long century of warfare that lasted from 1467 to 1573, "better than most" noble families.[10] Nonetheless, during this period all noble families found their hereditary landholdings encroached on by local strongmen and the remittance of revenues from these lands frequently interrupted; occasionally, aristocratic alliances with contending warrior factions involved flight from the capital and encampment in the provinces.[11] To make ends meet, aristocrats sold important manuscripts in their collections; they also made copies of manuscripts specifically for sale. The great court literatus and scholar of *The Tale of Genji*, Sanjōnishi Sanetaka (1455–1537), is perhaps the nobleman

8. Gyokuei's date of birth has been calculated as follows. Three of her four texts (the *Genji* poems and the two commentaries [see below]) include postscripts that record her age at composition. Calculating back from all three postscripts produces the same date of birth, Daiei 6 (1526). That she was still alive in 1602 we know from an undated manuscript of *Gyokueishū* in the Tōen Bunko, Tōkai University, which concludes with the notation "Keichō 7 [1602], fourth month, [blank] day Keifukuin Kaoku Gyokuei age 77," cited in the entry for *Gyokueishū* in Ii 2001, p. 63. This is the last known record of her life; we do not know when she died.

9. Gyokuei is identified as the daughter of Konoe Taneie in two similar texts from the mid–seventeenth century. One is the *Meikanshō*, a directory of styles (*gō*) compiled by a person or persons unknown during the reign of the Go-Sai Emperor (1637–85; r. 1654–63). The entry for Gyokuei appears in chapter 38, "Women Calligraphers" (*nyohitsu*), and reads "Keifukuin. Also known as Gyokuei. Daughter of Lord Konoe Taneie" (*Meikanshō*, 31 (*ge*):607). The other is the *Kendenmeimeiroku* (1688), a collection of capsule biographies compiled by the connoisseur of calligraphy Fujimoto Kizan (1626–1704) to aid the identification of calligraphers and calligraphy. The entry for Gyokuei reads "female religious of the southern capital [Nara], Keifukuin, daughter of Lord Konoe Taneie (nun)" (*Kendenmeimeiroku*, 2:392b).

10. For details, see Butler 2002, pp. 34–36. The quotation is from page 35.

11. Ibid., pp. 100–103. For one example, see the detailed analysis of Konoe Sakihisa's flight from the capital in Hashimoto Masanobu 2002.

best known for his (reluctant) participation in such trade.[12] But Gyokuei's father Taneie; her uncle, Taneie's younger brother Dōzō (1508–71); and her brother Dōchō (1544–1608) were no exceptions.[13] The family's commerce in manuscripts meant that Gyokuei would have grown up in a household where complete copies of *Genji*, as well as commentaries on the text, were readily available for reading and study. At this level of Japanese society, *Genji* was if anything more important than ever: for men of the Konoe and other aristocratic houses, *Genji* had become cultural capital that could be traded for cash.

Like calligraphy, manuscripts, and lessons in poetry, aristocratic wives were also in demand by upwardly mobile warriors.[14] Accordingly the daughters of the nobility, too, came to function as a form of cultural capital, traded not so much for cash as for the influence the warrior men they were entrusted to could have on the well-being of women's natal families in the capital. For a noblewoman groomed to make a politically advantageous marriage, therefore, knowledge of *The Tale of Genji* was an indispensible element of her aristocratic polish and thus her value as a trophy wife. The marriage, toward the end of 1558, of a daughter of Konoe Taneie to the ill-fated thirteenth Ashikaga shogun, Yoshiteru (1536–65), is one example of such an arrangement.[15] We cannot be absolutely certain that this daughter was Gyokuei, but it is a possibility.[16]

Four *Genji*-related texts by or attributed to Gyokuei survive. In order of composition, they are as follows.

---

12. Sanetaka is known to have sold complete manuscripts of *The Tale of Genji* at least three times over the course of his life, in 1506, 1520, and 1529. See Miyakawa 1999, pp. 415–16. In Sanetaka's diary entry for Eishō 3 (1506).8.22, for example, he notes the sale to "someone in [the province of] Kai" of a manuscript of *Genji* in his own hand for "five gold pieces." Quoted in Miyakawa 1999, p. 887.

13. See the examples cited in Ii 1969, pp. 14–15; Tsutsumi 1988, pp. 42–43; and Yanai 1993, pp. 468–82.

14. The literature on the history of marriage in Japan is voluminous. For summaries of the scholarship on intermarriage between aristocratic and warrior families, as well as some examples, see Butler 2002, pp. 51, 283–84; Kurushima 2004, pp. 233–38; and Kubo 1993.

15. The marriage of Yoshiteru to the daughter of Konoe Taneie is noted in chapter 328 of *Nochikagami*, entry for Eiroku 1 (1558).12.23, which reads in part, "That evening, a daughter of the Konoe (Taneie) house is made official consort" (*Nochikagami*, 37:687). The *Nochikagami* (Later Mirror, completed 1853) is a history of the Ashikaga shogunate that was commissioned by the Tokugawa shogunate and edited by Narushima Chikuzan (1803–54). I am grateful to Professor Hashimoto Masanobu, late of the Historiographical Institute, Tokyo University, for directing me to this source.

16. This possibility is explored in Rowley 2006. A different possibility is suggested in Rowley 2008. I should like to acknowledge my debt to Lee Butler, whose *Emperor and Aristocracy in Japan* first drew my attention to the subject of intermarriage between the Konoe and the Ashikaga.

1. A narrative picture scroll (*emaki*) in six scrolls dated Tenbun 23 (1554), now in the Spencer Collection of the New York Public Library[17]

2. A set of fifty-four poems on the chapters of *Genji* (*Genji kanmeika*) dated Tenshō 17 (1589)[18]

3. A four-volume commentary on *Genji, Kaokushō* (Kaoku's Gleanings), completed in Bunroku 3 (1594)[19]

4. A single-volume commentary on *Genji, Gyokueishū* (Gyokuei's Collection), completed in Keichō 7 (1602).[20]

It is these latter two texts, both classified by modern scholars as commentaries (*chūshaku*), that most directly concern us here.

Commentary is the closest form of reading short of translation—and the most gendered. Women did not write commentaries. Prior to Gyokuei, noblewomen had recalled their reading of *Genji* in *Sarashina nikki* (The Sarashina Diary, ca. 1059), recorded their discussions of *Genji* in *Mumyōzōshi* (The Nameless Notebook, ca. 1200–1201), advised their daughters to memorize *Genji* in *Menoto no fumi* (Letter from a Wet Nurse, ca. 1264), and relived whole scenes from *Genji* in *Towazugatari* (The Confessions of Lady Nijō, ca. 1306). In addition, one Yūrin (fl. 1450), a woman described by her contemporaries as a "*Genji*-yomi bikuni," a nun who traveled about reading aloud sections of the text and explicating them for her audience, had written a digest focusing especially on the poems in *Genji*.[21] But Gyokuei would seem to be the only woman in the premodern period to have written commentaries on *Genji* specifically for other female readers of the tale. This makes her work unique.

What, then, does Gyokuei's commentary tell us of what she thought of *Genji* and the way it should be read by women? "Commentary," as Stephen A. Barney aptly puts it, "accommodates a text to a presumed audience."[22]

17. On Gyokuei's *Genji emaki*, see Sorimachi 1978, pp. 18–19; Childs 1981; Thompson 1984; Murase 1986, pp. 91–97; Katagiri Yayoi 1989; McCormick 2006; and McCormick 2008.
18. For a transcription of the holograph, see Ii 2002.
19. For a printed edition, see *Kaokushō*.
20. For a printed edition, see *Gyokueishū*.
21. Yūrin is so described, for example, in the *Yasutomi-ki*, the diary of a low-ranking courtier and scholar of Chinese, Nakahara Yasutomi (ca. 1394–1457), which covers the years 1417–55. See the entry for Kyōtoku 3 (1454).7.5, cited in Ii 2001, pp. 441, 497. Yūrin's digest is entitled *Hikaru Genji ichibu uta* (Complete Poems of the Shining Genji) and was completed in 1453. For a printed edition, see *Yūrin*.
22. Barney 1991, p. viii.

Gyokuei's commentaries accommodate *Genji* to a female audience. They do this in a variety of ways. First, Gyokuei advocates reading *Genji* for pleasure, not as an adjunct to some other pursuit. Women are encouraged to read the fifty-four chapters straight through. The aim of *Kaokushō* and *Gyokueishū*, she writes, is to enhance the woman reader's enjoyment of this full-immersion experience, which is described in the afterword to *Kaokushō* in ecstatic terms.

> Of an evening in the fourth month, as she gazes out at the darkening sky, longing for the dim vestiges of the cherry blossoms of spring; or in summer, upon recalling the story of he who gathered fireflies as they flit past his window, she draws to herself this tale (*monogatari*).[23] And how much more so when she would seek consolation of an autumn evening, as the tints that move her so deeply one after another fade away; as the insects cry; as the evening sky, so beautiful she could die, all but breaks her heart. Or of a long winter's night, when she turns the lamp up high close to her bed, or next to the hearth spreads out the tale, what our young lady wants is just to enjoy herself—to read through the fifty-four chapters easily, entirely on her own, with nary a doubt, for this is the most important thing. After all, the reflection of the light of the moon in the waters of a shallow well is no different from that in a deep spring.[24]

Here Gyokuei sketches her ideal reader; she is a "young lady," sensitive to the changing seasons, who has no ambitions to a profound understanding of *Genji*, preferring "just to enjoy herself."[25]

The kind of reading Gyokuei advocates demands a different level of knowledge from that provided by mainstream commentaries. Anyone who has studied the earlier commentaries she cites approvingly—*Shimeishō*, *Kakaishō*, and *Kachō yosei*—must be struck by the vast distance between

---

23. This is a reference to a story from the *Meng Ch'iu* (J. *Mōgyū*), a Tang period primer in which rhyming four-character compounds are used to help students remember key stories about historical and legendary figures. The family of Ch'e Yin of the Chin (Qin) "was often too poor to buy oil for lamps, and so in the summer months he would fill a gauze bag with several dozen fireflies and use it to light his books, thus continuing his studies far into the night" (translator Burton Watson, in *Meng Ch'iu*, p. 120). Gyokuei's source may have been the *Mōgyū* itself, which had long circulated in Japan, or one of the many Japanese versions of the text. Murasaki Shikibu herself alludes to this very story in the "Otome" (The Maidens) chapter of *Genji*. See *Genji monogatari*, 3:20; and Tyler 2001, 1:383.

24. *Kaokushō*, pp. 447–48.

25. The word translated here as "young lady" is *shinsō*, literally "deep window," a reference to the distant interior of a house, where a proper young lady is supposedly raised.

them and her work.[26] Male-authored commentaries are larded with quotations from Chinese, "proof" that *The Tale of Genji* was a classic that could bear comparison with other classics, both Buddhist and Confucian. Such citations also served to demonstrate that the compiler of the commentary was engaged in a serious, scholarly, and therefore properly masculine enterprise.[27] Gyokuei was obviously familiar with these earlier commentaries, and she is not averse to borrowing from them when they can be of use to her.[28] More recent commentaries, however, she derides not only as unintelligible and irrelevant to an understanding of *Genji* but as mere displays of their authors' erudition. In *Gyokueishū*, for example, she complains:

> Many and various are the works compiled by recent commentators that tell one about even those things concerning which there is no doubt whatsoever. Some have eleven chapters, some twenty, others fifty-four. . . .[29] These people are only showing off their store of knowledge; endlessly adducing Chinese and Indian precedents in order to elucidate things that are of no particular use to a reader of *Genji*; with the result that gentlewomen are unable to make any sense of them, and in the end, their desire to know what the commentary is saying remains unsatisfied. I think all of this is totally unnecessary.[30]

Thus Gyokuei's second set of accommodations: in her own discussion of *Genji*, she cites no Indian, Chinese, or *kanbun* examples, proofs, or precedents. Rather, she selects only what she believes to be important or relevant to an understanding of the text.

Gyokuei's third set of accommodations to her female audience encompasses language, style, and tone. Both *Kaokushō* and *Gyokueishū* are written principally in hiragana; the only frequently used Chinese characters are those for the numbers one to ten; honorific *go*; *kokoro*, *koto*, *mono*, and *uta*; sentence finals such as *nari*, *haberi*, and *sōrō*; and the deferential auxiliary verb *tamau*. Gyokuei frequently translates words or phrases from *Genji* into contemporary Japanese. Her commentary on the "Kiritsubo" (The Paulownia

---

26. *Shimeishō* (Notes Explicating Murasaki, ca. 1293–94), compiled by the monk Sojaku (born ca. 1207–11, died after 1294); *Kakaishō* (Gleanings from the Rivers and Seas [of *Genji* Commentary], ca. 1362–67), by Yotsutsuji Yoshinari (1326–1402); *Kachō yosei* (Hints of Flowers and Birds, 1472), by Ichijō Kanera (1402–81).
27. This argument is elaborated in Rowley 2000, pp. 17–23. See also Cook 2008, esp. pp. 134–42.
28. Nakaba 2000 provides numerous examples of Gyokuei's borrowing from earlier commentaries.
29. See Ii 1969, p. 17, for suggestions as to which commentaries Gyokuei criticizes here.
30. *Gyokueishū*, pp. 121–22.

Pavilion) chapter in *Kaokushō*, for example, includes *kibiwa* (juvenile) glossed *yōchi naru koto nari* ("this means to be childlike").[31] She is also particular about how words ought to be pronounced, informing readers of *Kaokushō* that the word for maternal relatives (modern Japanese *gaiseki*), though written *gesaku* in kana, should be pronounced *geshaku* and that *sukuyō* (astrological divination) is properly pronounced *shukuyō*.[32] Gyokuei's concern with pronunciation suggests that at this time the ability to read *The Tale of Genji* aloud, to "perform" the text for listeners, remained as necessary a skill for noblewomen, and especially those serving as gentlewomen (*nyōbō*), as it had been three centuries earlier, when Abutsu (d. 1283) achieved renown for her accomplishment.[33] This impression is strengthened when one comes to the third section of *Gyokueishū*, which begins "I shall make a rough list of as many of those words [in *Genji*] I can think of that are exceptionally difficult to distinguish," that is, *kikiwakegataki*, literally "difficult to distinguish by ear." Gyokuei proceeds to provide an itemized list of seventy words, most of which are defined briefly in a line or less; a few words—less than a dozen—receive more extended explication. Some of the words she chooses to define are homonyms such as *okashū* ("usually a term of praise. Also the *okashiki* of laughter") and *karōjite* ("a word meaning at last. Also used about things that are troublesome"). In other cases she lists side by side different words that have the same meaning, for example, *yagate* ("means thereupon") and *sate* ("this also means thereupon"). Throughout both works, Gyokuei's tone is conversational, almost chatty. The sentence from *Gyokueishū* quoted above continues "though there are probably many more [such words], not having a text of *Genji* here at hand, I'll just write down the words I can remember."[34]

In all of the foregoing ways, Gyokuei's commentaries—indeed, we might better call them anticommentaries—are directed at female readers of *Genji*. She wants to make it easier for women to read *Genji* as a story rather than as an object of study or an aid to poetic composition. As she explains in her afterword to *Kaokushō*:

> And so for the sake of us foolish women, I have written this work and bound it up in four volumes. Of an autumn evening or a snowy morning, as you think back and your heart goes out to [the *Genji*], you can consult this in conjunction with the text.[35]

---

31. *Kaokushō*, p. 386.
32. Ibid., 385.
33. On Abutsu and *Genji*, see Ii 2008, pp. 165–66.
34. *Gyokueishū*, p. 156. The cited examples are from pages 156–57.
35. *Kaokushō*, p. 448.

Melissa McCormick has argued that the monochrome *Genji* picture scrolls (*hakubyō Genji emaki*) produced in the fifteenth and sixteenth centuries by Gyokuei and other (mostly anonymous) aristocratic women function as a form of commentary and succeed in reclaiming from male commentators a discursive space for women readers of *Genji*. Clearly, Gyokuei's *Kaokushō* and *Gyokueishū* are also part of this "female commentarial culture," which can be traced back at least to the early-thirteenth-century *Mumyōzōshi*.[36]

Gyokuei's commentaries continued to circulate in manuscript until 1936 (*Kaokushō*) and 1969 (*Gyokueishū*).[37] The extent to which they were read by their intended audience is a subject that awaits investigation; recent research has identified Gyokuei's niece, Chaa, as one recipient of her aunt's enthusiasm for *Genji*.[38] A modern reader may wonder why Gyokuei and her work have aroused so little interest over the centuries. Gyokuei herself probably provides the best answer to that question. "*Genji* is no amusement for the low-ranking (*Genji to iu koto wa gerō no moteasobimono nite nashi*)," she told readers of *Gyokueishū*, confident, we must assume, that they were of like mind.[39] Although she writes for women, her audience is avowedly an aristocratic one. The rest have no business even looking at *Genji*. Hers is a profoundly medieval view.

When Gyokuei wrote these words in 1602, however, the long process by which printing transformed *Genji* into a truly popular text was already under way. P. F. Kornicki has discussed the anxiety that the ready accessibility of *Genji* and *Tales of Ise* to a female readership aroused in male scholars during the second half of the seventeenth century.[40] Such worries went unnoticed in the Konoe house. Following the death of the retired Go-Sai Emperor in the second month of 1685, some of his personal possessions were distributed to relatives. Konoe Motohiro (1648–1722), Go-Sai's brother-in-law, listed in his diary seventeen items received, most of them furnishings such as folding screens and inkstone cases but also including five books and samples of calligraphy. All of the poetry-related effects went to Motohiro: the copy of the *Kokinwakashū* (Collection of Poems Ancient and Modern, ca. 905)

---

36. McCormick 2006. "Female commentarial culture" is borrowed from McCormick 2008.
37. Research on Gyokuei was pioneered by Ii Haruki, who prepared transcriptions of her texts (see *Gyokueishū*; and Ii 2002), as well as bibliographical introductions to them (see Ii 1969; and relevant entries in Ii 2001). Other scholarship on Gyokuei's commentaries is limited to Nakaba 1999; Nakaba 2000; and Tsutsumi 1988, who sees them as evidence for his argument that the system of secret transmissions concerning *Genji* (the so-called *Genji monogatari sanka no daiji*) was beginning to break down by the end of the sixteenth century.
38. See Niimi 2009; and Koyama 2010.
39. *Gyokueishū*, p. 121.
40. Kornicki 2005, pp. 152–62.

in the hand of Reizei Tamesuke (1263–1328), son of Tameie (1197–1275) and Abutsu; the hanging scroll with three poems in the hand of Fujiwara Teika; another with poems inscribed by Asukai Masatsune (1170–1221), one of the compilers of the *Shin kokinwakashū* (New Collection of Poems Ancient and Modern, ca. 1205). The tales, however, were bequeathed to the women in his life. His wife, Princess Tsuneko (1642–1702), Go-Sai's younger sister, received the late emperor's copy of *The Tale of Genji*, and Motohiro's daughter Hiroko (1661–1741), wife of Tokugawa Tsunatoyo (1663–1712, later the sixth shogun Ienobu), received the copy of *Tales of Ise* in the hand of the Go-Nara Emperor (1496–1557; r. 1526–57).[41] Although male scholars might inveigh against *Genji* and *Ise*, for women of the court aristocracy, these remained normative texts.

Rewards: Ōgimachi Machiko and *Matsukage nikki*

The life and work of Ōgimachi Machiko (1679–1724) exemplify the way that in the early modern period *The Tale of Genji* remained a requisite part of the cultural capital that noblewomen both embodied and transmitted. Machiko's *Matsukage nikki* (In the Shelter of the Pine, ca. 1710-12) furnishes a further example of a noblewoman employing *Genji* in a new text and in a manner calculated to enhance her position in the world she inhabited. Like so much literature by women of this era, aristocratic or otherwise, Machiko's writing has received little attention until recently.[42]

Machiko was born to a middle-ranking aristocratic family in Kyoto.[43] As Miyakawa Yōko has shown, both of her parents were descendants of the great Sanjōnishi Sanetaka.[44] In 1693, when Machiko was in her fifteenth year,

41. Sakai 2006, p. 7, citing the *Motohiro-kō ki* entry for Jōkyō 2 (1685).5.30. On Princess Tsuneko, see Segawa 2001; and Seigle 2002. On Konoe Hiroko, see Seigle 1999.
42. In Japanese, see the stimulating but overly salacious essay in Noguchi 1985, pp. 107–33; the more sympathetic account in Kado 1998, pp. 81–112; and Ueno Yōzō 2004. In English, a useful introduction is Bodart-Bailey 1979. The most reliable accounts in Japanese are Miyakawa 2002 and 2005, both now revised and reprinted in Miyakawa 2007. Quotations from *Matsukage nikki* below cite Miyakawa's 2007 edition of the text, based on Machiko's two holograph manuscripts in the Yanagisawa Bunko.
43. Machiko's putative date of birth (1679) is a back calculation from her age, given as forty-six, in the 1724 notation of her death in the Yanagisawa house record *Fukujudō nenroku*, cited in Miyakawa 2005, p. 12, n. 6; and 2007, p. 45, n. 3.
44. See the genealogy in Miyakawa 2007, p. 44. The evidence for Machiko's mother is presented in Miyakawa 2002; and 2007, pp. 33–35. Miyakawa 2005; and 2007, pp. 35–39, argue convincingly that Machiko's father was Ōgimachi Kinmichi (1653–1733) not Kinmichi's father Sanetoyo (1619–1703). Whether Machiko herself was aware of her real paternity is doubtful. In *Matsukage nikki*, Sanetoyo is described as *chichi*, "my father" (p. 554), and Kinmichi as *shōto*, "my elder brother" (p. 761).

her mother arranged for her to leave Kyoto for Edo so that she could become a concubine (*sokushitsu*) of Yanagisawa Yoshiyasu (1658–1714), the powerful adjutant (*sobayōnin*) of the fifth Tokugawa shogun Tsunayoshi (1646–1709; r. 1680–1709).[45] Machiko remained in Edo for the rest of her life; she died in 1724 at the principal suburban estate (*shimo yashiki*) of the Yanagisawa house, the Rikugien villa on the outskirts of the city at Komagome. It was while living at the Rikugien following Yoshiyasu's retirement there in the sixth month of 1709 that she wrote *Matsukage nikki*.

The reasons Machiko composed *Matsukage nikki* are intimately connected with her position as Yoshiyasu's aristocratic concubine, and thus it is with this relationship that any account of the text must begin. Machiko's own description of her move to Edo is as follows.

> I think it was when I was only about sixteen. Related as I was to Emonnosuke, who served in the Castle, she was good enough to urge me, time and again, "There is a place for you here in the East. Rather than go on as you are, make up your mind!" (554)

Despite her misgivings, she explains, "since people kept at me so, down I came" (555).

These few sentences in *Matsukage nikki* reveal something of how the arrangements were made for Machiko to become Yoshiyasu's concubine. Emonnosuke was not merely "related" to Machiko; she was her mother.[46] That she wrote to Machiko, "There is a place for you (*mi no oki-dokoro*) here in the East. Rather than go on as you are, make up your mind!" suggests that she had already broached the subject of her daughter to Yoshiyasu. Note also the phrase "rather than go on as you are" (*kakute aran yori wa*), which hints at Machiko's situation in Kyoto. The Ōgimachi family's annual stipend was a mere three hundred *koku*, less than a third of Emonnosuke's salary of one thousand *koku* in her position as administrative head of the Ōoku, the women's quarters of Edo Castle, and less than two-hundred-thirtieth of the more than seventy thousand *koku* that Yoshiyasu earned at the time Machiko became his concubine. Eventually, Yoshiyasu's emoluments would

---

45. Like most men of the warrior estate, Yanagisawa was known over the course of his life by a succession of names and titles; he was granted the use of the character "Yoshi" by Tsunayoshi only on 1701.11.26. For the sake of clarity, he is referred to as Yoshiyasu throughout the present essay.

46. The crucial connection between Machiko and Emonnosuke was discovered by Miyakawa Yōko. For details, see Miyakawa 2002; and 2007, pp. 33–35. The story of Emonnosuke's rise to a high position in the Ō-oku is told in two collections of biographies of Bakufu women. See *Gyokuyoki*, pp. 49–51; and *Ryūei fujo denkei*, pp. 174–78.

amount to some two hundred thousand *koku*.[47] In "rather than go on as you are," we hear Machiko's mother suggesting to her daughter that instead of continuing to live in genteel poverty in Kyoto she should choose economic comfort even though it would mean doing so as less than Yoshiyasu's official wife.

Yoshiyasu seems to have foreseen certain complications and moved to forestall them. A family of middle-ranking aristocrats, however genteelly impoverished, might be reluctant to consign one of its daughters to concubinage in a warrior house of humble origins, however rich. It was arranged, therefore, that Machiko should become the adopted daughter of one Tanaka Hanzō, a warrior with close court connections, from whose house she could enter the Yanagisawa house without disgrace. Yoshiyasu also had Machiko's father Kinmichi appointed *buke tensō* (court envoy to the military estate), whereupon his income increased tenfold. The messenger sent to express the family's gratitude to Yoshiyasu also escorted Machiko to Edo, completing the transaction.[48]

From a twenty-first-century point of view, such an arrangement might strike us as at the very least fraught with risk if not entirely unfathomable. For Yoshiyasu had never seen Machiko before she arrived in Edo, and even her mother had not seen her for at least a decade, perhaps as long as thirteen years, since leaving Kyoto to enter service in the *Ōoku*. We know from the passage in the *Matsukage nikki* quoted above that mother and daughter corresponded, but Emonnosuke certainly could not have vouched for her daughter's looks and bearing. Obviously, Machiko was attractive to Yoshiyasu for other reasons.

Why did Yoshiyasu go to such trouble to acquire an aristocratic concubine? First and foremost, Machiko was a potential conduit through which Yoshiyasu could gain direct access to the imperial court. Such access was important to him for reasons both political and personal, although the distinction between the two is perhaps more apparent to us than it might have been to him. His greatest political triumph involving the court was probably his arranging for Tsunayoshi's mother, Keishōin (1627–1705), to be awarded the first court rank during her own lifetime.[49] His greatest personal triumph was perhaps imperial perusal and assessment (*chokuten*) of

---

47. All income figures are from Miyakawa 2007, p. 40.
48. For detailed discussions of the arrangements outlined here, see Miyakawa 1990, pp. 407–9; and 2007, pp. 39–42. According to the list of *buke tensō* in *Shinpan Nihonshi jiten*, p. 1287, Kinmichi was appointed on 1693.8.16 and served in the position for six and a half years until 1700.2.6.
49. Keishōin was awarded highest court rank in the ninth month of Genroku 15 (1702). See Bodart-Bailey 2006, p. 123.

a number of his classically inspired *waka* by the retired Reigen Emperor (1654–1732; r. 1663–87). This Machiko was able to arrange for him through her Kyoto relatives, and she records the delicate negotiations that took place in "Aki no kumo" (Autumn Clouds), the sixteenth chapter of *Matsukage nikki*, which covers the period from spring through autumn 1703.

> The retired emperor [Reigen] is extraordinarily skilled [at poetry], not only by the standards of the present, but also those of the past. Even those court nobles whose families practice the way of poetry are forever entrusting [their compositions] to his imperial judgment. How then might he [Yoshiyasu] humbly request imperial correction? If only he might, with all due reverence, submit even one poem for his imperial judgment, how honored would be his efforts at poetry, he thought. The Ōgimachi Grand Counselor [Kinmichi], being a favorite of the retired emperor, is on familiar terms with him and constantly in attendance upon him. [Yoshiyasu] asked [Kinmichi] if, in the course of one of their private conversations, he might mention the matter. (602)

In the seventh month of 1703, Yoshiyasu's request was granted; both he and Machiko received letters from Kinmichi that transmitted the retired emperor's remarks. No less than twenty-six of his poems had been positively assessed, two of them even receiving the equivalent of "excellent" (*nagaten*) in the imperial hand. Yoshiyasu's expressions of gratitude were lavish, ranging from a silver incense burner and fragrant wood for the retired emperor to gold, silver, bolts of silk damask, sake, and edible delicacies such as salted bream for the others involved.[50]

As it turned out, then, Yoshiyasu had made a fortunate acquisition in Machiko. She provided him with access to the learning and immense cultural prestige of the court, and she was by anyone's standards a deeply learned woman herself. Her *Matsukage nikki* is studded with allusions not only to *Genji*, *Ise*, and the imperially commissioned anthologies of poetry but also to Chinese classics such as *Historical Records* (*Shiji*, J. *Shiki*) and the *Collected Works of Bo Juyi* (*Boshi wenji*, J. *Hakushi monjū*).[51] Such learning was of use to Yoshiyasu in various ways. One was in the writing of the *Matsukage nikki* itself. The work seems to have been created at Yoshiyasu's behest in order to transmit to his descendants a more personal and elegant version

---

50. Machiko's lengthy description of the saga, including Yoshiyasu's two best poems and the gifts sent in response, may be found in Miyakawa 2007, pp. 607–12.
51. Miyakawa 1990, pp. 429–30.

of the *Rakushidō nenroku*, the official (thus *kanbun*) record of the Yanagisawa house during Yoshiyasu's lifetime, and to emphasize that the flowering fortunes of the house were due to Tsunayoshi's favor.[52] As the Kyoto scholar and poet Ban Kōkei (1733–1806) noted in his copy of *Matsukage nikki*, the narrator's exclamation, in the "Yukari no hana" (Flower of Affinity) chapter, "Surely this too must have been due to the peerless favor of the pine!" (*Saru wa, matsukage no, taguinaki nimo yorikemu kashi*) is the origin of the title of the work: *matsu* from Matsudaira, the family name used by Tokugawa Ieyasu (1543–1616) until 1566 and granted to Yoshiyasu by Tsunayoshi in 1701; and *kage*, meaning the "shade" of the shogun's favor.[53] *Matsukage nikki* can be seen, therefore, as another, very material benefit of Yoshiyasu's acquisition of an aristocratic concubine.

Let us turn now to an examination of the different ways Machiko uses *The Tale of Genji* in the creation of *Matsukage nikki*.[54] Though arranged chronologically, *Matsukage nikki* is not a diary in the sense of a daily record. Like *Genji*, it is a narrative told by a female narrator who has not necessarily experienced all that she recounts. The first four chapters of *Matsukage nikki*, for example, cover the founding the Tokugawa shogunate, the history of the Yanagisawa house, and significant events that took place *before* Machiko became one of Yoshiyasu's concubines, such as Tsunayoshi's first visit to the Yanagisawa mansion at Kandabashi on 1691.3.22. Thereafter the narrator weaves together accounts of events at which she was present with events at which she was not. She also frequently interrupts her narrative to address the reader directly, a technique known as *sōshiji* (comments by the narrator) that is a distinctive feature of Heian period narrative fiction. In her history of the Yanagisawa house, for example, we read that

> twenty generations ensued before the present lord was born, it would seem.[55] At that time the world at large was in disorder, reign followed upon reign, and over the centuries, many events of an awesome nature occurred—but really, these are things no woman could ever hope to describe and they are best left to the writings of men. (117)

52. For a detailed discussion, see Miyakawa 2007, pp. 27–30.
53. Ban Kōkei's annotations are reproduced in Ueno Yōzō 2004. For this quotation, see pages 280–81.
54. For a discussion of correspondences between *Genji* and *Matsukage nikki*, see Miyakawa 1990, pp. 419–20; and 2007, pp. 24–26.
55. "The present lord" (*ima no kimi*) here refers to Yoshiyasu's father, Yanagisawa Yasutada (1602–87).

Another *Genji*-like feature of *Matsukage nikki* is the frequent occurrence of narrative ellipses (*shōhitsu*).[56] The majority of these are used to avoid long lists of gifts given and received. For example, "While indisposed, he [Yoshiyasu] received many things, day after day without fail, but there were so many it would be wearisome to list them (. . . *ito amari urusakute kakazu narinu*, 370). Poems are passed over in similar manner: "There were a great many poems by various people, but I have omitted them" (*hitobito no uta ōkaredo morashitsu*, 431). Like *Genji*, most chapters are given a title derived from one of the poems in that chapter. Twenty-six of the thirty chapters of *Matsukage nikki* have titles derived from poems; in *Genji monogatari*, some forty-one of the fifty-four chapter titles are derived from poems.[57]

Interestingly, the vast majority of quotations from *The Tale of Genji* in *Matsukage nikki* are from the so-called first part (the *ichibu* or *seihen*) of the tale, the thirty-three chapters from "Kiritsubo" (The Paulownia Pavilion) to "Fuji no uraba" (New Wisteria Leaves), which tell of Genji's birth, youthful transgressions, exile, return, and political and personal triumphs.[58] Machiko's brief seems to have been to depict Yoshiyasu's life as similarly exemplary, although he of course commits no errors, youthful or otherwise, and earns no one's ire; the tale she tells is of devotion to duty and services respectfully rendered, duly rewarded with promotions and shogunal praise. These rewards provided Yoshiyasu with sufficient power and wealth to live on a Genji-like scale. In "Tamakashiwa" (Jeweled Oak), the fourteenth chapter of *Matsukage nikki*, Machiko describes the rebuilding of the main Yanagisawa mansion after a disastrous fire in 1702 and concludes with the following observation.

> Each residence is of a different design; [he] gave orders that our wishes should be consulted as they were constructed. [He] made it possible to go to and fro between each other's residences. The splendid appearance is quite beyond words. (517)

"Our" and "each other" here refer to Yoshiyasu's women: his wife, Soshi Sada (1660–1713); and his concubines, of whom there were at least three in 1702, Iizuka Some (1667–1705), Machiko, and Yokoyama Shige (dates unknown).[59]

---

56. Miyakawa 1990, p. 421. For a genealogy of this rhetorical technique, see Tamura 2003, which notes that there are sixty examples in the fifty-four chapters of *Genji*. Ueno Yōzō 2004, pp. 498–507, lists all seventy-six examples in the thirty chapters of *Matsukage nikki*.

57. Miyakawa 1990, p. 422; 2007, p. 26.

58. Miyakawa 1990, p. 421.

59. Machiko is careful to dignify Yoshiyasu's other concubines by adding the aristocratic *-ko* suffix to their names, although neither was of noble birth. "Someko" first appears in

As Miyakawa notes, this passage closely resembles the description of the Rokujō mansion completed in the "Otome" (The Maidens) chapter of *Genji*.[60] Genji has the four quarters of his mansion "constructed to suit each resident's wishes" (*on-katagata no onegai no kokorobae o tsukurasetamaeri*),[61] just as Yoshiyasu has the various quarters of his mansion "constructed according to each resident's wishes" (*onegai no kokorobae o okitetsutsu tsukurasetamaeri*, 517). Likewise, at the Rokujō mansion, "in residences that were very close to ideal, the ladies exchanged letters with one another" (*itodo omou yō naru on-sumai nite, kikoekawashitamau*),[62] just as at the Yanagisawa mansion the ladies could "go to and fro between each other's residences" (*katagata ni on-sumai yukikayowashite*, 517).

There is much more to Machiko's allusions and narrative technique than the creation of a classically elegant effect, however. Such passages are not simply testaments to her profound knowledge of *Genji*. Machiko's narrativization of Yoshiyasu's life in the style of *Genji* rhetorically lifts him above his relatively humble origins, dignifies his rise to the heights of power, and at the same time suggests that she saw her own situation in terms borrowed directly from *Genji*. No mere concubine I, she seems to say. By describing the Yanagisawa mansion as a latter-day Rokujō estate, Machiko depicts herself as one of the Shining Genji's own ladies, a status she could never have achieved without her knowledge of *Genji*.

Conclusion

Kornicki argued in his "Unsuitable Books for Women" essay:

> The process by which *Genji* and *Ise* gradually came to be accepted as works valuable for women to read intersected with the larger sociological transformation of court culture in the seventeenth century as it passed out of the controlling hands of the aristocracy and ever more into the hands of those of lesser social status, such as the commoner compilers of the *Genji* commentaries or the

---

Matsukage nikki in the "Musashino" (Fields of Musashi) chapter when the birth, on 1687.9.3, of her first son by Yoshiyasu is noted (p. 128). "Shigeko" first appears in the "Chiyo no haru" (Eternal Spring) chapter when the birth on 1695.1.29 of her first child by Yoshiyasu, a daughter, is noted (p. 235). Yoshiyasu's wife is referred to as *kita no kata*, the usual designation for the principal wife of a ranking nobleman.

60. Miyakawa 2007, pp. 520–21.
61. *Genji monogatari*, 3:72. Translations from *Genji* here and below are my own.
62. *Genji monogatari*, 3:76.

commoner poets who challenged the aristocratic guardians of the
waka tradition.[63]

This is an important observation, but we must specify that the generic
"women" here means "nonaristocratic women." As we have seen, *The Tale
of Genji* had been essential reading for noblewomen from its inception. The
catalog of *Genji* chapters in the *Hakuzōshi* (1199–1201) indicates that familiarity with the tale was as fundamental to intelligent participation in day-to-
day court life as was knowledge of emperors and empresses, court titles, and
waka. Kaoku Gyokuei's commentaries (1594, 1602) were designed to make
such familiarity feasible for a later generation of noblewomen; in so doing,
they reaffirm the importance of the tale in their lives. Machiko's *Matsukage
nikki* (ca. 1710–12) is a vivid illustration of the way in which a knowledge of
Genji not only continued to provide noblewomen with materials for their
own artistic and literary productions but could also enhance their material
well-being. In short, throughout the thousand years since it was written *The
Tale of Genji* was required reading for aristocratic women.

Nonetheless, the evidence adduced here raises several questions. In
the larger context of writing by women in Japan, and especially in comparison with the Heian and Kamakura periods, it is striking that in the
five-hundred-some years that lie between the mid–fourteenth and mid–
nineteenth centuries we know of so few aristocratic women who wrote anything longer than thirty-one-syllable *waka*. One noblewoman who did write
at length was Princess Tsuneko, mentioned above as the younger sister of
the Go-Sai Emperor and inheritor of his copy of *The Tale of Genji*.[64] Why were
there not more like her? In the *sengoku* period, warfare was a decided deter-
rent, as were the impoverishment of the court and the consequent absence
of competing imperial consorts.[65] But why should the apparent silence of
noblewomen persist even through the Pax Tokugawa, when samurai women
and, after the turn of the eighteenth century, townswomen, too, produced
an enormous amount of writing? (Essays by Bettina Gramlich-Oka, Atsuko
Sakaki, and Anne Walthall in this volume discuss some of these women
writers.) A recent *Dictionary of Early Modern Women's Travel Diaries* lists more
than a hundred Edo period travelogues by women; only three, all composed

63. Kornicki 2005, p. 179. On the "commoner compilers of the *Genji* commentaries," see Harper
    1989. On the "commoner poets who challenged the aristocratic guardians of the *waka* tra-
    dition," see Thomas 1991.
64. Princess Tsuneko is the author of *Mujōhōin-dono gonikki* (The Diary of Mujōhō-in, 1666–
    1700, Yōmei Bunko manuscript). Segawa 2001 is a biography based on the diary.
65. This is the argument advanced in Tonomura 1996.

during the last years of the Tokugawa shogunate, are by noblewomen.[66] Further research is needed before satisfactory answers to these questions can be offered.

In the meantime, the question might usefully be reformulated from a different perspective: what enabled Gyokuei and Machiko to write what they did? First, it can be argued that both Gyokuei and Machiko were able to write at length precisely *because* what they wrote was either explicitly about *The Tale of Genji* or could be—indeed was—compared to *Genji*. (A later, alternate title of *Matsukage nikki* was *Azuma Genji*, "A *Genji* for the East Lands").[67] In the Heian and Kamakura periods, noblewomen had read *Genji* and written about, or on the model of, *Genji*; that women in later centuries did likewise is thus hardly surprising. Second, we might argue that Gyokuei was able to participate in a masculine genre—commentary—by disclaiming any intention of operating on the same terms as men.[68] By defining her audience as female and limiting her readership to aristocratic women, she was able to carve out a space for her own writing without in any way upsetting the natural order. In the case of Machiko, it seems clear that she did not take it upon herself to write such a long work on her own initiative but was commanded, or encouraged, to do so by Yanagisawa Yoshiyasu. Be that as it may, the women we glimpse in the interstices of *Kaokushō*, *Gyokueishū*, and *Matsukage nikki* serve to remind us that in early modern Japan *The Tale of Genji*—like great fiction in other places and times—continued to afford its female readers "scripts for living," means by which they might both shape and make sense of their lives.[69]

---

66. Shiba 2005.
67. Ikebe 1914, p. 8. Alas, Ikebe does not provide any examples of the use of this alternate title. This volume of *Kokubun sōsho* contains one of the first printed texts of *Matsukage nikki*.
68. I borrow this formulation from the discussion of Hildegard of Bingen's participation in the overwhelmingly male genre of theological writing in Flanagan 1989, p. 15.
69. "Scripts for living" is borrowed from Lynch 2004, p. xxiii, who writes, "One approach [Jane Austen's novel] *Persuasion* uses to explore how people live in time is to probe the paradoxical way in which books, though esteemed for transcending the immediacy of experience, still persuade readers that they are scripts for living."

3

Illustrated Classical Texts for Women in the Edo Period

Joshua S. Mostow

Thanks to Peter Kornicki's recent study, we now know quite a bit about the debates that occurred in the mid- to late seventeenth century over the appropriateness of *The Tale of Genji* (*Genji monogatari*) and *The Tales of Ise* (*Ise monogatari*) as reading material for girls and women.[1] My understanding of his conclusion is as follows: borrowing the concept of "kugefication" from Toshio Yokoyama, and extending it back into the seventeenth century, it would appear that, due to the overwhelming desire by members of both the warrior (*buke*) and townsman (*chōnin*) class for their daughters to acquire cultural capital associated with the aristocracy, the ability to read and compose *waka* became a sine qua non, and this desideratum had grown so strong by the beginning of the eighteenth century that it almost rendered invisible the previous morally based objections to the salacious content of the *Genji* and *Ise*.[2] In fact, debates about the appropriateness of the *Genji* and *Ise* were of relatively short duration. In the late sixteenth century, when the *Usuyuki monogatari* (The Tale of Light Snow), a tale replete with references

1. Kornicki 2005.
2. On "kugefication," see Yokoyama 2000.

to the *Ise*, was written, the debates had yet to begin.[3] By the middle of the eighteenth century, they were over, and it had become "a matter of course that women include *Genji* in their reading."[4] The debates were revived in the Meiji period, as scholars and educators struggled with the construction of a canon of national literature.[5]

Kornicki's study also traces the rise of genres of books published specifically for females. In this essay, I would like to look at this phenomenon particularly in relation to the *Hyakunin isshu* (One Hundred Poets, One Poem Each) and the *Ise* and to a lesser extent *The Tale of Genji*.[6] How were these courtly texts "packaged" for female consumers of the early modern period, and what can such packaging tell us about both the reception of such "classical" texts and the construction of femininity in the Tokugawa era?

The year 1608 marks the date of the publication of the *Saga-bon Ise monogatari* in movable type (*ko-katsuji*), the first example of Japanese belles lettres to appear in illustrated, printed book form (fig. 1).[7] This text went through a prodigious number of editions—especially after it was adapted to the single-block *kabuse-bori* format—and had a profound impact on all subsequent *Ise* illustrations. The original editions, however, were deluxe affairs with an extremely limited circulation.

The text was edited by Nakanoin Michikatsu (1556–1610), and the calligraphy of the *ko-katsuji* was based on that of Hon'ami Kōetsu (1558–1637), but the artist remains anonymous. The final section of Michikatsu's postscript reads:

> I was asked for a new critical and corrected edition of *The Tales of Ise*. Well, as Kyōgoku Kōmon [Teika] says in the colophon of one version: "The ancients gave various explanations about the origins of this tale and are not in agreement," and so forth. So I took the version that he gave to his granddaughter in the Tenpuku era and corrected it. Still, I fear that I have left errors in the corrections. Moreover, I have provided pictures to the two volumes based on the contents. Although these are not sufficient to move the feelings of amorous women, they will give some pleasure for the eyes of very small children.[8]

3. The story recounted in *Usuyuki monogatari* is reminiscent of tales of European courtly love. A man sees a young *buke* woman at Kiyomizu temple and falls in love with her. She is married, but he is undeterred and makes love to her anyway, insisting that such infidelities are the way of the world and studding a letter to her with references to *Ise monogatari*. See Noda 1960; Asakura 1985; and Mostow, 2009b.
4. Kornicki 2005, p. 179.
5. See Mostow 2000a.
6. For more on the role of the *Genji* in women's conduct books, see Mostow 2008, 2009a.
7. Reproductions can be found in Keyes 2006; Itō 1984; and Chino 1991a.
8. Katagiri 1981, p. 236.

Figure 1. *Saga-bon Ise monogatari* (1608), episode 1. Waseda University Library.

Visual evidence suggests that so-called *nara-ehon* versions of the *Ise* served as trousseaux objects in the late Muromachi (1392–1573) and Momoyama (1573–1603) periods. But no women appear to have been associated with *Saga-bon* production, and none of the other texts produced seems specifically designed for women. In fact, I would suggest that the *Saga-bon* edition of *Ise* represents a deliberate turning away from the text's previous association with women and their trousseaux. For example, illustrations for the first episode had previously always been set in spring (see the late Muromachi *Ono-ke-bon*), and that appears to be the case even in the *nara-ehon* closest to the *Saga-bon* in design, the *Hokuni Bunko-bon*.[9] But in the *Saga-bon*, the season has been changed to fall to resonate with the standard poetic association

9. For reproductions, see Itō 1984.

between deer and autumn foliage.[10] Such autumnal imagery is much less appropriate to the vernal celebratory mode required for trousseaux objects.

In 1609 Michikatsu edited the *Shōmonshō* (Shōhaku's Lecture Notes), a commentary on the *Ise*, for a Saga edition, but it appears to have had a limited circulation and no *kabuse-bori* exist.[11] Instead, it was commentaries on both the *Ise* and *Hyakunin isshu* by Hosokawa Yūsai (1534–1610) that achieved the greatest circulation in the Edo period. The first printed edition of Yūsai's *Hyakunin isshu* commentary, the *Yūsaishō*, appeared in 1631 and his *Ise monogatari ketsugishō* (The Commentary of Vacuous Questions) in 1634. (It was not until 1673 that a complete text with commentary edition of the *Genji*, the *Kogetsushō* [Moon over the Lake Commentary] of Kitamura Kigin, was published.) The first illustrated edition of the *Hyakunin isshu*, the *Soan-bon*, was published around 1620, analogous to the *Ise Saga-bon* in that it simply provided the text with images, in this case imaginary portraits of the poets, by an equally anonymous artist.[12]

These editions seem to have satisfied whatever market there was through the 1640s, as there appear to have been no new editions during this decade. Activity started up again in the 1650s with Yamamoto Shunshō's (1610–82) illustrated version of the *Genji*; Nonoguchi Ryūho's (1595–1669) *Jūjō Genji* (*Genji* in Ten Quires); and, in 1655, Asai Ryōi's (d. 1691) *Ise monogatari jokai* ([Waters] Drawn from the *Ise monogatari*), the first *Ise* to have both commentary and illustrations.[13] Despite this innovation, Ryōi's work was not influential. On the one hand, the illustrations simply follow the *Saga-bon*. On the other, his commentary is, according to Jamie Newhard, one of the most staunchly moralistic readings ever produced, and perhaps this is the reason why very few copies of this massive work survive.[14] Newhard suggests that the *Jokai* presents a moralistic reading of the *Ise* that is unrestricted in terms of gender; there seems to be no indication that this is a reading designed specifically for women or children, although it is very concerned with the raising of children and the propriety of the family.

The *Genji binkagami* (*Genji* Side-Lock Mirror) (fig. 2) of 1660 provides for each chapter a one-page synopsis, illustration, and haiku, among the last, as Kornicki has noted, three by women.[15] One might note in passing that there are no *chū-iri e-iri* editions of the *Genji* in the Edo period. In other words, there is no edition that presents the complete original text plus notes plus illustra-

10. Chino 1991b.
11. Newhard 2005, pp. 145–46.
12. For reproductions of the *Soan-bon*, see Mostow 1996.
13. Illustrations from Yamamoto Shunshō's version are reproduced in Seidensticker 1976.
14. Newhard 2005, p. 164. The translation of Ryōi's title is by Newhard.
15. Kornicki 2005, p. 167.

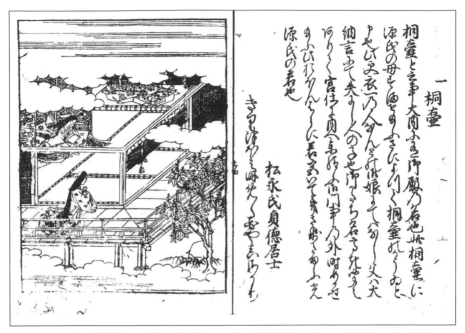

Figure 2. *Genji binkagami* (1660), "Kiritsubo." Aichi Prefectural University Library.

tions. There are either unannotated texts with illustrations, such as Yamamoto Shunshō's well-known *E-iri Genji monogatari* of 1650; paraphrases or synopses with pictures; or the text with notes but no illustrations. In the year 1660 the *Hyakunin isshu taisei* (fig. 3) was published, the first example of text, commentary, and poet-portrait; the woman in the frontispiece might suggest that this book was meant for a female readership, a question I shall return to below.

By 1670, as Kornicki has noted, booksellers' lists began to include the category of "woman books" (*josho/nyosho*).[16] Significantly, however, the court "classics" are not included in this category, and there are no editions of *Ise*, *Genji*, or the *Hyakunin isshu* in this group.

The *Ise* seems to have lagged behind in this march toward ever more popular and accessible editions. But finally, in 1674, we see the publication of what I shall term the first "plebian" commentary *and* the first illustrated and annotated edition of the *Ise*, the *Kashiragaki* (or *Tōsho*) *Ise monogatari shō* (The Tales of Ise with Headnotes).[17] The commentary is by one Sakauchi

16. Ibid., p. 160.
17. A microfilm of the text, which is owned by the Ishikawa Provincial Library, is held in the collection of the National Institute for Japanese Literature (Kokubungaku Kenkyū Shiryōkan).

Figure 3. *Hyakunin isshu taisei* (1660), frontispiece. From Ariyoshi 1994.

San'unshi (d. ca. 1711), a disenfranchised samurai who came to Kyoto in his youth to study *waka* and *haikai*. Noma Kōshin speculates that he may have had some connection to Kitamura Kigin.[18] San'unshi produced the commentary at the request of the bookseller Yamamoto Hiroyuki (Hachizaemon, active 1673–1704). San'unshi's was the first work published by Yama no Yatsu, as Yamamoto was known, whose shop became closely associated with erotica (*kōshoku-bon* and *shunga*) and actor critiques (*hyōbanki*).[19] Yama no Yatsu's inclusion of the *Ise* in his list reminds us that in Saikaku's *Kōshoku ichidai otoko* (The Man Who Loved Love, 1682), among the dildos and lubricants that Yonosuke packed on his final journey to the Isle of Women were three hundred copies of the *Ise*.[20]

In the *Ise monogatari hirakotoba* (The Tales of Ise in Plain Words) of 1678, we read in the postface that this vernacular translation has been created for "boys and girls" (*jijo*). However, as I have reported elsewhere, in his edition of the *Hirakotoba*, Imanishi Yūichirō insists that in fact these texts were not designed primarily for children but for commoner men who needed remediation in the classics so as to be able to participate in the *haikai* boom that was sweeping the country.[21] The *Hirakotoba* does appear "bowdlerized," as Richard Bowring calls it, and it may be that its author, Ki no Zankei (dates unknown) of Ōgaki, Minō Province, intended it for a juvenile audience.[22] The publisher, Kashiwaya Yo'ichirō (dates unknown), however, combined Zankei's text with the illustrations of Hishikawa Moronobu (d. 1694), and the latter most clearly have a comic intent, as seen, for example, in the frontispiece, which shows three manifestations of Narihira descending on *raigō-zu* (paradise-welcoming) clouds to bring sexual enlightenment to three aristocratic women. Moronobu's illustrations, the fact that Yama no Yatsu specialized in erotica, and Imanishi's argument about the real audience for the *Hirakotoba* all force us to take with a grain of salt declarations, verbal or visual, that insist that their texts' primary readership was children or women.

In 1678, the same year as his *Hirakotoba*, Moronobu provided illustrations for the *Hyakunin isshu zōsanshō* (One Hundred Poets with Portraits and Commentaries).[23] Again an argument against this text having been designed for women can be made on several fronts. Textually, the *Zōsanshō* is a nearly identical replica of the *Yūsaishō*, a thoroughly scholarly work with

18. *Nihon koten bungaku daijiten*, vol. 3, p. 95, s.v. "San'unshi."
19. Ibid., vol. 6, p. 96, s.v. "Yama no yatsu."
20. Screech 1999, p. 205.
21. Mostow 2003b, p. 9; Imanishi 1991, p. 384.
22. Bowring 1992, p. 478.
23. These are partially reproduced in Mostow 1996.

frequent references to Chinese texts, which thus uses language that even an educated woman might have found difficult. Visually there is evidence that at least some of Moronobu's *uta-e* derive from a *funpon* (copybook) by Kano Tan'yū (1602–74).[24] While Tan'yū's images seem to have been designed, at least partially, for *kuge* and *buke* trousseaux, we must keep class distinctions in mind.[25] Although it is true that women belonging to the highest echelon of *buke* brought deluxe copies of the *Genji, Ise, Hyakunin isshu,* and the imperially commissioned anthologies of poetry (*chokusenshū*) with them when they married, there is no evidence that this practice had yet extended to lower *buke* society, let alone to *chōnin.* The trickle down of classical culture was still largely limited to the male population. The *Onna Shoreishū* (Woman's Book of Ceremonies) of 1660 shows the kind of works included in a trousseau: *Kokin, Ise monogatari, Genji, Sagoromo, Ōgi no sōshi* (Book of Fans), *Hyakunin isshu,* and *Kasen* (the titles for all except *Hyakunin isshu* are given in kana).[26] But the class of woman addressed in this work is clearly that of a daimyo wife or daughter.

A year after his *Zōsanshō* and *Hirakotoba,* Moronobu produced his own edition of the *Kashiragaki Ise.* "Pirating" Kyoto editions was something of a regular thing for Moronobu, and we see him doing the same with Saikaku's *Kōshoku ichidai otoko.*[27] However, in all cases Moronobu replaced the illustrations with his own work. Consequently, his illustrations for the *Hirakotoba* and *Kashiragaki* were the first new visual interpretations of the *Ise* text since the *Saga-bon* seventy years earlier.

Nor was the Edo *Kashiragaki Ise* new only in terms of illustrations. Although Katagiri Yōichi claims that the commentary "follows" (*tōshū*) that of San'unshi's, there are plenty of differences.[28] For example, San'unshi's gloss for "*mukashi otoko*" is "*mukashi to yomite otoko to ku wo kirubeshi*" (which can be translated as "one should read 'in the past' and [then] 'man,' dividing the two [and not read it as '*mukashi-otoko*,' which was taken as a nickname for Narihira]"), whereas the Moronobu edition starts with a long quote from the *Shōmonshō* (1477–91) of Botanka Shōhaku (1443–1527) on the word *mukashi* alone. Clearly the Edo edition is meant for a more educated audience, which is not to say that it does not incorporate some elements of San'unshi's commentary. For example, at the end of episode 8 it also quotes a *Shin Kokinshū* (New Collection of Poems Ancient and Modern) poem by Asukai no Masatsune (1170–1221), an addition seen in none of the standard commen-

24. Ibid., pp. 416–17.
25. Mostow 2004.
26. This page of the *Onna Shoreishū* is reproduced in Trede 2003, p. 198.
27. See Mostow 1997.
28. *Ise monogatari zuroku*, vol. 2, p. 30.

taries such as those by Yūsai and Kigin. Nonetheless, the Edo edition is a considerable amplification of the Kyoto edition.

Again Katagiri insists that the *Shusho shinshō* (New Commentary with Headnotes) *Ise monogatari* of 1685, published in Edo by Izutsuya Tadaemon and others, is virtually identical in both notes and illustrations to San'unshi's and Moronobu's editions, except that this time the illustrations have been executed by Yoshida Hanbei (Sadakichi, fl. ca. 1660–92).[29] While in fact it is quite close to the San'unshi edition in its notes, the illustrations are usually closer to Moronobu's than to San'unshi's pale *Saga-bon* copies.

The San'unshi/Hanbei edition became one of the great standards of the Edo period under the title of *Shusho-iri* or *Denju-iri* (Including Secret Transmissions). Does this mean, then, that it was somehow able to transcend its *kōshoku* origins, and was it also a text given to or used by girls or women? I suspect the answer is no, at least for the former. Visually, the most striking example is episode 22. Compare the *Saga-bon* (fig. 4), San'unshi (fig. 5), Moronobu (fig. 6), and Hanbei (fig. 7), with Hanbei this time closer to the *Saga-bon*. However, Hanbei makes the analogy between the man and woman and cock and hen quite explicit, with the cock literally mounting the hen. Is this the sort of edition a father would provide his daughter? One wonders, in fact, whether the inclusion of the term *denju-iri* in the title was a gendered marker. Women, even among the aristocracy, were almost never entrusted with the "secret teachings" of the *Kokinshū* (Collection of Poems Ancient and Modern, ordered 905) or *Ise* (*Kokin* or *Ise denju*).[30] Given that *denju* were a form of patrimony, it seems to me likely that the very titles of these editions of the *Ise* may have indicated that they were not primarily intended for women.

The year 1685 was also the year of Moronobu's *Genji Yamato-ekagami* (*Genji* Mirror of Japanese Pictures), which, due to Moronobu's use of the term *nagusami* (amusement) and the fact that the copy in the British Library indicates that it was owned by a woman—at some point in time—Kornicki has suggested was "deliberately targeted at a female audience."[31] I cannot agree, however; at this point editions designed specifically for women are still about a decade away. Even Moronobu's *Sugata-e Hyakunin isshu* (Full-Figure Portraits of the One Hundred Poets), published in 1695, the year after his death, with its marked emphasis on *wakashu* (young men), is clearly

---

29. Ibid., p. 34.
30. One of the few examples I have learned of is Shimo Reizei Mochitame (b. 1401). When he died in 1454, he left his ten-year-old son Masatame (1445–1523) as heir, but the family's secret teachings were instead entrusted to Masatame's older sister. See Carter 2007, p. 157.
31. Kornicki 2005, p. 171. For reproductions, see Strauss and Bronze 1979.

Figure 4. Illustration to episode 22, in the *Saga-bon Ise monogatari* (1608). Waseda University Library.

intended for a male, and largely *buke*, audience.[32] Indeed, if one carefully examines Moronobu's pictures in his 1685 *E-kagami*, there seems to be a recurring figure that is clearly the male observer—often Genji himself—who serves as the subject position of these illustrations. Clearly we are meant to be looking over the protagonist's or male participant's shoulder, a standpoint that seems much more clearly designed for a male spectator than a female one. I would argue that the first printed edition of the *Ise* that suggests, through internal evidence, that it was designed primarily for women is the *Ise monogatari kaisei* (Revised *Ise monogatari*) of 1698. The *Kaisei* largely follows the San'unshi/Hanbei edition, but the notes at the top have been removed and replaced with supplementary texts and images. First pre-

32. See Mostow 1996, pp. 106–15, and selected reproductions. For more on *wakashu*, see Mostow 2003a.

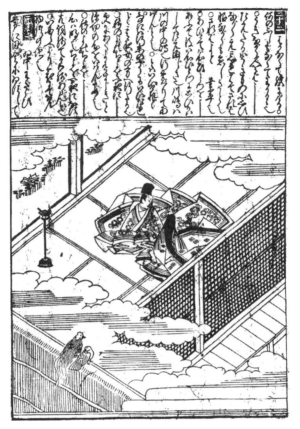

Figure 5. Sakauchi San'unshi's illustration to episode 22, in *Kashiragaki Ise mono-gatari shō* (1647). Ishikawa Prefectural Library.

sented is a drawing of a *tokonoma* with the portraits of the two saints of poetry, Hitomaro and Akahito. This is followed by an illustrated explanation of the famous poem of Soto'ori Hime—according to the Kana Preface of the *Kokinshū* the progenitor of the female line of *waka*. A picture of the Sumiyoshi shrine follows yet another depiction of the "three gods of poetry" (*waka no sanjin*). Then we have the *kanmei waka* or chapter poems of *The Tale of Genji*, followed by the *Genji-kō no zu* or *Genji* incense ciphers, and then (after two intervening poems), most significantly, the *Onna Kasen eshō*, that is, the Female Thirty-Six Poets, with one verse each, including a prose explanation and an *uta-e* (a picture illustrating the meaning of the poem).[33] It is only after all these that the standard "coed" Thirty-Six Poets appear.

33. For a reproduction of this picture, see Mostow and Mitamura 2004, p. 160.

Figure 6. Hishikawa Moronobu's illustration to episode 22, in *Kashiragaki Ise monogatari shō* (1679). Courtesy of the East Asian Library, University of California, Berkeley.

Figure 7. Yoshida Hanbei's illustration to episode 22, in the *(Denju-iri) Ise monogatari* (1685). Private collection.

Surely this favoring of the female version of this group of poets suggests a text "deliberately targeted at a female audience."

Beyond establishing that this or that particular edition was or was not designed with a female readership in mind, is there anything we can say about the *content* of the editions, that is, the kind of reading or interpretation they encouraged or enforced? Unfortunately, comparing the male-oriented *Denju* version with the female-oriented *Kaisei*, it appears not. For example, there is the treatment of the word *kaimami* (peeping). We see anxiety over this term in Yūsai's *Ketsugishō*: "It is a word common in such works as the *Genji*. It is a word that derives from the *Nihongi*. '*Kaimami*' means 'to peep through a space in a fence.' However, here, to see it as 'peeping' is not elegant, [so] it must mean 'to see through or over something' or 'to see faintly'".[34] The *Denju* gives "*Kaimami*: to see faintly" (*honoka ni mitaru*), while it is the female-oriented *Kaisei* that gives "to look through a gap in a fence" (*kaki no ma yori miru*). Arguably, it is the *Kaisei* that is less bowdlerized. (It also uses the vernacular *miru* over the classical *mitaru*.) Another example is the word *toburahi* in episode 4, which both the *Denju* and the *Kaisei* parse as "to have an illicit affair" (*mittsū suru*). The only evidence of bowdlerizing in the *Kaisei* is that the cock's leg has been erased (fig. 8)!

It is from the very end of the seventeenth century, then, that we see the boom in books designed specifically for women. The reason for this boom would seem to be due partly to wealthy *chōnin*, rich farmer, and low-ranking samurai families wanting to place their daughters in service.[35] This is suggested by the earliest *Ise* example that explicitly advertises itself for women, the *Shinpan e-iri shippō Ise monogatari daizen* (Newly Printed Illustrated Seven Treasures *Ise monogatari* Compendium) of 1708.[36] Here the upper register is given over to the "bedding that someone who serves in a palace must have" (*miyadzukahe suru hito kokorohe aru-beki shingu*) and other explanations of the rules and practices of the polite female lifestyle. This is also the case for the 1721 (*Zōho eshō*) *Kagyoku Ise monogatari* ([Enlarged Illustrated] Flower and Jewel *Ise monogatari*), which shows a young woman instructing a girl on the methods of letter folding according to the Ogasawara style.[37] Note that

---

34. Horiuchi and Akiyama 1997, p. 240
35. The *Onna Chōhōki* of 1692 was also compiled to meet the demands of girls going into service as maids (*jochū*). It includes the chapter titles of *The Tale of Genji* and their *Genji-kō* ciphers but no other excerpts or illustrations of classical literature. As G. G. Rowley suggests in her essay in this volume, knowing the chapter titles seems to have been the degree zero of familiarity with the *Genji* expected of women.
36. *Ise monogatari zuroku*, vol. 2, p. 50.
37. Ibid., pp. 54–55.

Figure 8. *Ise monogatari kaisei* (1698), episode 22. Private collection.

while there are many depictions of contemporary life in the frontispiece and upper register, the *Ise* figures are still depicted in Heian-style costume.

This orientation toward service is also seen in the 1737 *Banka Hyakunin isshu tama-bako* (Cornucopia One Hundred Poets Jewel Box), which has the subtitle *"Jochū manpō* (Ten Thousand Treasures for Maids)."[38] Nishikawa Sukenobu (1671–1750) provided the pictures for this text, but it includes no *uta-e*. These appear three years later in the 1740 *Ehon Ogura nishiki* (Picture-Book Ogura Brocade) by Okumura Masanobu (1686–1764).[39] Here, for the first time since Moronobu in 1695, *Hyakunin isshu* poets are depicted in a contemporary setting. The populating of these pictures exclusively with female *bijin* would have appealed to both a male and female audience. The text also includes humorous reworkings of the second half of the poems (*kyōka shimo no ku*).

In regard to the *Ise*, we see several simultaneous trends. One is a return to bare texts without annotation. This was apparently due to the widening of publishers' rights.[40] At the same time, the illustrations start to disengage from the text, ending up far removed from the episodes they supposedly illustrate; nor are the poems inscribed on the pictures meant to illustrate them, as was the case in the *Kaisei*. Finally, these bare texts exhibit a cloying style of illustration that suggests overwhelmingly that they were marketed to young women. One example is the *Daiji seishō Ise monogatari taisei* (Big Print Revised *Ise monogatari* Compendium) of 1753, with pictures by Terai Shigefusa (fl. 1744–64).[41] Here we still see the poems inscribed on the pictures working against the distance from their intended *dan*. But we also see them isolated, and grouped together, away from their respective episodes.

This return to *Ise* as trousseau object, or the domestication of the *Ise*'s *kōshoku* quality to serve regular matrimonial relationships, can be seen in Nishikawa Sukenobu's 1756 edition, where in the first episode the young man is no longer really confronted with two women, only one.[42] Cute illustrations and bare text were also produced by Tsukioka Tange (Settei) (1710–86) in the very same year in Osaka and later by Shimokōbe Shūsui (fl. 1764–89) in 1756 (fig. 9).[43]

---

38. Atomi 1995, pp. 220–221. It is not clear whether the term *jochū* should be taken to mean "maid" in an aristocratic or daimyo household or simply "wife" (*fujin*), a meaning that the word takes on in the early 1600s. See *Nihon kokugo daijiten*, vol. 11, s.v. *jochū*.
39. It is reproduced in *Nihon fūzoku zue* 1914.
40. Ichiko Natsuo 1996, p. 39. I am indebted to Yokota Fuyuhiko for bringing this article to my attention. This widening of publishers' rights had an effect on annotated editions. Ichiko notes the virtual disappearance of new annotated editions of *Tzurezuregusa* (Essays in Idleness) after 1701 (pp. 35–36). See also Kornicki 1998, pp. 181–82, 245–47.
41. *Ise monogatari zuroku*, vol. 2, p. 60–61.
42. Ibid., pp. 62–63.
43. Ibid., pp. 64–65.

Figure 9A. Shimokōbe Shūsui (Jūsui). *(Shinpan) Ise monogatari* (1756). Private collection.

Shūsui's text exemplifies the characteristics enumerated above: bare text, cute pictures, and the lumping together of the pictures so that they can be printed on one page, as well as the intrusion of contemporary garb. The acme of this trend is probably Katsukawa Shunshō's (1726–92) polychrome book, *Fūryū nishiki-e Ise monogatari* (Elegant Brocade-Print *Ise monogatari*) (1770–72). It seems no accident that this edition consists only of poems from the *Ise* with no inclusion of the prose text; as with the *Genji*, a fair amount of the text's lascivious quality could be elided by eliminating the poems'

Figure 9B. Shimokōbe Shūsui (Jūsui). *(Shinpan) Ise monogatari* (1756). Private collection.

contextualizing prose.[44] Shunshō's edition, as I have suggested elsewhere, has a decidedly *jokun* orientation.[45] What these characteristics suggest is that either these texts were once again trousseaux objects with little practical use intended or they were used in conjunction with an instructor, as seen in the frontispiece of Tange's 1756 *Ise monogatari* (fig. 10). By the mid–

44. See Mostow 2008.
45. Mostow 2002, pp. 37–38. Shunshō's entire work is reproduced in *Ise monogatari zuroku*, vol. 6.

Figure 10. Tsukioka Tange (Settei). *(E-iri) Ise monogatari* (1756), Woman teaching. Waseda University Library.

eighteenth century even the *Kaisei*'s minimal interlinear notes disappear. In other words, we may be witnessing the results of a widespread gradual rise in the level of female education.

As we saw above, there were few substantive differences between the glosses provided in the male-oriented San'unshi/Hanbei edition of the *Ise monogatari* and those of the *Kaisei* version. But now, with bare texts, it is impossible to discern any gender-specific reception. It is at precisely this time, however, that moralized versions of *Ise* and *Hyakunin isshu* begin to appear. Shūsui, for instance, the illustrator of the *Shinpan Ise*, also illustrated *shingaku* texts, and the 1780 *Ehon Ama-yadori* (Picture Book: Sheltered from the Rain) includes illustrations related to both *Ise* and *Hyakunin isshu* (fig. 11). The Tatsuta Mountain poem scene has by this point become an icon of wifely forbearance.

Another example of a moralized version of a classical text appears to be entitled *Joyō fukuju-dai*, or "The Foundation of Happiness and Longevity for the Use of Women" (1785), written by Takada Masanori.[46] The illustrations are by Takehara Shunchōsai (fl. 1772–92), who is known chiefly for his contributions to illustrated gazetteers of Kyoto and Kansai such as the

---

46. His other works include *Nihon shioji no ki*, or *Record of Japan's Salty Tracks* (1787), and *Gosha bakkin* or *Selected Brocade from Five Cartloads of Books* (1822).

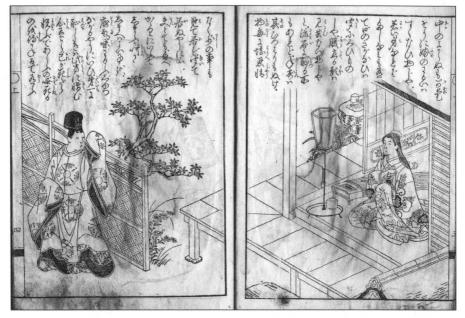

Figure 11.   Shimokōbe Shūsui. *Ehon Ama-yadori* (1780), "Tatsuta Mountain." Private collection.

Yamato meisho zue (Illustrated Landmarks of Yamato, 1791). The copy of the *Fukuju-dai* that I have found seems to be missing a quite considerable number of pages. Nonetheless, its structure remains clear: a fairly standard presentation of the *Hyakunin isshu* is followed by a selection of poems from the *Hyakunin isshu* and other sources, accompanied by commentary. What is unusual about this work is that after a generally typical paraphrase of the poem the author goes on to draw a moral lesson from the poem specifically applicable to housewives (*fujin*). So, for instance, the first poem (fig. 12), the *Hyakunin isshu* poem by Emperor Tenji, is said to relate to a housewife's ordering of her own home, and that the most important thing in this regard is to have sympathy for one's underlings, as in the illustration, which depicts the young mistress's forbearance with a clumsy maid. Among the forty-one poems extant in this section, six are from the *Ise*. Some of these, such as the exchange in episode 84 between Narihira and his aged mother, are rarely seen in other illustrated versions. But others include the famous Tatsuta Mountain poem from the continuation of episode 23. Not surprisingly, the moral of this story is that a wife should not complain even if her husband takes up with prostitutes or another woman; the wife's fidelity will bring her husband back. However, as the process of "kugefication" continued, such moralizing adaptations were no longer needed, and, as we have seen, editions designed for women presented fairly standard interpretations or none at all.

This brings us to the best-selling *Onna daigaku takara-bako* (Treasure Box of the Women's Great Learning), originally published in 1716. This was one of the most popular editions of *Onna daigaku*, attributed (incorrectly) to Kaibara Ekiken (1630–1714), and a wonderfully ironic one at that. Kornicki quotes from Ekiken's *Wazoku dōjikun* (Teachings of Japanese Ways for Children), published in 1710: "One must be selective in what one allows young women to read. . . . One should not readily allow them to read such books as *Ise monogatari*, *Genji monogatari*, and their ilk, which, although possessed of a literary elegance, depict licentious behavior."[47] Yet here, in the *Takara-bako*, we have the *kanmei waka* of each chapter of the *Genji*, with illustrations borrowed from Yamamoto Shunshō's 1650 edition. These lead *directly* to *Onna daigaku* itself, capped with repeated images of female literacy. It is followed by the entire *Hyakunin isshu*, with *uta-e* in the top register, stories about Chinese paragons of virtue in the middle register, and

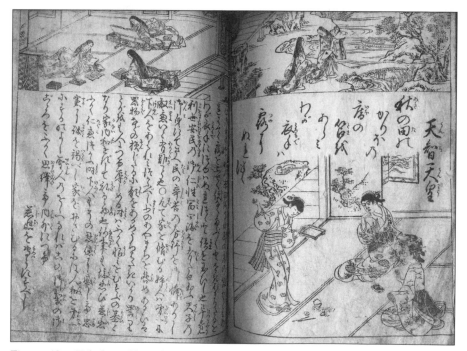

Figure 12.   Takehara Shunchōsai, illus. *Joyō Fukuju-dai* (1785), "*Aki no ta no.*" Private collection.

47. Kornicki 2005, p. 158. The translation is from Rowley 2000, p. 31.

in the lower register a text called *Yotsugigusa* (Grasses of Succession), by Suzuki Shigetane (1812–63), which, according to Sasaki Kiyoshi, proclaimed the sanctity of life and expressed deep distress at the practice of abortion and infanticide.[48] By Yokota Fuyuhiko's calculation, less than half of *Takara-bako* is devoted to morally uplifting items such as the *Onna daigaku*, or "The Twenty-four Chinese Exemplars of Filial Piety" (*nijūshi kō*), and a full 20 percent is given over to items of literary education such as the *Genji* and *Hyakunin isshu*.[49] Moreover, Janine Sawada notes that "as a single work, *Onna daigaku* in block-print form dates only from 1790," and the *Takara-bako* is in fact the oldest printed edition.[50] Moral medicine apparently required quite a bit of sugarcoating!

But where, amid all this, is the *Ise*? There is not one text or image in this edition of the *Takara-bako* that refers to it. And if we look at "the catalog of books profitable for maids to read" (*jochū no mi-tamahi eki aru shomotsu mokuroku*), of the sixty-seven titles listed, thirteen are editions of the *Hyakunin isshu* or include it; six include the *Genji* in some fashion; and only four include the *Ise*. Among these are two editions of the *Ise*, one with the *Kokinshū* and one with the *Usuyuki monogatari*. There appears to be not one annotated edition of the *Ise*. An examination of other massive compendia for women yields similar results. The hundreds of pages of the *Jokyō manpō zensho Azuma kagami* (Women's Education Ten-Thousand-Treasure Complete Eastern Mirror) first published in 1829 and reprinted into the Meiji period, find space for the *Kokin rokkasen*, *Genji-kō no zu*, *Ōmi hakkei* (Eight Views of Ōmi), *Jūni tsuki imyō narabi waka* (Variant Names for the Twelve Months with Poems), *Sanjūrokkasen eshō* (Pictorial Commentary of the *Thirty-six Immortal Poets*), *Hyakunin isshu*, *Onna sanjūrokkasen eshō*, *Kyōkun iroha-uta taiga* (Educational ABC Poem with Corresponding Pictures), *Nana Komachi-zu no eika* (Compositions on Pictures of the Seven Komachis), and *Roku Tamagawa no waka onajiku zu* (Poems on the Six Tama Rivers with Pictures as Well) but room for only two images from the *Ise*—hardly "*zensho*" at all. The Meiji-produced *(Nichiyō takara-kagami) Kijo no shiori* ([Daily-Use Treasure-Mirror] Lady's Bookmark) (Meiji 28/1895) still finds room for the *Genji-kō no zu* and *Hyakunin isshu* amid home economics, world geography, and practical English but has no room for the *Ise*. In short, it would appear that by the late Edo-period the *Ise* had been largely dropped from women's education at the most general level, represented by the compendia listed above, slipping between the floorboards of the *Genji* and the *Hyakunin isshu*. As seen in the

48. Sasaki Kiyoshi 2000.
49. Yokota 1995, p. 365.
50. Sawada 1993, p. 183.

Jokyō manpō zensho Azuma kagami, the only scenes or episodes regularly encountered in late Edo period texts for or by women are the "Tatsuta Mountain," and Narihira and Mount Fuji from the "Azuma-kudari" episode.[51]

There were, of course, specific reasons for the continued, and in fact increased, popularity of the *Genji* and *Hyakunin isshu*. For the former, there was Ryūtei Tanehiko's (1783–1842) *Nise Murasaki inaka Genji* (Phony Murasaki, Bumpkin Genji) of 1829–42, illustrated by Utagawa Kunisada (1786–1864). For the latter, there was the wildly popular 1833 *Hyakunin isshu hitoyo-gatari* (Nightlong Stories about the One Hundred Poets), which led to a veritable *Hyakunin isshu* boom with *nishiki-e* (polychrome wood-block print) series by Hokusai, Kuniyoshi, and Kunisada. It should be noted, however, that the *Genji* had not in fact been especially popular before Tanehiko and Kunisada's intervention; as pointed out by G. G. Rowley, no new printed edition of the complete *Genji* appeared between 1706 and 1890.[52] And, while copies of Kigin's *Kogetsushō* may have been available, Richard Bowring notes that in 1696 a copy "was selling for well over twenty times what it cost to buy a work of contemporary fiction, well beyond the reach of the average reading public."[53] As Rowley concludes, throughout most of the Edo period "demand for printed editions of other works in the classical canon, particularly *Kokinshū*, *Ise monogatari*, and *Tsurezuregusa*, seems to have been far greater than demand for *Genji*."[54] In other words, the *Genji* was in general little read by all but scholars, and, despite the inclusion of its chapter-title poems in most texts for female education, there were no editions of it produced specifically for women.

On the other hand, if the *Ise* was omitted from texts for women, we can also discern a certain "masculinization" in its reception in the late Edo period. The only new wood-block edition of note is the *Ise monogatari zue* (Illustrated *Ise monogatari*) of 1825 by Ichioka Takehiko (d. 1827) and illustrated by Gyokuzan (1737–1812). Takehiko was a student of Motoori Norinaga (1730–1801), and one can sense a certain *kokugaku* (national learning) quality to the *Zue*. For example, since the reign of Tokugawa Ieyasu (1542–1616) the shogunate had forbidden the aristocracy to hunt, maintaining it as a prerogative of the shogun and daimyos. While showing Narihira hunting on horseback had not been uncommon in Muromachi-Momoyama depictions of episode 1, such depictions disappear in the Edo period until the *Zue*,

---

51. Indeed, as the research of Laura Nenzi makes clear, women traveling along the Tōkaidō regularly invoke the "Azuma-kudari" in their travel accounts. See Nenzi 2008.
52. Rowley 2000, p. 23.
53. Bowring 1988, p. 92, cited in Rowley 2000, p. 23.
54. Rowley 2000, p. 23.

suggesting a degree of reassertion of the martial qualities of the *kuge*.[55] In tandem, a political interpretation of the *Ise* can also be seen on the stage. Plays about Prince Koretaka (844–97), in the form of an *o-ie sōdō mono*, or "great family dispute drama," first appear in 1775 and are revived in the 1820s.[56]

By contrast, the *Hyakunin isshu* stays central to women's education and beyond. One can suggest three reasons for this. First, as noted by Koizumi Yoshinaga, the *Hyakunin isshu* was a fundamental part of female education, frequently produced in the *ōrai* format and specifically designed for girls. However, as he cautions, and as the *senryū* has it, *Imagawa ha chichi, Hyakunin isshu haha oshie*, that is, it was the mother of the household who taught the *Hyakunin isshu*, but she taught it to both her sons and her daughters.[57] Certainly *karuta*, too, with its courtly connection, has something to do with the *Hyakunin isshu*'s continued popularity, although one must note that there were card versions of the *Genji* and *Ise* as well. The third way the *Hyakunin isshu* stayed culturally relevant was through *ishu hyakunin isshu*, or "Variant One Hundred Poets," of which Senryū V (Ryokutei Senryū, 1787–1858) made something of a one-man industry throughout the 1840s and 1850s, often illustrated by Katsushika Hokusai (1760–1849) and others such as Kunisada.

We have seen that there were debates in the early Edo period about the appropriateness of the *Genji* and *Ise* as reading material for women, but I know of only one case in which bowdlerized versions of either text were made.[58] However, in the Meiji period at least two versions of the *Hyakunin isshu* were produced that specifically removed all the love poems and replaced them with seasonal verses. According to Iwai Shigeki, criticism of love poetry actually started in the late Edo period, but it became fully entrenched in the Meiji period.[59] Certainly, as far as I know, there are no love poems among the tens of thousands written by Emperor Meiji.

The other reason for the censoring of the *Hyakunin isshu* was that *karuta* were now being played in public in coeducational groups. It was the idea of young men and women reading suggestive verses *together* that was the problem.[60] The predominant image of the game being played, however, remains thoroughly feminine, though less and less lively, as seen in the frequent

---

55. The picture is reproduced in Mostow and Mitamura 2004, p. 165.
56. *Ise* motifs appear in various *haikai* collections, but again the motifs are limited to an extremely few and hackneyed number, as in, for example, *Ise monogatari e-iri haikai higagoto shū* (1831). See *Ise monogatari zuroku*, vol. 8, pp. 46–47.
57. Koizumi 2005, p. 66.
58. Goi Ranshū (1697–1762) produced *Seigotsū* (Understanding the *Ise*) for his daughter, excising all but 47 of the *Ise*'s 125 episodes. See Newhard 2005, pp. 262–79.
59. Iwai 2005, p. 47.
60. Ibid., pp. 48–51. I have never, however, seen any example of these bowdlerized versions in *karuta* form.

treatment of this theme by Miyakawa Shuntei (1873–1914).[61] At some point, coeducational meets must have been banned; today the annual competition is divided by gender. In the twentieth century, *ishu hyakunin isshu karuta*, or "variant One Hundred Poets card sets," such as those based on the poems of Emperor Meiji, made their appearance in the Taishō period, capped by the infamous *Aikoku* (Patriotic) *hyakunin isshu* of 1943 (fig. 13). Presumably during the Pacific War there were no complaints about the love poems in the Ogura version. A Shōwa 13/1938 cartoon (fig. 14) reads, "karuta-kai ni mo hyaku-pāsento gunkokuchō" (Even at the card meet, 100 percent in uniform), referring to the women as well as the men.

The *Ise*, on the other hand, is given a new lease on life in the Meiji period; Narihira is declared a patriot who supported the proper candidate for emperor against the usurping Fujiwara.[62] But the *Ise* is still banned from the educational curriculum. And it is not returned to women until the Taishō period, when, to the best of my knowledge, the first commentary written by a woman (Kobayashi Eiko, 1871–1952) appears, as well as a modern translation by Yoshii Isamu (1886–1960), with illustrations by Takehisa Yumeji (1884–1934).[63]

Conclusion

I have focused on the way three classical texts—the *Ise monogatari*, *Hyakunin isshu*, and, to a lesser extent, *Genji monogatari*—were made available to and for female readers in Japan from the seventeenth through the nineteenth centuries. The *Hyakunin isshu* was a fundamental part of feminine education from the late seventeenth century onward. Throughout the Edo period both bare and annotated texts, mostly illustrated, are produced, and the anthology is included in compendia for women well into the late nineteenth century. It was not until the Meiji period that there seemed to be any concern about the moral qualities—or lack thereof—of its poems.

The *Ise monogatari* followed a very different trajectory. As soon as it was published in the mid–seventeenth century, along with the *Genji* it was embroiled in debates about its appropriateness for female readers. The increasing importance of *waka* as a feminine accomplishment across a widening social spectrum, however, meant that this debate was largely occluded by the mid–eighteenth century. Despite the arguments against the appropriateness

---

61. For a biographical sketch of Shuntei, see Merritt and Yamada 2000.
62. Mostow 2000a.
63. On the former, see ibid., pp. 105–6. On the latter, see Mostow 2000b, pp. 93–95.

Figure 13.   Anonymous, Nihon Bungaku Hōkokkai, ed. *Aikoku Hyakunin isshu*. Osaka: Hakusuisha, 1943. Private collection.

Figure 14.   Sakuma Shirō. "Hijōji no haru," Japanese weekly (January 1938).

of *Ise* as a book for women, annotated editions of the text were produced in large quantities in the first half of the Edo period, and illustrated editions catering to a specifically female market continued to be produced throughout the eighteenth century. However, the *Ise* seems to have gradually disappeared from the female curriculum by the beginning of the nineteenth century. This decline is also seen in the way episodes and motifs from the *Ise* feature less and less frequently in women's didactic texts. Meanwhile, the *Genji monogatari* was for the most part either reduced to a collection of the fifty-four poems associated with its chapter titles or known almost exclusively through the parody by Tanehiko with its amazingly popular illustrations by Kunisada. In short, while the *Hyakunin isshu* remained, like flower arranging, fundamental knowledge with which a woman could present herself as feminine and cultured, female readers would have to wait until the Taishō period and such vernacular translations as Yosano Akiko's *Shin'yaku Genji monogatari* (A New Translation of the *Genji*) of 1912–13 or Ishii and Takehisa's 1917 translation of the *Ise* to make these texts once again their own.

4

The Woman Reader as Symbol: Changes in Images of the Woman Reader in Ukiyo-e

Itasaka Noriko

It is well known that in the Heian period male bureaucrats were required to have extensive familiarity with Chinese canonical texts, while women's reading was for the most part confined to poetry, Buddhist texts, educational works for their children, and the fictional literature known as *monogatari*.[1] In this and the succeeding periods, however, it needs to be remembered that women readers were confined to the highest classes of society. It was only in the Edo period, when educational institutions for commoners became widespread and the literacy rate began to rise, that commoner women acquired the leisure to read and the habit of reading. The woman reader soon began to feature in art, and in this essay I propose to consider how the image of the woman reader as it appeared in ukiyo-e, pictures of the floating world, changed over the course of the Edo period.

Before the Edo period, painters had not sought to present an accurate image of something directly visible but instead incorporated conventional mechanisms and styles of depiction in their works. By the seventeenth

---

1. As Minamoto no Tamenori wrote in *The Three Jewels* (*Sanbōe*, 984), "There are the so-called *monogatari*, which have such an effect on the ladies' hearts" (Kamens 1988, p. 93).

century, however, historical or imaginary subject matter was giving way to contemporary urban scenes as depicted by urban artists. Thus did ukiyo-e come into being with a new focus on representing changing social mores, including the minute details of everyday life. Needless to say, other impulses such as idealization, fictionalization, and the creation of designs for visual effect were also at work, but these, too, allow us to glimpse contemporary visual values.

Reading women were depicted by a huge number of artists, including Hishikawa Moronobu (d. 1694) in Edo and Nishikawa Sukenobu (1671–1750) in Kyoto in the early history of ukiyo-e, and by other artists right up to the end of the nineteenth century. Given that the term ukiyo-e covers both paintings and prints, to say nothing of illustrations in printed books, the quantity of depictions is enormous. In this essay I shall focus on a database of some three hundred ukiyo-e single-sheet prints from which the main features and trends can be identified. Illustrations found in conduct books for women and in fictional works will not be considered here.[2]

Ukiyo-e depictions of reading women and women with books seem to fall easily into three periods. The first covers the period stretching from the works of Hishikawa Moronobu and Nishikawa Sukenobu up to but not including the work of Suzuki Harunobu (1725–70); during this period colorful paintings were produced, but prints were predominantly in black and white. The second period covers the decades from the emergence of Harunobu to the work of Kitagawa Utamaro (1753–1806) at the end of the eighteenth century when color prints came into their own. And the third covers the activities of the Kitao School, Tōshūsai Sharaku (fl. 1794–95), Katsushika Hokusai (1760–1849), and the Utagawa School for the remainder of the Edo period and the beginning of the Meiji period when ukiyo-e achieved their highest level of social penetration. This tripartite division mirrors that often used for ukiyo-e as a whole, but it has its own justification in the decisive shifts in the depiction of women reading that we can identify when surveying the whole range of depictions from the seventeenth to the nineteenth centuries.

The Early Period

During the seventeenth century many images of women reading are to be found in illustrated books, but the depictions are for the most part closely associated with *waka* poetry. Take, for example, Moronobu's *Bijin ezukushi* (Pictures of Beautiful Women, 1683), in which the poet Ise (ca. 877–ca. 940)

---

2. On illustrations in fiction, see Itasaka 2006.

has a book open in front of her on a desk as she gazes into the garden, while Sei Shōnagon (ca. 966–ca. 1017), compiler of the *Pillow Book* (*Makura no sōshi*, ca. 1001), is depicted indoors with other women and they have a book open in front of them. In *Bijin ezukushi*, the images of the women occupy the lower half of the pages, leaving the upper half for their poems and explanations of who they are. The women are shown wearing costumes approximating to those of the Heian period, but, with the exception of conduct books for women, this kind of historicizing approach is not common. Gradually it became the norm to depict women in the contemporary costume of the seventeenth century. For example, in Moronobu's *Sugata-e hyakunin isshu* (Portraits of the One Hundred Poets, 1695; fig. 15), the upper part gives a poem from the *Hyakunin isshu* (One Hundred Poets, One Poem Each, ca. 1230)

Figure 15. "Sagami" from Hishikawa Moronobu's *Sugata-e hyakunin isshu* (1695). Private collection.

anthology together with a commentary, while the lower part depicts the poet Sagami (fl. ca. 1050) as a beauty in contemporary fashions and reading with a young girl.

It should be noted that Sagami is reading with the book balanced on her knee, which is a common pose depicted in the seventeenth century and seems intended to indicate a relaxed mode of reading. In the scene supposed to show Fujiwara no Okikaze (fl. ca. 900), he, too, is reading in the same pose. But the important point is that they are depicted with all the appearance of figures from the Edo period, and this increasingly became the usual mode of depiction. Thus in Okumura Masanobu's (1686–1764) *Ehon Ogura nishiki* (Picture Book of Ogura Brocade, 1740), the illustration for a poem by Ōnakatomi Yoshinobu (921–91) shows a woman leaning out of a mosquito net reading a book by the light of fireflies, and she is unmistakably presented in terms of dress and hairstyle as a woman of the Edo period. The same transformation is seen in single-sheet prints as well. In Masanobu's print "Ukiyo Suma" (Suma of the Floating World), Murasaki Shikibu (973?–1014?), looking out onto Lake Biwa from her desk, is shown as a contemporary beauty. The rejection of historicism for contemporary styles and fashions even in parodic *mitate* pictures supposedly based on scenes from the past is to be found not only in ukiyo-e but in fact in all Japanese painting of the Edo period.[3]

As Joshua S. Mostow has shown in his essay in this volume, *Hyakunin isshu* had a close connection with illustrated books for women produced in the seventeenth and early eighteenth centuries. A painting by Torii Kiyomasu II (1694–1716) reflects this with its depiction of a young girl standing on a veranda and reading an illustrated edition of *Hyakunin isshu* (fig. 16).

What kind of woman is being depicted in these early representations of reading women and what are they reading? In Moronobu's *Wakoku hyakujo* (One Hundred Women of Japan, 1695), we see high-ranking women of a daimyo household reading books such as *Kokinshū* (Collection of Poems Ancient and Modern, ca. 905), *The Tale of Genji*, and *Tales of Ise* while the daimyo himself is away from home.[4] Similarly, in Sukenobu's *Hyakunin jorō shinasadame* (One Hundred Women Classified according to Their Rank, 1723), the wife of a high-ranking samurai has a book in front of her and a daimyo's daughter is looking at a book on the floor (fig. 17).

On the other hand, far more frequently depicted are courtesans, particularly in colorful paintings. Thus in "Ensaki sugakaki no zu" (Playing Music on the Veranda) by Okumura Toshinobu (1709–43), a courtesan is

3. For a definition and discussion of *mitate-e*, literally "look and compare pictures," see http://www.viewingjapaneseprints.net/texts/topictexts/faq/faq_mitate.html (accessed 9 May 2009).
4. Illustrated in Kornicki 2005, p. 169.

playing the samisen with a songbook on her knee. Similarly, in Nishimura Shigenaga's (1697–1756) triptych "Utsutsu no asobi" (Real World Pastimes, n.d.), two out of the three courtesans shown have books on the floor in front of them, and in Sukenobu's series *Hyakunin jorō shinasadame*, too, there is a scene showing courtesans leafing through books. In other words, at this stage reading and the presence of books are associated with courtesans and

Figure 16.   Painting by Torii Kiyomasu II of a young girl reading *Hyakunin isshu*. Private collection.

the women of daimyo and aristocratic households. It might be supposed that this is naturally because they were the only kinds of women to appear in ukiyo-e, but that is not so; *Wakoku hyakujo* and *Hyakunin jorō shinasadame* both depict many other kinds of women, though rarely in the act of reading.[5] Rather than courtesans and high-class women representing opposite extremes, however, Nakano Setsuko has argued that in women's conduct books "the manners and lifestyle of aristocratic women were idealized and retained their traditional distinctiveness alongside the manners and lifestyle of courtesans".[6] Thus aristocratic women, daimyo women, *and* courtesans were all appropriated as glamorous representatives of womanhood.

But are the women depicted in ukiyo-e really representative of the women they are supposed to be? It might be objected that the poses of those depicted in *Wakoku hyakujo*, for example, are too slovenly, even though the daimyo is away from home. Recall, however, that urban artists such as Moronobu cannot be supposed to have been blessed with opportunities

Figure 17. Scene from Nishikawa Sukenobu's *Hyakunin jorō shinasadame* (1723). Private collection.

5. In works such as the print "Shikishi tanzaku-uri," attributed to Masanobu, in which a woman is shown peddling books and *tanzaku* (rectangular strips of paper or card stock used for writing poems), it is clear that women are being imagined in male roles rather than being shown in roles that women actually undertook.
6. Nakano 1997, p. 86.

to glimpse the private lives of upper-class women; these scenes are surely imagined rather than drawn from life. Similarly, the courtesans are so gorgeously appareled that it is difficult to distinguish them from other women, and that suggests the possibility that the depictions of daimyo women and aristocratic women are in fact modeled on courtesan fashions—and perhaps even manners, too—not the other way around.

When it is possible to identify the books the women are depicted reading, either from the accompanying text or from the illustrations themselves, they mostly consist of collections of *waka* poetry, particularly the *Hyakunin isshu*, and various *monogatari* such as *The Tale of Genji*. In other words, the focus is on the kind of books that for several hundred years had been held up as those that a young woman with social rank ought to study in order to acquire the desired level of familiarity with Japanese literary traditions. Courtesans are depicted either with these books or with musical scores or songbooks. Furthermore, it is noticeable that women are depicted reading in relaxed rather than formal postures, and in some cases books are piled up in alcoves (*tokonoma*) or on the floor, conveying the impression of cultured women who not only read but also possess their own books.

The Middle Period

The development of the use of color, hitherto confined to ukiyo-e paintings, in the prints of Suzuki Harunobu ushered in a shift from black and white ukiyo-e to the polychrome *nishikie*, and the entrepreneurship of Tsutaya Jūzaburō (1748–97) led to the publication of luxurious color-printed albums. Reading women in the ukiyo-e of this period are dominated by courtesans of the Yoshiwara licensed quarter, particularly in the case of albums in which a *waka* poem or haiku is attached to each courtesan. Tomikawa Fusanobu's (fl. 1750–80) album *Hana yosooi* (Dressed in Flowers, 1765) is a pre-*nishikie* work with black and white illustrations, but here one hundred courtesans are depicted, of whom fourteen are reading a book.[7] The courtesan Michinoku is reading the *Kokinshū*, Kikuzono the *Shinkokinshū* (ca. 1205), and Hitoe *Essays in Idleness* (*Tsurezuregusa*, ca. 1330); it is not clear what Azumaya is reading, but behind her are boxes containing *The Tale of Genji*, the late-fourteenth-century historical chronicle *Taiheiki*, and the first eight imperial anthologies of *waka* poetry (the so-called *hachidaishū*, comprising *Kokinshū* through *Shinkokinshū*). Other courtesans are looking at songbooks. They are all depicted reading books that relate either to the musical skills

7. See the facsimile in Satō 2006.

they are supposed to have among their accomplishments or to their literary pretensions.

Harunobu's *Ehon seirō bijin awase* (Picture Book: Competition of Bordello Beauties, 1770) furnishes some examples in full color; here 166 Yoshiwara courtesans are depicted with haiku they are supposed to have written, and eleven of them have books in their hands. The books in question are *The Tale of Genji* in the case of Tokiwado, *Essays in Idleness* in the case of Chiyozuru, and the imperial anthology of *waka* poetry *Fūgashū* (ca. 1349) in the case of Nishikigi, while once again others have songbooks in their hands. Thus the appearance is one of the continuation of age-old reading tastes and practices. Nonetheless, there are some striking exceptions. Utagawa is reading Hiraga Gennai's (1728–79) satiric novel *Nenashigusa* (Rootless Weeds, 1763), Agemaki is reading Harunobu's own recently published *Ehon fukujin ukiyobukuro* (Picture Book of a Floating World Bag of Lucky Gods, 1770), and Morokoshi is reading a Yoshiwara handbook, the *Yoshiwara taizen* (Yoshiwara Compendium, 1768). In all these cases, then, courtesans are depicted with the latest reading matter. This was not, however, a line followed in *Seirō bijin awase sugata kagami* (Bordello Beauties Compared in a Mirror, 1777), an album jointly produced by Kitao Shigemasa (1739–1820) and Katsukawa Shunshō (1726–93) (fig. 18).

Here the courtesans are reading *Kokinshū,* as well as other anthologies of *waka* poetry, *Kinjitsushō* (probably a book of koto music), and *Kogetsushō* (1673), Kitamura Kigin's edition of *The Tale of Genji* with selections from the major commentaries. In all, of the forty-three scenes in this book, eleven either depict courtesans reading or show books among the objects near the courtesans. Whereas Harunobu had reflected current reading, the focus here is on traditional reading matter. This is also true of single-sheet prints, such as Isoda Koryūsai's (1735–90) series *Hinagata wakana no hatsu moyō* (Models of Fashion: New Designs as Fresh as Young Leaves, 1776–84), in which Michinoku of the Tsutaya is depicted reading the *Hyakunin isshu.*

In this period we see not only courtesans reading but also new types of women such as those from samurai households or from the upper reaches of the merchant class. For example, in Harunobu's print "Zashiki hakkei: Kotoji no rakugan" (Eight Indoor Views: Descending Geese over Koto Bridges, ca. 1766) a maid in a samurai household has a book of music for the koto open in front of her, and in his "Eika (*mitate* Murasaki Shikibu)" (Murasaki Shikibu Writing Poetry, ca. 1767) a young girl is represented as Murasaki Shikibu facing Lake Biwa, and on the desk lies a copy of *Meidai waka zenshū* (Complete Collection of Poems That Clarify Topics, fifteenth century), a popular anthology first printed about 1660 and subsequently re-

Figure 18.   Katsurano reading *Kinjitsushō*, from *Seirō bijin awase sugata kagami* (1777).
Private collection.

printed many times throughout the Edo period. In Shunshō's series of twelve
ukiyo-e paintings showing women in different months of the year, which
bears the title *Fujo fūzoku jūnikagetsu zu* (Pictures of Women Attired for the
Twelve Months, 1783) and of which ten are preserved in the Museum of Art
in Atami, books are shown in three of the paintings. In *The Fourth Month* a
copy of the eleventh-century *Tale of Flowering Fortunes* (*Eiga monogatari*) lies
close to a girl in her bedchamber, in *The Fifth Month* several girls have books
in their hands, and in *The Eleventh Month* a woman in a *kotatsu* is showing a
cheap picture book to a child. In another painting by Shunshō (fig. 19), two
women are reading *The Tale of Genji* using a pointer in what appears to be a
reading lesson.

 In some cases more everyday scenes are depicted. In Kitao Shigemasa's
black and white album *Ehon yotsu no toki* (Picture Book of the Four Seasons, 1773) there are four scenes showing women with books, and in one of

them books and clothes are being hung out to air, a traditional practice that helped prevent insect infestation. A similar scene is depicted by Shunshō in a painting entitled *Woman Airing Books and Clothes* (n.d.) in the Freer Gallery, and there the women are reading the books as they hang them up to air.

As mentioned above, the eleventh-month scene in Shunshō's set of paintings shows a woman with the sort of cheap picture book generically known

Figure 19.   Painting by Katsukawa Shunshō. The original is in the Tokyo National Museum but shown here is a later copy from a private collection.

as a *kusazōshi*. It seems that the earliest depiction of this kind of mass-market book in ukiyo-e is to be found in a print from Torii Kiyonaga's (1752–1815) series *Hakone shichitō meisho* (Seven Hot Springs of Hakone, 1783; fig. 20).

It shows a woman reading a recently published work of light fiction in the genre known as *kibyōshi*, namely, Iba Kashō's (d. 1783) *Bakemono hakoiri*

Figure 20. "Kiga" from Torii Kiyonaga's series *Hakone shichitō meisho* (1783). Private collection.

musume (Ghostly Well Brought Up Daughters, 1781), for which Kiyonaga himself had provided the illustrations; he is clearly advertising one of his own works in this print. The important point, however, is that reading is represented here no longer as a form of cultural education but rather as a pleasurable activity to be enjoyed in one's spare time such as at a hot springs resort. In a similar way, in a single-sheet print entitled "Rokkasen Henjō" (Six Immortal Poets: The Monk Henjō, ca. 1788), Hosoda Eishi (1756–1829) shows young women in leisurely poses reading light fiction on their knees, and Kitagawa Utamaro, in his series *Edo kōmei bijin* (Famous Beauties of Edo, 1792-93), depicts a young beauty called O-chie reading light fiction as a token of her up-to-date sensitivity to the tastes of her age.

In this period, then, it is courtesans that predominate among the reading women depicted in ukiyo-e. They have replaced the aristocratic and high-ranking samurai women of the early period, who are now rarely to be found. Some merchant-class women are depicted, too, but mostly they are shown with maids in attendance and are clearly intended to be far removed from the world of the ordinary town dwellers. Like their forebears, courtesans, too, are mostly shown reading works of classical literature or songbooks, which were all part of the essential training of those who aspired to high rank in the profession. Nevertheless, the message is clear. Book reading is no longer an elite activity, and nothing makes this clearer than the occasional appearance, in the hands of women readers, of contemporary fiction, books about the Yoshiwara licensed quarter, and other ephemeral works published in Edo.

The Later Period

In this period the figure of the reading woman appears in the works of the Utagawa School, Toyokuni (1769–1825), Kunisada (1786–1865), and Kunichika (1835–1900), and in the works of Kikugawa Eizan (1787–1867) and Keisai Eisen (1790–1848). Reading women do not appear particularly frequently in the works of Katsushika Hokusai (1760-1849), and, as might be guessed from his preferred subject matter—landscape—they are rarely to be found in the works of Utagawa Hiroshige (1797–1858). Courtesans and songbooks continue to appear, as in two of Keisai Eisen's series, *Yoshiwara hakkei* (Eight Views of the Yoshiwara) and *Keisei Edo hōgaku* (Courtesans of Edo in All Directions), both produced during the Bunsei era, 1818–30, in which the courtesan Shichinin appears with a samisen and a songbook. In his later series *Edo onkyoku uta awase* (Song Contest of Edo Tunes, Tenpō era, 1830–44), many music books are featured, as the title suggests.[8] Collections of *waka* poetry and other works of classical literature continue to feature, too. Toyokuni's triptych *Hatsuyume* (First Dream of the Year, ca. 1801) shows a courtesan dreaming her first dream of the new year with a copy of *The Tale of Genji* on the desk beside her while the younger courtesan close by is looking at what appears to be the *Hyakunin isshu* contained in a conduct book for women. Katsukawa Shunkō's painting *Kinki shoga zu* (The Four Accomplishments, 1806) shows a courtesan writing a *waka* poem with *Kogetsushō* on her desk.[9] And Kitao Masayoshi's (1764–1824) painting *Waka o yomu bijin zu* (Beauty Composing *Waka*, 1806, Freer Gallery) shows a similar scene with what appear to be books of *waka* poetry on the desk. It is perhaps significant, however, that such scenes are now more commonly to be found in paintings rather than printed ukiyo-e.

In this period fictional works are much more likely to be the object of a reading woman's attention. Chōbunsai Eishi's (1756–1829) series *Shichikenjin ryaku bijin shinzō-zoroi* (Beautiful Apprentices as the Seven Sages of the Bamboo Grove, 1795) contains a print showing a courtesan called Tokiuta and her apprentice reading works of popular fiction, and similar scenes are to be found in the works of Kikugawa Eizan, for example, in a print in his series *Fūryū hokku gosekku* (Four Courtesans in Festival Garb, ca. 1810), where the courtesan is reading standing up, and in his triptych *Seirō bijin haru no tamakura* (Bordello Beauties: Spring Pillow Sleeves, ca. 1804–18), where several young courtesans are killing time with books, including what seem to be popular works of current fiction. Some paintings also show more contemporary reading tastes such as Chōbunsai Eishi's *Yoshiwara jūnidoki emaki* (Twelve Hours of the Yoshiwara Picture Scroll, ca. 1804–18, Ōta Kinen Bijutsukan).

Ordinary merchant-class girls loom much larger in nineteenth-century ukiyo-e. As the following few examples show, the books they are shown reading cover all the categories so far mentioned. Kikugawa Eizan's series *Azuma sugata Genji awase* (Genji Match in the Eastern Style, 1818) includes one print entitled "Momiji no ga" (Festival of Autumn Leaves, fig. 21) in which a young woman is sitting by a lamp engrossed in an *Itchū-bushi* songbook. *Itchū-bushi* was a style of *jōruri* singing much in vogue at this time; other styles, such as *Shinnai-bushi*, were also popular. The ability to perform

---

8. For translations of the titles of this and other Yoshiwara-related materials, I am indebted to Seigle 1993.
9. See Yamaguchi 1982, plate 32. The present location of this painting is not stated. The "four accomplishments" are calligraphy, painting, playing the koto, and playing the game of go.

Figure 21. In "Momiji no ga" from the series *Azuma sugata Genji awase* (1818) by Kikugawa Eizan, a young woman is engrossed in an Itchū-bushi songbook. Private collection.

jōruri was a useful one for girls seeking a position in service and it was common for parents in the nineteenth century to make sure that their daughters possessed this skill. Such accomplishments were therefore something that courtesans and ordinary city girls had in common.

Scenes showing ordinary young women reading works of classical literature are not common, but there are some showing older women. One example depicting a younger woman is a painting by Hokusai in the possession of the Cincinnati Art Museum, *Ensō no bijin* (Beautiful Girl at a Round Window, ca. 1805).[10] Rather more common are prints reflecting the quantities of conduct books and similar sorts of semieducational books that flooded the market in the nineteenth century. Utamaro's five-sheet print "Gosekku" (Five Seasonal Festivals, ca. 1785), for example, shows a young girl with *Onna daigaku* open in front of her.[11]

There is no gainsaying the fact that in the nineteenth century the various genres of vernacular fiction known at the time as *gesaku* appeared with ever greater frequency in ukiyo-e, depicted in scenes where women are toying with books or reading them. Kunisada, for example, produced many prints of this kind such as the one shown in figure 22.

A particularly interesting example is Utagawa Sadakage's (fl. 1818–44) triptych *Edo jiman bijinzoroi* (Pride of Edo: Gathering of Beauties, 1831), in which a young girl is shown with a copy of the latest part of Ryūtei Tanehiko's (1783–1842) enormously popular serial novel *An Imposter Murasaki and a Rustic Genji* (*Nise Murasaki inaka Genji*, 1829–42). Another version of this triptych, *Edo jiman zenseizoroi* (Pride of Edo: Gathering of Stars, 1831), shows the same scene only with popular courtesans instead of young girls, and this makes it clear that when it comes to reading there is little difference between the treatment of courtesans and the treatment of ordinary young women in prints. Keisai Eisen made several prints showing ordinary young women reading or handling books; in one a girl is handing a child a volume, and

---

10. For examples of scenes containing *The Tale of Genji* and other classical literature, see Chōbunsai Eishi's *Kisen hōshi* (The Monk Kisen) in his series *Fūryū ryaku rokkasen* (The Six Immortal Poets Depicted à la Mode, ca. 1795), Toyokuni's album *Ehon imayō sugata* (Picture Books of Modern Figures of Fashion, 1802), Keisai Eisen's print "Chiryū" in the series *Bijin Tōkaidō* (Beauties on the *Tōkaidō*, 1842), Utagawa Toyokiyo's series *Imayō bijin musume awase* (Match of Beautiful Daughters in the Contemporary Style), and Kunisada's triptych *Fūryū haru no kyō* (Elegant Spring in the Capital, ca. 1850).

11. See also Utagawa Yoshitora's (fl. 1850–80) "Gosekku no uchi fumizuki" (Seasonal Festivals: The Seventh Month, ca. 1850) and Gyokuransai Sadahide's (1807–73) "Sōshiarai Komachi." See Kunisada's triptych *Mutsuki wagayu no zu* (Bathhouse in the First Month), his print "Nihonbashi" in the series *Shōkei kagami* (Mirror of Beautiful Scenery, ca. 1820), and his triptychs *Shoshun no ashita* (New Year Morning), and *Ki no au dōshi haru no tanoshimi* (Lovers Enjoy Spring, 1854).

Figure 22. Utagawa Kunisada, "Arigatai miyo no kage-e" (ca. 1850). Private collection.

in another a woman is standing reading a work of illustrated fiction.[12] Note that in all these depictions the young women are not reading at a desk but in snatched moments—standing, at night by a lamp, or while doing something else—and their poses are always suggestive of leisure.

The Readers of Edo Fiction

The most significant point about the depiction of women readers in the later period is undoubtedly the presence in ukiyo-e of books known as *kusazōshi*, a generic term for the lighter genres of Edo fiction. Illustrated fiction of the Edo publishing world ranged from *sharebon* (witty stories set in the licensed quarters) at the end of the eighteenth century to *kokkeibon* (humorous stories about townspeople and their lives), *ninjōbon* (sentimental stories), and *yomihon* (adventure stories) in the nineteenth. The genres lumped together as *kusazōshi* included *akahon, kurohon, aohon, kibyōshi,* and *gōkan,* all except the last being names derived from the color of the covers, which underwent changes from decade to decade. In all these different types of *kusazōshi,* illustrations dominated the page, and the text—almost entirely in *hiragana* and with very few Chinese characters—is squeezed in around the figures. *Kusazōshi* texts were uniformly small in size and required a relatively low level of literacy. In the eighteenth century it is fair to say that the imagined audience for these works was a predominantly male one based in Edo. In the nineteenth century, however, among professional authors and commercially minded publishers alike, there was growing consciousness of the potential female market. This is apparent not only from the rise of the sentimental *ninjōbon* but also from the runaway success of Tanehiko's *Nise Murasaki inaka Genji,* which re-created *The Tale of Genji* in a Muromachi period setting. In *gōkan* (popular serial fiction) like this it became common for authors to make explicit reference to their expected women readers, and thus reading women often figured on the covers or in the illustrations for *gōkan* (fig. 23).

If the common view is that female readers only came into play as a market force in the nineteenth century, as suggested above, there is nevertheless evidence to suggest that the rise of the woman reader of *kusazōshi* can be taken back a little farther. For example, Santō Kyōden's (1761–1816) *kibyōshi* entitled *Kiji mo nakazu wa* (Pheasants Don't Cry, 1789), illustrated by Kitao Nariyoshi, begins with an imaginary account of the reaction from women

---

12. These are the single-sheet print "Kusazōshi" (Light Reading) and the diptych *Ezōshi o yomu machimusume* (City Girl Reading an Illustrated Romance), both Tenpō era, 1830–44.

Figure 23.   The covers of part 11 of Santō Kyōsan's *Nyōbō katagi* (The Character of Housewives). Private collection.

readers to the work itself. And, as we have seen, ukiyo-e from the late eighteenth century often depict women reading *kusazōshi*.

The Symbolic Meanings of the Woman Reader

The meaning of the woman reader in ukiyo-e is conveyed by the books she is depicted as reading, by the social class of the woman depicted, and by her reading environment and posture. In the early period, the books were classical, the readers were of high status, and their encounter with books was in the midst of leisure. Reading was thus presented as a mark of social rank and an indicator of a cultured upbringing. In the eighteenth century, there was something of a shift as the focus of depiction turned toward courtesans and to some extent toward other women who were not of high status but were well-to-do. The only alteration in the reading matter shown was the inclusion of songbooks, which were more practically related to courtesans' professional lives, alongside the full range of classical literature. The association established in ukiyo-e between courtesans and works of classical literature meant that such books—formerly markers of high status and cultured backgrounds—were now losing that sheen of exclusivity.

The major shift really comes at the end of the eighteenth and in the nineteenth centuries, when commercial fiction and conduct books come to replace older genres in the hands of the women depicted, who themselves cover an even wider social spectrum and are shown reading in a wide variety of situations indicative of leisure reading. Leisure reading was not, of course, restricted to women, but it is overwhelmingly women that form the subject of ukiyo-e depictions of reading. This is just as true of erotic prints and books (*shunga* and *shunpon*), in which, perhaps surprisingly, reading is a common activity depicted and books are often present.[13]

Utamaro's print "Kyōkun oya no mekagami: rikōmono" (A Parent's Moralizing Spectacles: Clever One, 1802) shows a girl lying on her back reading *Ehon taikōki* (Illustrated Records of the Imperial Adviser), a novelistic version of the life of military leader Toyotomi Hideyoshi (1536–98) published 1797–1802, and she is labeled a *rikōmono*, "clever one."

The accompanying text reads as follows.

> Tomoe's courage is not that of a woman. When Ki no Aritsune's daughter married the Middle Captain, she was not jealous of her husband's visits to Kawachi but recited a poem: "as the wind blows, the white waves rise as high as Mt Tatsuta and there in the middle of the night will go my lord alone".[14] This turned her husband's heart and he ceased thinking about going to Kawachi. *Women's sincerity is always [the equivalent of] men's courage. It may seem clever to resort to useless passions or write unconvincing letters, or to neglect one's needlework or to be skilled in music, but these all go too far.*

Thus the text criticizes the "clever" young woman shown reading and suggests that needlework and housekeeping are more important. This is by no means an isolated case.

According to the celebrated Edo period writer Kyokutei Bakin (1767–1848), one of the results of the great popularity of his serial fiction *Keisei*

13. See, for example, the scenes from works by Moronobu reproduced in the journal *(Kikan) Ukiyo-e* 41 (1970): 81, 87, 42 (1970): 80, 107, 61 (1975): 64–65, 88–89; and in Hayashi and Lane 1995–2000, vol. 11, 20–21, 24–25; vol. 22, 14, 38–39.
14. The story appears originally in *Tales of Ise*, section 23. For the Japanese text, see *SNKBT* 17, p. 105. The quoted poem was later collected in *Kokinshū*, no. 994. The translation used here is from Rodd 1984, p. 335 (emphasis added).

suikoden (A Courtesans' *Water Margin*, 1825–35) with women readers was that "when people see a tough-minded woman, they say, 'Oh, there's a *Keisei suikoden*.'"[15] Elsewhere he said that "girls should be gentle and yielding, able to weave and to sew clothes, and good at handwriting and housework".[16] And women who became "tough-minded" through reading lots of popular fiction, he said, "are rough in all that they do and have their husbands under their thumb, and thus much harm is caused".[17] An unknown author sought to depict precisely such a situation in a *kibyōshi* entitled *Shinsaku iroha tanka* (A New ABC of Short Poetry, ca. 1820), showing a woman so immersed in the latest fiction that she neglects the housework, presenting her as a typical bad wife.[18] Similarly, *ninjōbon* were perceived as dangerous reading matter for women. In 1878 Utagawa Kunichika produced a series entitled *Kaika ninjō kagami* (Mirror of Enlightenment Feelings). "Yamome" (Widow), one of the illustrations in this series, shows a young widow immersed in a *ninjōbon*; she already has a lover and is shown as a woman whose passions are aroused by reading romantic novels. Reading is by no means presented as a good thing for ordinary women in the nineteenth century.

Even the reading of classical literature, for centuries an essential part of the education and tastes of aristocratic and high-ranking samurai women, was not immune. The cultural pretensions of townswomen readers, for example, are ridiculed in Shikitei Sanba's (1776–1822) comic novel *Ukiyoburo* (Bathhouse of the Floating World, 1809–13). Two women (named after two species of duck whose names happen to coincide with two verb endings commonly found in classical poetry, "Kamoko" and "Keriko") encounter each other at a public bathhouse and chat about their recent reading. One claims to be "collating" texts of the late-tenth-century *Tale of the Hollow Tree* (*Utsuho monogatari*); the other is "annotating" her copy of *Genji* with the aid of Edo period commentaries.[19]

Keriko: "Kamoko-san. What are you perusing these days?"

15. Letter to Tonomura Jōsai of 23 November 1827, reproduced in Shibata and Kanda 2002.
16. Kyokutei Bakin 1850, *fugen*.
17. Ibid.
18. Only one published copy of this text is extant. Although the author is not identified in the surviving copy, the artist was Utagawa Kunimaru (fl. 1800–1830). See Itasaka 2003.
19. The translation is from Markus 1982, pp. 29–30, as slightly adapted in Rowley 2000, p. 28. The original can be found in Shikitei Sanba, *Ukiyoburo*, ed. Nakamura Michio, *NKBT* 63, p. 220. See also Aoki 2003. The commentaries "Keriko" claims to be consulting are Kamo no Mabuchi's (1697–1769) *Genji monogatari shinshaku* (A New Exegesis of *The Tale of Genji*, ca. 1758, first published in 1816) and Motoori Norinaga's (1730–1801) *Genji monogatari tama no ogushi* (*The Tale of Genji*: A Little Jeweled Comb, 1799).

Kamoko: "Well now, just as I was thinking that I might reread *Utsuho*, I was lucky enough to find an edition in movable type and so I am collating the texts. But I have been interrupted by this and that since last year and so I put it aside having got as far as the latter half of the 'Toshikage' chapter [the first chapter of *Utsuho*]."

Keriko: "You have got your hands on something nice."

Kamoko: "Keriko-san. I expect you're still with *Genji*?"

Keriko: "Yes indeed. With the Venerable Kamo's *Shinshaku* and the Great Motoori's *Tama no ogushi* as my guides, I had just begun annotating it, but what with all the distractions of the mundane world, I have hardly had time to pick up my brush."

As Sugano Noriko and Mara Patessio show in their essays for this volume, in the Meiji period reading reacquired serious connotations. There was a difference, however. Utagawa Kunichika, Tsukioka Yoshitoshi (1839–92), and other artists depicted girls or young women in more formal poses engrossed in books, but now the books are Western books: prints by Utagawa Kunichika titled "Kaika ninjō kagami: Benkyō" (Mirror of Enlightenment Feelings: Study, 1878; fig. 24), and by Yōshū Chikanobu (1838–1912) titled "Gentō shashin kurabe: Yōkō" (Magic Lantern Comparisons: Journey to the West, 1885; see front cover image) both show young Japanese woman reading Western books, the latter in some unidentified overseas setting.[20]

Schopenhauer once wrote, "One of the conditions for reading what is good is that we must not read what is bad," having already declared that "inferior books are intellectual poison; they ruin the mind".[21] In Edo period Japan, as in nineteenth-century Europe, however, books acquired an aura of "badness" by being associated with women readers, or, to put it another way, gender was part of the question, and what was "poison" for women readers was not necessarily seen as so for male readers. Furthermore, the growing engagement of women with commercial fiction in the Edo period, as depicted in *ukiyo-e*, can be seen as an incipient assertion of autonomy. In this sense it is precisely the phenomenon of the woman reader with her own tastes in fiction that is surely responsible for the anxieties about women readers that we have seen expressed in the *ukiyo-e* discussed in this essay.

20. See also Tsukioka Yoshitoshi's print "Mitate taizukushi: Yōkō shitai" (Collection of Desires: I Want to Travel Overseas, 1878).
21. Schopenhauer 1974, vol. 2, pp. 557–58.

Figure 24.   Utagawa Kunichika, "Kaika ninjō kagami: Benkyō" (1878). Private
collection.

5

In the Shadow of Men:
Looking for Literate Women
in Biography and Prosopography

Anna Beerens

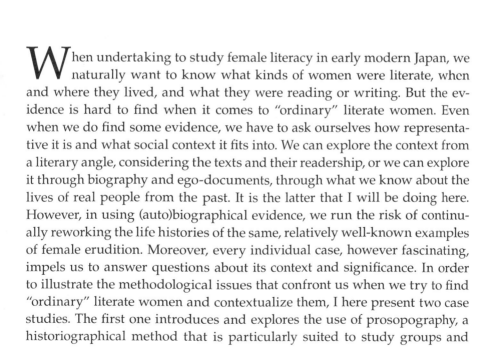

When undertaking to study female literacy in early modern Japan, we naturally want to know what kinds of women were literate, when and where they lived, and what they were reading or writing. But the evidence is hard to find when it comes to "ordinary" literate women. Even when we do find some evidence, we have to ask ourselves how representative it is and what social context it fits into. We can explore the context from a literary angle, considering the texts and their readership, or we can explore it through biography and ego-documents, through what we know about the lives of real people from the past. It is the latter that I will be doing here. However, in using (auto)biographical evidence, we run the risk of continually reworking the life histories of the same, relatively well-known examples of female erudition. Moreover, every individual case, however fascinating, impels us to answer questions about its context and significance. In order to illustrate the methodological issues that confront us when we try to find "ordinary" literate women and contextualize them, I here present two case studies. The first one introduces and explores the use of prosopography, a historiographical method that is particularly suited to study groups and communities. The second one, derived from a set of biographies included in a collection of *waka* poetry from the late Tokugawa period, highlights the problems we face when dealing with defective biographical material. My purpose is not so much to come up with new findings as to discuss ways to approach sources and matters of source criticism.

My first case study is based on my previous work on a set of biographical data relating to a group of individuals who were active in various fields of scholarship, literature, and art between 1775 and 1800.[1] For this investigation I used the prosopographical method, and this case study is based on these same data and my experience of handling them. Prosopography involves the comparative study of biographical data relating to a group of individuals from the past in order to demonstrate common characteristics or patterns in their life histories. As Lawrence Stone described it in his classic article on the subject, "The method employed is to establish a universe to be studied, and then to ask a set of uniform questions. . . . The various types of information about the individuals in the universe are then juxtaposed and combined, and are examined for significant variables."[2] Prosopographers stress the importance of preserving the individuality of every person within the chosen collective; the aim is certainly not to write the "biography of a group." One historian aptly described prosopography as "the study of biographical detail about individuals in an aggregate."[3] Prosopographers generally deal, for instance, with the members of a society, guild, fraternity, or organization, an occupational group, the pupils of a certain teacher or school, the members of a family or interrelated families, circles of friends, or members of a distinct social elite, but the method can also be used to study a group that is less clearly delimited.

Because it includes both the individual life history and its context, prosopography can present both the common and the exceptional. Findings can be used to support general claims but also to call into question widespread assumptions and prejudices. Prosopography tends to move at the surface levels of behavior because the size of the collective to be studied usually precludes in-depth research.[4] Also there is one important point about the prosopographical method that should be made absolutely clear: prosopography as such cannot tell us what motivated people. Prosopography is about

1. Beerens 2006.
2. Stone 1971. See also Beerens 2006, pp. 36–43.
3. Smythe 2000, p. 85.
4. Depending somewhat on the nature of the aggregate and the questions to be asked, between 75 to 100 individuals seems to be a minimum for a collective. On the other hand, we have prosopographies like that of Wolfgang Reinhard (1996), which contains 1,545 entries.

how people acted, about patterns of behavior, but it cannot reveal *why* they did whatever they did. In order to find out about motives and opinions, we have to turn to ego-documents of various kinds.[5] Although the results of prosopographical investigation may suggest topics and guidelines for further research, matters relating to what Lawrence Stone called "minds and manners" have to be approached separately.[6]

So there are limits to what prosopography can do. On the other hand, it can help us answer questions that could not be answered otherwise because it enables us to draw conclusions even when the evidence is meager or defective. One does not need a complete biography of every member of the group under scrutiny in order to answer certain questions about the group as a whole. Usually there is an imbalance between well-documented individuals and those about whom we know relatively little. The prosopographer should determine what questions can be reasonably asked of the evidence and should try to strike a balance between what can actually be inferred and measured and what is deemed essential and significant.[7] When investigating the social background of brewers in seventeenth-century London, for example, we must establish whether the person we are dealing with was a brewer in London at that time and whether something is known about his social background. We do not even need to know the exact dates of his birth and death, let alone whether he was happily married. We cannot write his biography, but in a prosopographical account we can use the available evidence about him.

After establishing boundaries of time and space and developing proper working definitions, I ended up with a network of 173 interrelated intellectuals—scholars, poets, painters, authors, and medical men, both professionals and nonprofessionals—active between 1775 and 1800. This group of intellectuals at first sight seems rather diffuse, but in fact it is not: it is a network of various overlapping smaller networks of friends and acquaintances. Social contacts and interaction were an integral part of the research because this group was not a self-defined entity.[8] If it is the historian who establishes the group to be studied, there must be some common factor that connects the members of this collective because there should be something that justifies asking the "set of uniform questions" of this particular aggregate of

---

5. The term *ego-document* was coined by the Dutch historian Jacques Presser in the early 1950s. He defined the term, which covers all kinds of autobiographical writing (including diaries and letters), as "those documents in which an ego intentionally or unintentionally discloses, or hides itself" (quoted in Dekker 2002, p. 7).
6. Stone 1971.
7. Roorda 1984.
8. Beerens 2006, pp. 19, 29.

individuals. In this case, that common factor was their mutual contact; the required "set of uniform questions" mentioned by Lawrence Stone in his definition included matters such as place of birth, status, sources of income, teachers, and intellectual activities.

I did not set out to look for literate *women* but rather literate individuals; nevertheless, there were women in my network of intellectuals. Of the 173 individuals, 5 were women, just 2.8 percent. These 5 women were not the smallest minority in this network, for there were only 4 individuals connected to the imperial court (1 imperial prince and 3 people from *kuge* families), just 2.3 percent; moreover, the whole network contains only 3 persons from families of Shinto priests (1.7 percent). In what way these figures are significant is an extremely complex matter. To begin with, there were, of course, considerably more women around in eighteenth-century Japan than there were *kuge* or Shinto priests. But the figures do invite us to rethink questions surrounding social mobility and visibility. It may have been the case, for instance, that Shinto priests were even more tied to certain locations and lifestyles than women were.

So five women were given separate entries in my prosopography. Two of them, Fushimatsu Kaka (1745–1810) and Tani Kankan (1770–99), were from samurai families.[9] Kaka was a *waka* and *kyōka* poet, the wife of the author Akera Kankō (1738–98). Kankan was the first wife of the painter Tani Bunchō (1763–1840) and a fine painter in her own right. As for the other three, they are Ike Gyokuran (1727/8–84), Rai Baishi (1760–1843), and Kō Raikin (dates unknown). Gyokuran was the illegitimate daughter of a samurai and the Kyoto teahouse owner and *waka* poet Yuri (1694–1764). She was married to the painter Ike Taiga (1723–76), almost as famous as her husband as a painter and calligrapher, and definitely the better *waka* poet of the two. Rai Baishi, a highly accomplished woman, was the daughter of a scholar (Inooka Gisai, 1717–89), the wife of a scholar (Rai Shunsui, 1746–1816), and the mother of a scholar (Rai San'yō, 1781–1832).[10] The background of Kō Raikin, painter, calligrapher, and *kanshi* poet, is unknown.[11] It *is* known, however, that before her marriage to the scholar Kō Fuyō (1722–84), she worked as a servant in the house of Itō Tōsho (1730–1804), who headed the Kogidō academy founded by his grandfather, Itō Jinsai. As such she is representative of a tendency within

9. For Kaka, see *Nihon koten bungaku daijiten*, s.v. Fushimatsu Kaka. For Kankan, see Fister 1988, pp. 86–87, 94–96; and Chance 2003, pp. 78–79.

10. For Gyokuran, see Takeuchi 1992; and Fister 1988, pp. 74–75, 86–90. For more on Baishi (and her younger sister, who married the scholar Bitō Nishū, 1745–1813, and is also mentioned in my prosopography), see Bettina Gramlich-Oka's contribution to this volume.

11. For Raikin, see Fister 1988, pp. 86, 91–93, 96 n. 7.

samurai households and upper-class commoner families to engage talented and educated women as servants.[12]

Now, of course, these women are relatively well known, well documented and well researched, which brings to mind the problem of continually meeting the same examples of female erudition. But then there are other literate women mentioned in my prosopography, even if they did not have their own entries. Naturally, the biographical sketch of the physician Ema Ransai includes his talented daughter Saikō (1787–1861), and that of the polymath Kudō Heisuke mentions his daughter Ayako (1763–1825), who, using the name Tadano Makuzu, was a writer in her own right.[13] However, the biographical sketch of the scholar Adachi Seiga (1726–92) brings to our attention a lesser-known daughter of a scholarly father. One of Seiga's *kanshi* students was Shūzan, the daughter of the painter Sakurai Sekkan (1715–90). Very little is known about her, but we *do* know that she wrote a book on her father's painting method called *Gasoku* (The Rules of Painting).[14] Every biography of Takizawa Bakin mentions O-Michi, his widowed daughter-in-law, who assisted him with his writing as his blindness grew worse. However, my prosopography reveals a similar case, that of the famous blind *kokugakusha* and poet Hanawa Hokiichi (1746–1821), who received much help in his scholarly work from his daughter and his second wife.[15]

Speaking of literate wives, we find that both the first and second wives of the painter and *haikai* poet Matsumura Goshun (aka Gekkei, 1752–1811) were accomplished *haikai* poets; they were both former courtesans. The wife of Goshun's friend, the painter Ki Baitei (1734–1810), was also active as a *haikai* poet.[16] Another of Goshun's friends was the novelist and scholar Ueda Akinari (1734–1809), whose wife Tama, although she is not mentioned as such in my prosopography, was likewise an educated woman.[17] Tama may have been acquainted with the wife of Morikawa Chikusō (1763–1830); Chikusō, who had his own calligraphy academy in Osaka, was a friend of Akinari's and also of the Osaka brewer, collector, and sage Kimura Kenkadō (1736–1802).[18] Chikusō's wife was one of the first to enroll as a calligraphy

---

12. Leupp 1992, p. 63; compare Dore 1992, pp. 268–69.
13. For Saikō, see Fister 1988, pp. 100–103; and 1991. For Makuzu, see Gramlich-Oka 2001 and 2006b.
14. Chance 2003, p. 65.
15. For Hanawa Hokiichi, see, for instance, *Kokushi daijiten*, s.v. Hanawa Hokiichi.
16. French 1974, pp. 31–4; Itsuō Bijutsukan 1982, pp. 5, 10.
17. For Ueyama Tama, see Young 1982; and Ushiyama 1985, chapters 1–4. Two short essays written by Tama, describing episodes of her married life, *Tsuyu wake goromo* and *Natsuno no tsuyu*, can be found in Kokusho kankōkai 1969, pp. 135–41.
18. See Miyoshi 2000, s.v. Morikawa Chikusō.

pupil when he set up his academy. She was a competent painter and gave her husband painting lessons. I have so far found no further information about her except that she died in 1810 and her family name was Kagawa, but she evidently moved in talented circles.

My prosopography also reveals a number of literate mothers, such as the mother of the priest and *kanshi* poet Rikunyo (1734–1801), who wrote *waka*.[19] The famous *waka* poet Momozawa Mutaku (1738–1810) was the son of a village headman in the region of Ina in Shinano province; he turned to *waka* after meeting his mother's *waka* teacher, the priest-poet Chōgetsu (1714–98) from Kyoto, who visited the Ina region in 1760.[20] The biographical sketch of the scholar Irie Masayoshi (1722–1800) takes us to the world of commerce. Masayoshi was the second son in a wealthy family of Osaka money changers. He lost his father when he was in his third year. The business was conducted by his mother until Masayoshi's elder brother was old enough to take over. Another example from the commercial milieu is Santō Kyōden's younger sister, Yone, who wrote *kyōka* and *kibyōshi* but died in her eighteenth year. Kyōden's biographical profile in my book does not mention that his other sister, Kinu, was married to a man called Iseya Chūsuke, Iseya being the name of an important publishing house with which Kyōden was in contact.[21] I assume both sisters were educated, even if Kinu apparently lacked her siblings' creative talent. The case of Kyōden's father, the owner of a pawnshop, would then support Ronald Dore's contention that, as far as the education of commoners was concerned, "merchants were perhaps the most likely to be willing to spend money educating their girls, since shop-keepers' wives needed to read and write in order to help in the shop."[22] There must have been many businesswomen in the cities of early modern Japan; how literate these women were greatly depended on the nature of the business, on the actual role they played in it, and on their personal ambitions and inclinations. Nevertheless, the businesswoman is a category not to be neglected.[23]

The methodological point I wish to make is that my prosopographical research shows that we find literate women in the margins of the life histories of literate men where they might easily be overlooked. Information

---

19. For Rikunyo, see Kurokawa 1990.
20. For Mutaku, see, for instance, Ichiko Teiji 1993–99, s.v. Momozawa Mutaku.
21. See Devitt 1979, p. 255.
22. Dore 1992, p. 254.
23. Takizawa Bakin's wife O-Hyaku, who conducted a footwear business, is of course a case in point. She is hardly known for her erudition, to say the least, but it is known that she and Bakin's daughters possessed basic literacy. Bakin's daughter-in-law O-Michi was the daughter of a physician.

about female literacy is often given cursorily and inconspicuously and, because the rhetoric of the writing directs our attention to the hero of the biography, these bits of information often remain unnoticed. However, even a simple entry in a biographical dictionary concerning a male author, artist, or scholar can put us on the trail of interesting cases of female literacy.[24] Many of these women remain anonymous, but the information we have is by no means useless because the biographies of their sons, husbands, and fathers give them a milieu and context so that, despite their anonymity, they can serve as examples or reveal the tips of various interesting icebergs.

The prosopographical method also lays bare the enormous diversity in social background behind this aggregate of eighteenth-century intellectuals so that these biographies of literate men actually provide us with information about literate women *from many different walks of life*. We find women from samurai families and daughters of scholars and physicians but also women with a commercial background and wives of rural worthies. This reflects the changes that took place in the cultural climate during the Tokugawa period. Commoners were very much part of the cultural and intellectual scene, and they had come to stay. By the beginning of the eighteenth century, "culture" had become an eminently marketable product, and among both producers and consumers of cultural commodities there was an increasing number of people from social groups that had never had access to such commodities before. My own prosopographical research also shows that in matters of the intellect there was free interaction going on between members of different status groups. Women were very much a part of all this. Moreover, when considering educated women with a commoner background it should be kept in mind that, on a practical, day-to-day level, there was no very sharp distinction between the world of commerce and the world of learning and cultivation. Conducting a private academy, a medical practice, or a painter's or calligrapher's studio was very much like having a business.[25] In fact, it *was* a business. There were patients, pupils, or apprentices to attract and attend to, work to be sold, commissions to be obtained, publishers to be dealt with, materials to be bought, and administrative and financial matters to be handled. The educated wife of the physician or Confucian scholar was just as useful to her husband as was the educated shopkeeper's wife. Besides,

---

24. In this sense the works of Mori Senzō (1895–1985) have much to offer. Although he is sometimes maligned for his antiquarian approach, his works contain an enormous amount of biographical information on intellectuals from the later Tokugawa period. See Mori 1988–89.

25. See Beerens 2006, pp. 220–22.

when trying to "sell" scholarship, literature, or art the skills and erudition of one's womenfolk could be used as an advertisement.

Handling biographical material on a large scale in the context of prosopographical research has made me sensitive to the fact that (literate) women hide in the life histories of (literate) men. A prosopographical investigation of a group of scholars, a shopkeepers' guild, a poetry circle, or a pupils' register will no doubt mostly concern the lives and careers of men. But it might also reveal new examples of female scholars, shopkeepers, or poets and, for instance, give us insight into how many male scholars or shopkeepers were married to educated women or gave their daughters a proper education. The best results will certainly be obtained if one is able to compare several similar aggregates in different regions and different periods. Such prosopographies will inevitably contain the life histories of *both men and women*; we should be wary of constructing prosopographies of women. As I have already stated, prosopographical research requires an aggregate that in some way is internally connected by common factors. Not every list of names and not every compilation of indiscriminate biographical data can be called a prosopography. And even if we do not have to know everything about the individuals in the aggregate under scrutiny in order to answer certain questions about the collective, there must at least be enough information to compose a reasonable "set of uniform questions." If data are too capricious and arbitrary, this cannot be done. The prosopographical method can be very useful in tracing literate women who can be used as examples and illustrations, but a prosopography consisting only of women will be a rare thing indeed in the context of premodern Japan.

Prosopography is a method we can use when approaching a group, but what about the individual biography? By "individual biography," I do not mean the full biography of the well-documented individual. What I am speaking of are biographical sketches and snippets we encounter in various sources. Here, too, we find literate women in biographies of literate men. Obviously, some women have their own biographies, but our expectations concerning such biographies of women should not be too high for all too often they are no more than veiled accounts of the careers of the men in their lives.

My second case study is about a collection of such biographical sketches and about the problems we face when trying to make sense of them. It concerns an anthology of *waka* poetry entitled *Oka no agata shū* in the possession of Fukuoka Prefectural Library.[26] This anthology contains *waka* composed

26. Itō Tsuneashi 1915. I would like to thank Professor Peter Kornicki for bringing this collection to my attention. My thanks also go to Nobuko Karthaus-Tanaka (formerly of Leiden

over a number of years by people from, roughly, the region of the river Onga in northern Kyūshū, compiled and edited by one Itō Tsuneashi in 1827; he reedited the collection in 1835. It was subsequently again corrected and enlarged, and wherever possible life histories of the poets were added. It was printed in 1915, and a facsimile of this final edition appeared in 1980. *Oka no agata shū* presents 1,262 poems composed by 271 persons, 39 of them women. Its supplement contains the biographies (written in *kanbun*) of 214 men and 37 women. It is because of these 251 small biographical sketches that *Oka no agata shū* is of interest to students of local history and genealogy and to social historians of the Tokugawa period. The biographies can be studied for information on social and geographical mobility, career patterns, marriage and adoption strategies, and the role of family relationships.

A careful study of the biographies in the supplement can tell us a lot about social structures and strategies in a provincial setting in the late Tokugawa period. But it cannot be turned into a prosopography because, even though some of them were related, these individuals do not really belong together. As will be shown below, they were not a coherent group, and therefore this source can only be studied as a set of individual biographies. Now at first sight a set of 251 biographies of *waka* poets would seem to be an ideal source for studying aspects of literacy; the fact that there are 37 biographies of women makes it even more attractive in the present context. However, we find that *Oka no agata shū* tells us little about these people *as waka poets*. Apart from data about names and region of origin, the biographical information centers on social status and career developments.

Moreover, the source has other major drawbacks that appear to be especially obstructive where matters of (female) literacy are concerned. *Oka no agata shū* is a very subjective source. It is not a membership list or a pupils' register; it is a selection of *waka* poems, and the authors' biographies are in it first and foremost because their poetry was available to and appreciated by Itō Tsuneashi and later editors. All kinds of factors may have played a disruptive role here. To begin with, *Oka no agata shū* seems very much a showcase for a regional elite: samurai, tradesmen, manufacturers, physicians, local dignitaries, and members of the Buddhist and Shinto clergy. Is this because the compilers were, consciously or unconsciously, being elitist and only selected the work of those belonging to the upper and middle classes?

University) and Sasaki Motoe (of Johns Hopkins University) for their help in obtaining a photocopy of the material. *Oka no agata shū* may be translated as "Collection of the Hill County." The *oka* (hill) supposedly refers to Fukuoka, and *agata* is an old administrative term indicating a rural district. For general information on the collection, see Itō Tsuneashi 1915, pp. 3–4; and Nakama Shishi Hensan Iinkai 1992, pp. 484–88.

Or is it because the lower classes did not produce *waka* (let alone *waka* that was above average) from which to choose? And if the latter is the case, was this because the lower classes were hardly literate or because they did not have the inclination, leisure, and/or funds to engage in *waka*?

There were doubtless many more literate individuals in the region at that time. But not all of them composed *waka*. And if they did, for whatever reason their work may not have been available to Itō Tsuneashi or his successors. And if it was, the compilers may have chosen to ignore it because it (or its author) was somehow deemed inferior. These subjective aspects should be firmly kept in mind when evaluating any findings on literacy, cultural life, or levels of education, whether they concern the men or the women. What about, for instance, the male-to-female ratio of the source? The collection contains poems by 232 men and 39 women (that is, 85.6 and 14.3 percent, respectively, out of a total of 271) and the biographies of 214 men and 37 women (85.2 and 14.7 percent of a total of 251). It is, of course, no surprise that the collection is dominated by men, but is this ratio in any way representative of the rate of female literacy there and then? Would the percentages of women have been higher if their poetry had been better or if some of the more talented female poets in the region had not been, say, courtesans but physicians' wives? Perhaps proportionately more *waka* composed by women were lost because of a general sense of the inferiority of women's achievements. Perhaps parents did not wish their daughters' names and work to appear in print. Unfortunately we do not know the answers to these questions, and the value of the percentages remains doubtful.

We find ourselves faced with other difficulties when trying to deal with the chronology of *Oka no agata shū*. The various editors decided to use the *iroha* order to arrange the biographical sketches, although they knew (and apparently regretted the fact) that any chronology would be lost in that way.[27] They also decided not to give dates of birth or death unless a person died before his or her thirtieth year (so that the reader would deplore the early demise of so talented a person) or after his or her seventieth year (so that the reader would rejoice in his or her longevity). The biographical sketches of the men frequently mention the dates of highlights in their careers such as succession to the family headship or the bestowal of court rank and title. Such data and the careful study of family relationships allow us to reconstruct something of a chronology for the biographical supplement, but if we detach the life histories of the women (who had no careers) from the rest, we have almost nothing left. At most we can get some idea of the time range of the women's biographies. The biography of Ishii Namiko tells

27. Itō Tsuneashi 1915, p. 3.

us that she died in 1797 at the age of eighty-one, so she belongs completely to the eighteenth century. As a possible terminus ante quem we have 1847, for in that year Hatano Nakako died at the age of eighty.[28]

However, in order to establish, for instance, whether or not we find indications of an increase in female literacy in this region during the early years of the nineteenth century the source is totally unsuitable. Not only is it impossible to say anything on the basis of only thirty-seven biographies of women, but the uncertain chronology is also definitely unhelpful. Moreover, we should take into account the likelihood that compilers had more material from later periods at their disposal. This could create the (possibly false) impression that "more was happening" in the early nineteenth than in the late eighteenth century. We cannot but conclude that the supplement is unfit for investigating long-term trends and tendencies.

Oka no agata shū abounds in geographical detail. The poet's region of origin is given in virtually every instance.[29] Often geographical movements in the context of marriage or career are recorded or can be reconstructed with the help of other biographies in the supplement. But what did such movements mean to these men and women? And how did they impact them as literate persons, as *waka* poets? In order to evaluate the significance of locality for the lives of our individuals, male or female, much more research is needed. How big were the towns and villages mentioned in the biographies? What was their regional function? How about opportunities for education and local cultural life? And how "provincial" were these people actually? The biographies of the men contain quite a lot of information about travel, but as far as the women are concerned there is only Hatano Nakako, who in 1825 went on a journey through various provinces together with her husband, the Shinto priest Hatano Haruki. Very likely, many of the women poets of *Oka no agata shū* never left the province and perhaps never even traveled far from their region of birth. What was their outlook as "provincial women"? The only thing we can say so far (an obvious but significant conclusion) is that in their case a small town or village environment does not seem to have been an impediment to literary self-cultivation. This, I suggest, is very much in line with what I said about the general availability of cultural commodities in the late Tokugawa period.

Nevertheless, we have here thirty-seven concrete examples of literate provincial women from the late Tokugawa period, and I have argued that such examples may help us to fill in the "general picture." So let us see what we *can* infer from these thirty-seven biographical sketches even if the result

28. We also have dates for Hatano Tokuko, who died in 1828 at the age of seventy-eight, and for Hosaka Naoko, who died in 1824 at the age of seventy-nine.
29. We learn, for instance, that Haga Michiko was born in Buzen province.

is somewhat disappointing. When looking at the women's biographies, we find again that it is mostly the men in their lives that give these women their context and milieu. The women are invariably "the daughter of X" and "the wife of Y." The majority of the biographies of the women consist of only one or two lines, mainly devoted to the names, sources of income, and places of origin of their fathers and husbands. Sometimes we find the date of the individual's death and at what age she died. Only very rarely do we find other information. In the case of Hatano Tokuko, for instance, it is recorded that she bore her husband fourteen children, and in Hatano Nakako's biography we find the journey mentioned above. Twenty-four women have at least one male relative who is also in the collection, and some have several. In these cases the biographical sketches of their fathers and/or husbands elsewhere in the supplement are absolutely indispensable to constructing biographies for the women in question.[30] The supplement provides information about the source(s) of income of the fathers of thirty-three women and the source(s) of income of the husbands of virtually all of them. This information allows us to make a survey of their social backgrounds (see table 4).[31] The result of this investigation is predictable because of the elitist character of the source; we already know that they were relatively prosperous women, and it is to be expected that such women could read and write and would take part in cultural activities. Nevertheless, the women's biographies from *Oka no agata shū* confirm that this was also the case in a provincial setting.

Throughout this essay I have argued that we find (literate) women in the shadow of (literate) men. This also appears to hold good for the women of *Oka no agata shū*. Apart from the fact that we should constantly keep in mind what kind of a source we are dealing with, we definitely need the rest of the supplement (the biographies of the male poets) to get the whole picture; the biographical sketches of the women contain too little information to use them as they are. What we have been taught by the prosopography of 173 intellectuals also holds good for these 251 biographies; in order to get to know women in a male-dominated society we must, paradoxically, study the men. The prosopographical method may help us not only to *find* the women in their lives but also to *find out* about them. Moreover, in order to phrase the right questions and be neither discouraged nor overly optimistic we should maintain a critical attitude toward the sources we use.

30. Sometimes the supplement contains quite a few members of the same family. We have, for instance, nineteen individuals carrying the name of Hatano (a family of Shinto priests). Moreover, Shinagawa Masao, Shioda Asako, and Yamamoto Satoko also belonged to the Hatano family. It appears that material in the possession of a member of the Hatano family was used for one of the revised editions of *Oka no agata shū* (Itō Tsuneashi 1915, p. 3).
31. The occupation of the second husband of Hatano Kameyo is unclear; he most likely was a Shinto priest.

TABLE 4
Backgrounds of Women Poets Contained in *Oka no agata shū*

Name	Occupation of Father	Occupation of Husband
Abe Sayaka	Physician	Physician
Akieda Ieko	Unknown	Merchant/ local administrator
Akieda Ikuko	Farmer	Senior local administrator
Akieda Kuniko	Sake brewer	Physician
Akieda Nakako	Local administrator	Senior local administrator
Haga Michiko	Shinto priest	Local administrator
Hamanaka Kumeko	Farmer	Rice merchant
Hatano Kameyo	Shinto priest	1. Port official, 2. Shinto priest (?)
Hatano Masako	Physician	Shinto priest
Hatano Nakako	Shinto priest	Shinto priest
Hatano Namio	Shinto priest	Shinto priest
Hatano Tokuko	Shinto priest	Shinto priest
Hatano Yumiko	Shinto priest	Shinto priest
Hosaka Iwako	Unknown	Physician
Hosaka Naoko	Physician	Physician
Hosaka Sanoko	Local administrator	Physician
Ichida Utako	Senior local administrator	Senior local administrator
Ishii Namiko	Physician	Samurai
Itaka Tomiko	Merchant	Shinto priest
Itō Naoko	Senior local administrator	Physician
Kita Tomiko	Unknown	Merchant
Kuroyama Sumako	Local administrator	Shinto priest
Kuwabara Hisako	Local administrator/ farmer	Rice merchant
Matsura Matsuko	Local administrator	Pottery merchant
Monji Tsugiko	Farmer	Merchant
Nakazawa Satoko	Samurai	Samurai

(continues)

TABLE 4 (*continued*)

Name	Occupation of Father	Occupation of Husband
Oda Hisako	Local administrator/ sake brewer	Fish merchant
Oda Ibeko	Merchant/shopkeeper	Merchant/shopkeeper
Oda Matsuko	Shinto priest	Soya manufacturer
Oda Sakuko	Soya manufacturer	Soya manufacturer
Ōta Kiyoko	Sake brewer	Sake brewer
Shinagawa Masao	Shinto priest	Merchant/shopkeeper
Shioda Asako	Shinto priest	Merchant
Takasaki Yaeko	Unknown	Senior local administrator
Wada Takeko	Merchant/shopkeeper	General merchant
Yamamoto Satoko	Shinto priest	Dyer
Yoshinaga Tatsuko	Local administrator	Merchant

Notes: "Shinto priest" is used as a translation for the term *shinkan*, "farmer" for *nō*, "local administrator" for *risei*, "senior local administrator" for *dairisei*, "merchant" for *shō*, and "general merchant" for *yorozuya*. The readings of personal names are given in the supplement by way of a system of rhyming characters. All three samurai mentioned in the table were in the service of the domain of Fukuoka. Abe Sayaka's father was the second son of a farmer who became a physician, Kuwabara Hisako's father also manufactured glazed paper (*rōgami*), and Yoshinaga Tatsuko's husband sold *tawaramono*, goods packed in straw bags. We have the trade names of the fathers of Oda Ibeko and Wada Takeko and of the husband of Shinagawa Masao, but we do not know the exact nature of their businesses. Abe Sayaka, Hatano Nakako, Hatano Tokuko, Ichida Utako, Oda Ibeko, Oda Sakuko, and Ōta Kiyoko all married their fathers' adopted sons.

6

A Father's Advice:
Confucian Cultivation for Women
in the Late Eighteenth Century

Bettina Gramlich-Oka

What did it mean for a woman to be educated or cultivated in Tokugawa Japan? There can be no single answer to this question, of course, but an unusual source—a didactic text composed in 1782 by a father for his daughter—provides us with a valuable contemporary discussion of the subject.[1] When Rai Shizu (1760–1843) left her hometown of Osaka for Hiroshima, her father, Inooka Gisai (1717–89), gave her a set of instructions that he hoped would guide her over the years ahead. Entitled *Yakakusō* (A Sentinel's Notes), the text describes a daughter's education, how she should use her education, and what this father understood as the necessary conditions for a woman to be considered cultivated. At the same time, *Yakakusō*

---

1. I am not aware of any other didactic text written by a father for his daughter. There is one example where the lord of the Yonezawa domain Uesugi Yōzan (1746-1822) on the occasion of the marriage of his granddaughter wrote a didactic guide, called *Momo no wakaba* (Young Leaves of a Peach). For a discussion, see Lindsey 2007, chapter 2. In the case of mother to daughter, from a much earlier period there is a text known as *Menoto no fumi* (The Nursemaid's Letter, ca. 1264), written by Abutsu-ni (d. 1283) for her daughter. On this text, see Laffin 2009.

is also an index of those didactic texts this father regarded essential to a woman's learning.

A Family of Scholars

The family at the center of my discussion is not an obscure one but a well-known if not well-studied one. Today Rai Shizu is best known in Japan as the mother of Rai San'yō (1780–1832), the famous painter, poet, calligrapher, scholar, and author of *Nihon gaishi* (General Outline of Japanese History, 1827). Some may also know of Shizu's husband, the Confucian scholar Rai Shunsui (1746–1816), who shaped the curriculum at the domain school in Hiroshima and whose scholarship linked him to Matsudaira Sadanobu (1758–1829) and the "ban on heterodox doctrines of the Kansei period" (Kansei igaku no kin, 1790). Some may have heard of Shizu's epic diary, which spans the fifty-eight years from 1784 through 1842 and is called simply *Baishi nikki* (the Baishi Diary) after her nom de plume, Baishi.[2] Shizu is also the author of travelogues and hundreds of poems. Research on San'yō in Japan is voluminous; there is less on his father and uncles and almost nothing on his maternal grandfather. Several biographies of Shizu have been written, mostly to explain the familial circumstances of her son. Only recently has Minakawa Mieko introduced Shizu and her diary to the academic world in a monograph.[3]

Outside Japan, the Rai family has yet to be discovered.[4] Shizu's father, Inooka Gisai, was a native of the merchant city of Osaka. He made his living as a Confucian scholar and town physician. Although we do not have much in the way of biographical data, we know that he was born into a family of

---

2. Most of the *Baishi nikki* became available in print when it was included with her son's collected works, published in 1931, but the portion covering the last ten years of the diary is still only available in manuscript. The diary manuscript is held by the Rai San'yō Museum (Rai San'yō Shiseki Shiryōkan) in Hiroshima. The Rai family carefully preserved Shizu's diary, and we may assume that until its partial publication in 1931 only family members had read it. There is no evidence that further copies were made. Early on, the diary was edited, although we do not know by whom or when. Of the fifty-eight years, only two—1813 and 1814—are incomplete, although in the first fifteen years some shorter periods are missing. Minakawa (1997, p. 98) surmises that it is not so much that pages have been lost as that they never existed. An older diary, known as *Baishi ko nikki* (the Baishi Old Diary), is missing many entries. It is difficult to establish exactly when Shizu began keeping a diary; the extant version of *Baishi ko nikki* covers the period 1784.7.21 through 1785.5.12 and is also held by the Rai San'yō Museum. For publication details, see *Baishi nikki* and *Baishi ko nikki*.
3. Minakawa 1997. See also Ōguchi 2001, a compilation by students of the vast Rai family archive of articles related to Shizu's diary.
4. For an introduction to Shizu and her diary, see Gramlich-Oka 2006a.

physicians but lost his parents when still young. After having probed various Confucian schools of thought, among them Ishida Baigan's (1685–1744) Shingaku (School of Mind), Gisai determined to study in depth the Song Confucian teachings of Zhu Xi (1130–1200), and it was this school in which he also instructed his daughters.

Gisai's interests in scholarship and poetry made him well connected. At the center of his network was the Chinese poetry (*kanshi*) society, the Kontonsha (Confusion Society), which was established in 1765 and chaired by Katayama Hokkai (1723–90). Through this network he met Rai Shunsui, a promising young scholar who, at the age of only twenty-eight, had opened a private school, the Seizansha, in Osaka.[5] Gisai was so impressed with the young man's scholarship that he encouraged Shunsui to marry his older daughter, Shizu. Their mutual acquaintance Nakai Chikuzan (1730–1804), of the Osaka merchant academy Kaitokudō, acted as go-between. The marriage took place in 1779, when Shunsui was thirty-four and Shizu twenty years old. Shizu and her younger sister, Nao (1763–1832), were Gisai's daughters by his second wife, Jū (d. 1784), and the only two of his children to survive childhood.[6] His first wife gave birth to three children who all died young, as did she.[7] In 1793, Gisai's younger daughter also became the wife of a scholar, Bitō Nishū (1747–1813), a teacher at the Shōheikō shogunal academy in Edo from 1791 until his death. Thus, not only was Gisai part of a network of scholars—Shunsui, Chikuzan, and Nishū were all members of the Kontonsha—but his two daughters were also linked to these scholars through marriage.[8]

Gisai was devoted to his daughters. That he made sure they were well educated and possessed the requisite poetic capital for the marriage economy we can conclude directly from the sources. As an early example, on the occasion of Shizu's first meeting with her father-in-law, the dyer Rai Kōō (1707–83), she accompanied him, her husband, and her husband's youngest brother, Rai Kyōhei (1756–1834), on a sightseeing tour to the old capital of Kyoto.[9] Afterward Shizu drafted an essay, *Yūrakuki* (Leisure Trip to Kyoto,

---

5. Ages are given by traditional Japanese reckoning, one or two years older than by Western count.

6. Jū was the daughter of Kurushima Chōji. Some biographers read her name as Sawako and give Kijima for her family name. At the time of her death on 1784.7.21, she was in her sixty-second year.

7. Rai Tsutomu 2003, p. 568.

8. Evidence that the group had more than poetry in common is provided by the fact that the Kansei ban on heterodox doctrines was principally a creation of Osaka scholars participating in the Kontonsha, demonstrating again that poetry and politics cannot be separated at this time. For further discussion, see Ooms 1975, pp. 135–37.

9. There was another brother, Rai Shunpū (1753–1825), who also became a scholar of renown.

1779), the earliest literary testimony by her, in a style that was common among poets of her time and reflects her comprehensive training in classical literature.[10] Various collections of Shizu's poetry provide further evidence that Gisai had endowed his daughter with a thorough poetic education; embellished by her obvious talent, this education proved to be a good investment. In other sources Shizu mentions that her father-in-law and later her son also concerned themselves with her poetic education, introducing her to poets such as Ozawa Roan (1723–1801) and Kagawa Kageki (1768–1843), both of whom were central figures in Kyoto poetry circles and continued to instruct her in the newest poetic trends.[11]

In 1781, soon after Shizu's marriage, Asano Shigeakira (1743–1813), daimyo of the Hiroshima domain, offered Shunsui a position as teacher at the new domain school, which was to be opened the following year.[12] That Shunsui received the offer is no coincidence. The establishment of domain schools was a growing trend, and scholars were needed to staff them. Shunsui, who had proved his erudition in Osaka, was certainly recognized in his home province. It was an excellent opportunity, since it provided him, a commoner, with quasi-samurai status and a regular income. Shunsui took up his new employment at the end of 1781. In the fourth month of 1782 he returned to Osaka to settle his affairs. Two months later, on the ninth day of the sixth month, he left again, this time with his wife Shizu and their three-year-old son San'yō (or Hisatarō as he was then called). It was on this occasion that Gisai, who was then sixty-six years old, gave his twenty-three-year-old daughter a set of instructions that would provide her with advice in the future when he would not be there to guide her directly.

YAKAKUSŌ

The title Gisai chose for his instructions, *Yakakusō*, is taken from a poem by the famous Tang poet Bai Juyi (772–846), which describes how the crane at night broods over its chicks in the nest.[13] The poem refers to a mother's

---

10. For a printed version of the essay, see *Baishi nikki*. Over the course of her life, Shizu composed a total of six travel diaries. They are reproduced in Rai Seiichi 1941. See also the bibliography in Ōguchi 2001, pp. 135–39.
11. See Azuma 2001, p. 54.
12. According to the entry for "Hiroshima-han: Hankō" in *Kokushi daijiten*, vol. 11, p. 1093, upon the opening of the new domain school buildings in 1782 some 280 students were registered.
13. The poem "Wu xian tan" is included in *Quan Tang shi* (Collected Poems of the Tang), *juan* 426. Gisai refers to the ninth verse: "Ye he yi zi long zhong ming." I thank Maria Rohrer for this information. The Sino-Japanese dictionary *Daijisen* renders the first two lines of the ninth verse in Japanese as "*Yakaku ko o omoi kochū ni naku / yakaku midari naki.*"

love for her children, and Gisai apparently saw it as befitting the title of this collection of advice in which he expressed his affection for his daughter. On an evening of light summer rain (*samidare*), Gisai put *Yakakusō* together and probably gave it to Shizu before she left for Hiroshima. It consists of a thirty-four-page booklet, only one copy of which has survived, comprising a preface and 111 points, most of them couched in the form of *waka* poems.[14] Gisai adds some poems he had written not long before, for instance, one dated the fifth day of the third month, but he also includes poems that he probably wrote some time earlier. Between the poems, Gisai provides some instructions for Shizu in prose.

Persuasive Formulas

In general, the text illuminates the designs of a father for a daughter who is about to move to a new town where she will rise in social status. Fore-grounded is not the notion that a wife should follow her husband blindly in the manner recommended by *Onna daigaku* (Greater Learning for Women, early eighteenth century); rather, the emphasis is on a wife doing as her husband does (*otto no gotoku naraba*) and being so outstanding that she will be remembered in the future, which in turn will reflect well on her parents.[15]

Gisai begins his admonitions with a discussion of Shizu's new role. Since Shizu's extraordinarily gifted husband Shunsui has risen in rank through a summons to teach at the domain school in Hiroshima, it is now up to her to sustain him in his new position. Gisai knows that it is difficult to part from one's parents and hometown, but, "woman though you be, you must screw up your courage and be stalwart and assiduous in the pursuit of your duties" (*onna nagara mo yūmō no ki o okoshite mamoru beshi tsutomu beshi*). In truth, if she is deeply concerned to honor her parents, she cannot give them greater joy than to make every effort to become accustomed to her new place and to put into practice the Way (*michi o okonai*).[16]

Already the opening passage of the text hints at the core of the problem. Shizu most likely did not want to go to Hiroshima, a town some ten days'

The term *yakaku* seems to have been popular among fathers at the time, and Matsudaira Sadanobu also used it as the title of a collection of advice for his son, Sadanaga (1791–1838), entitled *Yakaku hissō*.

14. The manuscript is held by the Rai San'yō Museum in Hiroshima. The title of the printed version is *Yakaku midari naki*, which is the second line of Bai Juyi's poem. For a printed edition, see Inooka 2001b, pp. 121–26.

15. Ibid., p. 121. In *Onna daigaku* it is stated, for example, that a woman "must look to her husband as her lord, and must serve him with all worship and reverence" (*Onna daigaku*, 38).

16. Ibid.

journey from Osaka, whether her husband rose in rank or not. In order to convince Shizu that it would be advantageous *to her* to move to the castle town, Gisai came up with a series of arguments. First, once she is away from home, Shizu will be able to prove her courage and strength. She can venture to make a mark of her own by putting the Way into practice. This is an important point, since it is mentioned repeatedly by Gisai, and I shall return to it below. Embedded in the platitude that her moral conduct will in the end reflect on her parents is Gisai's attempt to persuade her to look positively on the move away from home.

Another strategy Gisai utilizes is to paint Hiroshima in its most favorable colors. Gisai, who had probably never been to Hiroshima himself, knew that Shizu was reluctant to leave her sheltered life in Osaka. As the wife of a Confucian scholar in Hiroshima, she will have to put her fondness for the culture of the Osaka–Kyoto Kamigata region—from ancient times, the cultural center of Japan—to one side. In an attempt to sound convincing, Gisai argues:

> In the countryside the sincere and ancient Way is still alive. There are few distractions. Your determination to deport yourself properly and to strive for virtue will arise of its own accord. People with strong resolve go voluntarily to the countryside. Already in ancient times, there were those who left the noisy capital, who never again longed for the ways of Kamigata.[17]

Gisai makes the case that only the countryside can offer the proper environment for self-cultivation. He repeats the same argument further on, emphasizing that it should be Shizu's goal, too, to take this opportunity for self-improvement.

> In the Kamigata region there are too many distractions, so that it is difficult to focus on learning (*gakumon*). From now on, you should resolve to strive for learning and to embark upon the Way, to cultivate your mind and to behave properly (*mi o osamu*).[18]

Obviously in Gisai's view the temptations of the city keep young women like Shizu from learning about the ancient Way, for which the countryside is the perfect place. Before discussing whether Gisai was successful in cheering up Shizu as she prepared to leave Osaka for Hiroshima, his paternal concerns about more concrete matters deserve closer examination.[19]

---

17. Ibid.
18. Ibid., p. 122.
19. Ibid., p. 124.

Useful Advice

Gisai addresses various points in *Yakakusō*, most of them common to educational texts for women. Superficially, Gisai plays on the tenets of *Onna daigaku*, but his tone is different, being that of a loving father giving advice to his spoiled daughter. First, the way of man and the way of woman (*onna no michi*) are different, and the distinction between them must be strictly observed. In particular, chastity (*teiretsu*) is imperative; in the absence of her husband, Shizu "must not meet with" (*aumajiki*) any other man.[20] Second, Gisai commands, garments should be kept simple. Shizu is no longer in Osaka but in a castle town, living as the wife of a domain scholar he regards as a member of the samurai class. Frugality and simplicity are the virtues proper to a warrior's wife. Gisai also emphasizes upholding the virtues of propriety and righteousness, decency and shame (*reigi renchi*).[21] Third, servants should be treated with compassion. Henceforward, Shizu will most likely head a larger household with more servants than she has been accustomed to.[22]

The fourth point Gisai makes is about literature that should be avoided. In a short excursion, he explains why some texts give cause for concern.

> [T]hese days daughters and wives read *Tales of Ise*, *The Tale of Sagoromo*, and *The Tale of Genji*; they compose love poetry, play the koto and strive shamelessly to emulate their betters. Likewise do they follow the way of the Buddha and thus lose sight of the Great Way, which makes them subject to bodily ills, disorders their minds, and wreaks ruin in their households.[23]

This critique of the three great works of classical Japanese fiction, which due to their content were often regarded as "unsuitable books" for women, is a common feature of educational tracts for women, and thus it is not surprising to see it here.[24] Gisai simply reiterates a well-known list of works to be avoided. Based on his conviction that learning the Way is essential for women as well as men, Gisai recommends a predictable set of literature. Women should study the way of the ancients by means of the Confucian primer *Xiao xue* (J. *Shōgaku*, Elementary Learning, 1187) and the Japanese

---

20. Ibid., p. 122. Gisai probably did not expect that Shizu's husband Shunsui would be absent for more than ten years during the course of their married life. The separation of the sexes, discussed in *Onna daigaku*, is mentioned in *Mencius* Bk. 3,1,4,8, which reads "between husband and wife, attention to their separate functions" (*Mencius*, pp. 251–52).
21. Inooka 2001b, p. 124.
22. Ibid., p. 122.
23. Ibid., p. 123.
24. For a comprehensive discussion, see Kornicki 2005.

Himekagami (Mirror for Young Women).[25] Indeed, he continues, both texts should be read repeatedly. As a result, the "way of the woman" will be neither frightening (*kowaku*) nor dreadful (*osoroshiki*). Instead, Gisai argues, "she will be graceful (*miyabiyaka*), solemn (*shizuka*), upright (*tadashiku*), gentle (*yasashiku*), and humble (*shiorashii*)."[26]

Consolation

Gisai's more personal advice is presented in his poems—over a hundred of them—and he suggests that Shizu should console herself by (re)reading them from time to time. Gisai records some he regards as elegant (*ga*) and some he considers rather more vulgar (*zoku*).[27] Examples include:

Waga kokoro	Once you know
minamoto shireba	your heart well,
kanashiki mo	sad and
tsuraki mo nami no	difficult matters
mizu no awa naru	become as foam on the waves.[28]

Yo no naka ni	There is much
kanashiki koto wa	sadness
ōkeredo	in the world,
michi ni tagau ni	but nothing
shiku mono zo naki	compares to the Way.[29]

The lower hemistich of the oft-quoted last poem in the collection, translated below, has been used as the title of a recent biography of Shizu:

Yo no naka ni	Whatever in the world
michi yori soto wa	lies outside
nanigoto mo	the Way,
supporapon no	throw
pon ni shite oke	away![30]

The greater part of Gisai's text consists of such personal messages to his daughter. By choosing to couch his advice in the form of poems, he seems to

---

25. *Himekagami*, by the Kyoto scholar Nakamura Tekisai (1629–1702), bears a preface dated 1661 but was not published until 1709–12 (Kornicki 2005, p. 159).
26. Inooka 2001b, p. 124.
27. Ibid., p. 122.
28. Ibid.
29. Ibid.
30. Ibid., p. 126. For the biography, see Minobe 2000.

want to convey feelings of closeness, feelings he hopes will comfort Shizu and reassure her that it is only physical distance that separates them.

Shizu

Was Gisai successful in making Shizu feel better about leaving Osaka and moving to Hiroshima? Fortunately, a variety of sources inform us of succeeding events. First, Shizu stayed in Hiroshima for only a little over one year. Before the family could settle into its new life, Shunsui was ordered to move to Edo to instruct the domain's young heir apparent; he would have to leave his wife and son behind. Worried about how they would manage alone in what was to them still an unfamiliar place, he asked his lord for permission to allow them return to Osaka.[31] His request, founded upon three excuses—one of which was Gisai's and another Shizu's "frail" health—was granted, and in 1783 Shizu was able to return to her natal house with her young son San'yō while Shunsui continued east to Edo. Now she was back at home with her parents and younger sister Nao.

Shortly after her return to Osaka, Shizu was drawn back to her former pastime, namely, taking lessons in the koto. This is rather amusing since in *Yakakusō* Gisai expresses his disapproval of the recent fashion for the "way of the strings" (*ito no michi*), which he regards as not in accord with the simple, ancient way of life.[32] Who would have thought that his own daughter was a follower of just this fashion? Gisai goes so far as to suggest explicitly that Shizu "should resolve to put an end to her studies of the koto. People look at the wife and daughter of a scholar and wonder that she is so lost to the way of the strings."[33] Evidently Shizu disregarded Gisai's admonition. The sources tell us that she learned the koto before she went to Hiroshima and took it up again upon her return to Osaka. She discontinued her lessons when her mother died the following year but resumed them after the seventy days of mourning were over. Yet Gisai seems to have praised his daughter in front of Nakai Chikuzan, the well respected Kaitokudō scholar and the couple's go-between, claiming that Shizu was good at needlework and did not play the koto.[34] One wonders how Gisai managed to keep Shizu's practicing a secret.[35]

31. For Shunsui's letter, see Yoshida Yuriko 2001, pp. 33–34.
32. Inooka 2001b, p. 123.
33. Ibid., pp. 121–22.
34. Minakawa 1997, p. 64.
35. Shunsui, too, was apparently not overly fond of her playing since he was not very responsive when Shizu consulted him about buying a new instrument (Minakawa 1997, p. 64, reading from the *Baishi ko nikki* and letters).

While in Osaka, then, Shizu lapsed back into life as an indulged daughter, a life far removed from the responsibilities of being female head of a household. As well as her lessons in koto and her study of poetry and calligraphy, Shizu recorded in her diary the many outings she took to enjoy what the city had to offer. When she had to return to Hiroshima two years later, she must have been miserable.[36] Indeed, a letter from Gisai to Shizu written in the seventh month of 1785, two months after her departure, suggests how wretched she must have felt about leaving Osaka again. Gisai repeats his admonition that since Shizu is now the wife of a warrior she must rise to her "new" status. He seems to feel that her time in Osaka had made her forget that Shunsui's promotion had in fact taken place three years ago and as a consequence her status had already changed. As we have seen, Gisai refers repeatedly to Shizu's new status, even though the reality may have been rather different since becoming a domain scholar did not necessarily mean becoming a samurai. In his view, however, and perhaps in the perception of many, this fine distinction is ignored. Implying that Shizu should start over, Gisai declares that since her roots are those of a commoner she is not prepared for the task of being the wife of a samurai. But if she perseveres and practices the Confucian Way even more rigorously—and here Gisai's earlier list of guidelines should be of assistance—she will manage. Nonetheless, Shizu will need to develop some special qualities (*kakubetsu na tokoro*), and by that Gisai means

> Observe the Way (*michi o mamorite*) and be brave. Do not show others your weeping face (*gunya gunya nakitsura*), but meet others calmly and with courage. . . . If you feel sorrow, free your heart by composing poetry (*urei no omoi areba, utaute kokoro o hanazubeshi*). Do not let your heart be worried. If you dwell on [your worries], you will become ill. Do not forget this remedy! You should develop a heart that has cast aside all [worries] (*zuberapon no pon to kokoro o yaru beshi*).[37]

It seems that Shizu followed her father's advice. Her writings, published in 1941, include a vast number of *waka*, as well as various essays.[38] Perhaps she also had a lot of worries. After Shizu left for Hiroshima the second time, she was not to return to Osaka except for short visits.

36. Shizu was back in Osaka between 1783.8.16 and 1785.5.5.
37. Letter dated 1785.7.23, cited in Minobe 2000, pp. 34–35.
38. These are reproduced in Rai Seiichi 1941. See also the bibliography in Ōguchi 2001, pp. 135–39.

Various Forms of the Way or Various Ways?

Gisai stresses repeatedly that a woman is capable of cultivating herself and, moreover, can do so on her own. A husband must be respected, even revered, because such reverence is a crucial pillar of society. Nevertheless, Gisai allows Shizu—and by implication other women, too—direct, full agency over her own intellectual abilities. She can practice the Way herself. She can be cultivated.

> Since olden times in our country people say that a woman's erudition is dreadful, but this is only because they do not know the way of the sages.[39] That she is dreadful with reason (*michimichishiku osoroshiki wa*) is because a woman is easily distracted and sidetracked. . . . But when a woman studies sincerely the way of the sages, she will arrive at the point where she can understand accurately.[40]

It is easy enough to deduce from this passage that Gisai assumed women were sufficiently qualified to learn the Way. But how should a woman study the Way? Gisai's discussion of the Way in *Yakakusō* is most ambivalent.[41] His recommended literature indicates that, even though he acknowledges women's ability to pursue the way of the sages, he nevertheless refers to a woman-specific way (*onna no michi*).[42]

Shizu's pursuit of self-cultivation through learning (*gakumon*) also appears to have been woman specific. Although she kept a diary for over fifty years, precise information concerning her actual reading practices is sparse. We can only speculate about her study of Confucian texts from those books mentioned in her diary. While she was in Osaka, Shizu borrowed a copy of Liu Xiang's (79–8 BCE) *Biographies of Women* (*Lienü zhuan*, J. *Retsujoden*) from a friend of Shunsui.[43] The work consists of examples of Chinese women who displayed virtuous behavior, and in choosing to study this text she followed her father's instructions. Later, back in Hiroshima, Shizu made copies of

---

39. The entire sentence reads "*onna no michimichi wa osoroshiki yō ni ieredo, sore wa michi shiranu yori omoi narawaseshi nari*" (Inooka 2001b, p. 123).
40. Ibid.
41. Gisai uses the term *michi* eighty-four times with various meanings in *Yakakusō*. See the "Kaidai" to *Yakakusō* in ibid., p. 126.
42. Ibid., p. 124.
43. See entries in the *Baishi ko nikki* for 1784.9.14 through 10.10 cited in Minakawa 1997, p. 63. According to Minakawa, Nakamura Tekisai borrowed many parts of *Retsujoden* for his *Himekagami*.

a variety of texts, among them the well-known collection of didactic tales (*setsuwa*) *Kojidan*.[44]

More than anything else, however, it was Shizu's pursuit of poetry that qualified her as cultivated. In Osaka, Shizu studied with Shunsui's friend Eda Hachirōemon (d. 1795), who corrected her poetry. Through the good offices of another poet, Shizu and her sister Nao were introduced to Hino Sukeki (1737–1801), a wealthy court poet from Kyoto whose fees were correspondingly high.[45] Nonetheless, the sisters became his official students. According to Nao, Gisai was quite proud of his daughters' accomplishments with the brush, calligraphy as well as composition, and therefore we must assume that he did not mind the cost of their lessons.[46] Father and husband alike supported—and probably also expected—Shizu to follow the "way of the poet."

Once embarked upon that path, however, Shizu carved out her own literary space.[47] In her practice of poetry, she did not stick strictly to the course Gisai had set out in his instructions. Shizu mentions reading a collection of poetic theory by the court poet Mushanokōji Sanekage (1661–1738), and this effort exemplifies the huge personal investment she made in poetry.[48] She also read the *Kogetsushō* (1673), an annotated edition of *The Tale of Genji* compiled by Kitamura Kigin (1624–1705). *Genji* had been required reading for poets at least since the twelfth century, and so we may assume that Shizu had enhanced poetic competence in mind when she embarked upon the tale. Nevertheless, *Genji* was precisely the kind of reading her father had warned against.[49] In a further departure from Gisai's instructions, while

44. *Baishi nikki*, entry for 1797.4.3. *Kojidan* was compiled by Minamoto no Akikane between 1212 and his death in 1215. The other texts Shizu mentions are an illustrated book (*ehon*, entry for 1786.4.10); the poetry collection *Kanshin'eiga*[shū] (entry for 1786.2.27); the unidentified *Shinkikigaki* (literally "New Transcripts of Conversations," entry for 1787.6.24); and *Matsukage nikki* (In the Shelter of the Pine, ca. 1710–14) by Ōgimachi Machiko, which Shizu copied in early 1793 at Shunsui's request (entries for 1793.1.10 and 1793.1.17). On Ōgimachi Machiko and *Matsukage nikki*, see the essay by Rowley in this volume.
45. Gisai mentions in his diary entry for 1785.3.27 that both Nao and Shizu became students of Hino through the introduction of a certain Kojima Masao. Gisai's diary, *Hibi sōkō* (Daily Notes), covers the same period as Shizu's old diary, but we can assume that he had already been keeping his for some time before she began hers. Extant portions of Gisai's diary date from 1785.2.28 through 1785.5.15, overlapping the period when Shizu was in Osaka staying with him.
46. See Nao's letter of 1786.1.6, cited in Minakawa 1997, p. 66.
47. On the "liberties" available to the woman poet, see, for example, Walthall 1998.
48. *Baishi nikki*, entry for 1786.2.21. The text is *Shirinshūyōshū*, compiled by Sanekage's disciple Jiun (1673–1753) and dated 1739. It is a record of Sanekage's discussions on court (Tōshō, also read Dōjō) *waka* practices, secret transmissions, and so on. Several abridged versions also circulated as manuscripts under a variety of titles. I thank Lawrence Marceau for this information.
49. *Baishi nikki*, entry for 1786.5.20.

Shizu composed poetry together with the family physician's wife on a regular basis, men too occasionally participated in their poetry circle. During the year 1788, for example, she held Chinese poetry parties even during her husband's absence, again going against her father's injunctions to keep the "way of man" and "the way of woman" strictly separate.[50]

In Hiroshima, Shizu also practiced the Way by educating others. She appears to have had her own school. We know that beginning as early as 1785.9.2, she taught reading and writing to Hayashi Ai, the daughter of their physician; later she taught her the aforementioned Song Confucian primer *Shōgaku*, which the thirteen-year-old girl studied for two years.[51] While we do not know any of her other students by name, there must have been a number of them since Shizu notes in her diary entry for 1788.1.15, "Today I received permission to have a study room (*keiko shitsu*)."[52]

Shizu's principal achievement, however, and the one for which she is best known today, is her diary, *Baishi nikki*. She began keeping it in Osaka when she returned there from Hiroshima, and she would keep it more or less continuously for the next fifty-eight years until shortly before her death. The diary was an outlet for her emotions: her worries, anger, and anxiety. Keeping a diary was, like composing poetry, also an important means by which she could continue to cultivate her mind and body. Gisai told her in *Yakakusō*:

> My sole hope for you is that you will devote yourself to the study
> of the true Way; clarify meticulously in your own mind the quali-
> ties of virtue and duty (*dōtoku giri*); rectify your errors and trans-
> form them into goodness; and, every day anew and every month
> upon month with greater precision, follow the Way that a per-
> son ought to follow; and shine forth as a mirror of what a woman
> ought to be (*onna no onna taru kagami o teraseyokashi*).[53]

Writing a diary was certainly nothing extraordinary for men or women at the time. Shunsui and Gisai both kept diaries. The extant manuscript of Shunsui's diary shows that he began to record daily events on 1781.12.16, the day he was appointed a domain scholar, and continued keeping the diary

50. Ibid., entries for 1786.2.9, 1786.2.14, and 1786.2.16. For the presence of men, see the entries for 1788.3.8 and 1788.10.20. In 1788 Shizu experienced a difficult pregnancy with her second child, her daughter Tō (1789–1826), and subsequently took an extended break from the poetry circle, which lasted for some nine years, until 1797.
51. The catalog of the family library contains various versions of *Shōgaku*, one copy from 1787 (no. 531).
52. Suzuki Yuriko 1993, pp. 154–55. Shizu would continue to mention children she taught.
53. Inooka 2001b, p. 122.

for thirty-four years; the last entry is dated 1815.12.2, only two months before his death. Just like her father and husband, Shizu, recorded her duties day by day.

Once the domain school had been established, Shunsui sought to make his household into a model Confucian home. It was crucial that Shizu successfully fulfill her role. Before he went away from Hiroshima to serve in Edo for his third posting, in 1788, Shunsui left behind instructions. He meant for Shizu to perform daily service to the ancestors; safeguard their son and heir, now nine years old, and provide him with an elementary education; keep the library aired and clean; be thrifty; and stop smoking.[54] Shizu may not have given up smoking, even though her husband urged her to do so, but she did everything else as instructed, and, most important, she recorded her fulfillment of these duties in her diary. Two years later, on his fourth posting to Edo, Shunsui also left behind instructions, but this time they differed.[55] Service to the ancestral spirits was still in first place, but the education of San'yō, who was by then eleven years old and whose studies took place outside of the house, was no longer second. In place of this duty were instructions for dealing with the finances of the growing household, a practical matter not considered by Gisai in *Yakakusō*.

When Shunsui died in 1816, Shizu's life changed. She retired from her duties as female head of the family, and poetry became her main pursuit. Her diary, which she continued to write for twenty-seven more years, became interspersed more extensively with prose and poetry. She accompanied her son San'yō on journeys to meet other poets, and she composed accounts of these travels.

We see, then, that Shizu took her father's advice and practiced the Way as they both understood it. Her poetry was one part of this pursuit of the Way; her diary was another. As we have seen, in Osaka Shizu lived a carefree life of comparative leisure. Gisai knew that she would not be able to live this way in Hiroshima, where she was expected to fulfill the role of female head of the household. Shizu had to grow into this role. By keeping a diary, she attempted to portray herself as the daughter of a scholar who knew propriety and followed her father's instructions; later the diary came to have a second function, namely, to depict the daily life of a Confucian wife in a model Confucian household. In her diary, she demonstrates her accomplishment as a woman of virtue.

As noted above, Gisai's advice to his daughter acknowledges Shizu's ability to cultivate herself through *gakumon* (learning). This means study-

---

54. The instructions are dated 1788.9.14 (cited in Yoshida Yuriko 2001, p. 35).
55. These instructions are dated 1790.9.13 (cited in ibid., p. 36).

ing the classics, keeping a diary, and practicing the way of the poet. We should be careful, however, to distinguish between the self-cultivation necessary for the female head of a properly Confucian household and the self-cultivation required of a scholar. When we compare Gisai's written advice to his son-in-law, which was written, like *Yakakusō*, when Shunsui and Shizu first left Osaka for Hiroshima, we encounter a different text altogether. In *Bōgosō* (Notes of a Foolish Old Man), Gisai addresses Shunsui as one scholar to another. Rai Shunsui was most certainly not his son, and his education was never in Gisai's hands. For this reason, "cultivation" does not need to be mentioned unless it is in reference to their role as teachers of cultivation to others. And it is on this subject—how Shunsui should perform his new role as a domain scholar—that Gisai directs warm words of encouragement to him.[56] The difference between *Bōgosō* and *Yakakusō* is that Shunsui is the gentleman (*kunshi*) whose duty it is to order the people (*tami*), while Shizu is "the people." Cultivation is possible for women, but in the end it differs from cultivation for men. There is certainly no equality of the sexes; rather, there are separate or different spheres for each. A scholar's daughter could cultivate herself by practicing the way of the poet and observing ancestral rites within the scholar's household, but the way of the scholar itself remains a male undertaking.

Yakakusō *as Keepsake*

Yakakusō remains ambivalent about woman's pursuit of the Way, even within the scholar's household. Although the text echoes commonplace phrases about womanly virtue familiar from didactic books and describes some of the practical aspects of a woman's education, it cannot be compared to any scholarly treatise of the time that deals with the subject.[57] For *Yakakusō* is principally a personal testimony; it is not a text that Shizu was supposed to copy and circulate. In 1792, however, when her sister Nao married the Confucian scholar Bitō Nishū, Shizu sent a copy of *Yakakusō* to her.[58] Gisai had died three years earlier, and Shizu seems to have taken it upon herself to present their father's instructions to Nao for her trousseau in his stead.[59] Nao certainly would have read the text with different eyes. In the first place, the piece was originally meant for her older sister, and Nao did not move to

---

56. Inooka 2001a, pp. 130–32.
57. Kornicki (2005) discusses a variety of educational texts for women. Gisai's set of instructions is certainly not such a text.
58. *Baishi nikki*, entry for 1792.8.7.
59. What happened to this copy of *Yakakusō* is unknown. It is also unclear whether Shizu passed the text on to her daughter Tō when she was married on 1808.4.22. Rai Tsutomu (2003, pp. 573–74) notes that apparently Nao handed it on to her daughter.

the countryside but rather to Edo, which by the 1790s was a cultural center for scholars and poets alike. What probably did have the same significance for both sisters was the text's aim of providing comfort and direction to a new wife in her unaccustomed role.

An important purpose of *Yakakusō* was, therefore, to be a keepsake, and perhaps many didactic works for women encompassed this function. The texts that Gisai recommended Shizu should read were intended, he argues, to make the way of the woman less "dreadful" (*osoroshi*). They served not simply to teach or reinforce the subordinate and inferior place of woman in society; they also offered readers consolation and strength as they faced the unfamiliar and the "dreadful." Such texts were replete with words women had grown up with, words that she in turn could fill with various layers of meaning attuned to her new role as the wife in a specific household, words she could later teach with confidence to other women. Perhaps we can think of these conduct books as a sort of childhood memento in a bride's trousseau, books that when opened would remind a woman of her childhood, her parents, and, most important, the reason why she is where she is.

Yakakusō is a case in point. Shizu's life is embedded in a specific social structure. In the household of a scholar, a daughter needed to be educated beyond mere primers for it was her duty to be the link between two scholars, father and son: she had to be prepared to educate the offspring. As a daughter, she needed to acquire the knowledge—the intellectual capital—that would enable her to fulfill her social function in this male-dominated marriage economy. Primers alone would never have sufficed to meet Gisai's expectations for his daughter. Shizu had to cultivate herself morally. For that, other literature was needed. Shizu was trained in more than the basics; eventually, her education surpassed that which Gisai had prescribed in *Yakakusō*. By the time Shizu passed *Yakakusō* on to Nao, therefore, the text itself had become a keepsake. Behind the general advice about how to live a virtuous life, it was the expression of Gisai's devotion, his affirmation of love for his daughter, that had become the most important reason why Shizu held on to her father's letter in Hiroshima.

The relationship between father and daughter, which I have encountered in other scholarly families as well, invites further investigation. Daughters Ema Saikō (1778–1861), Tadano Makuzu (1765–1825), and Rai Shizu all benefited from a solid education, supported by their fathers, that went well beyond the basics. It is striking that Tokugawa women themselves often point to a strong father-daughter relationship while their mothers remain in the background. Even though Shizu's mother was alive and well at the time Gisai wrote *Yakakusō*, no writings by her survive. We do know that when Shizu first left for Hiroshima she was accompanied by her mother, who helped her daughter settle into the new environment, suggesting that her mother was just as concerned for her welfare as was her father. And yet mothers are largely absent from the records of these women's lives. Their absence serves as a further reminder of how male dominated Tokugawa society was. Just as the encouragement of female self-cultivation remained a male endeavor, for a woman to succeed in society the help of men was essential. Shizu would seem to have understood this. When her father Gisai fell ill, she wanted to return to Osaka, but the weather did not permit her to travel. Instead, in her diary entry for 1788.8.5 she recorded the following appeal to the gods in the form of a poem.

Ametsuchi mo	Take pity on me
aware to omoe	O gods of heaven and earth
tsuma to oya	and carry me who
waga mi hitotsu o	is divided between
hakobu kokoro o[60]	a husband and a father.

Note

An earlier, short version of this essay was published in English and Japanese in Shirane 2009.

60. *Tsuma*, written here in hiragana, is used in its old sense of "spouse" and can refer to either partner or both husband and wife.

7

Nishitani Saku and Her Mother: "Writing" in the Lives of Edo Period Women

Yabuta Yutaka

In this chapter I take up the case of Nishitani Saku in order to bring further evidence to bear on the kinds of lives commoner women led in the Edo period and the kinds of education they received. These are questions that Takai Hiroshi, in his book on the educational experiences of boys and girls in the Tenpō era (1830–44), has already sought to address with evidence from the Yoshida family, but the Nishitani family furnishes a somewhat different perspective.[1]

Let us first consider the Yoshida family, which is the focus of Takai's study. They were a family of weavers in Kiryū, one of the leading silk-producing areas in the Kanto region. Takai focuses on the upbringing of the daughter Ito, born in 1824, and the son Motojirō, born in 1828, presenting the data from the perspective of their father, Seisuke. Ito started attending a local school in 1831; this school was run by Tamura Kajiko, who was the wife of a local merchant and provided an education for girls intending to go into service in samurai households. There Ito learned to read and write, received

---

1. Takai 1991.

training in etiquette, and acquired a basic knowledge of *waka* poetry. She appears to have left this school in 1838, but by that time she had also learned to play the koto and the samisen and had taken lessons in flower arrangement and the tea ceremony, presumably from private teachers.[2] A year or two later Ito was sent for a time to the home of Tachibana Moribe (1781–1849), a Kokugaku scholar living in Edo, and the letters she exchanged with her father provide particularly valuable insights into the upbringing of girls at this time. The contrast with the upbringing of her brother Motojirō provides a gendered perspective, showing the different educational expectations and horizons of rural women at this time.

By contrast, the case of Nishitani Saku furnishes us with a different perspective on the multiple literacies of the Edo period and on the connections that linked women with the acts of writing and reading. In fact, it was my discovery of her diary in 1979 that first drew my attention to the importance of female literacy for the study of the Edo period. Subsequently, many other documents came to light, and what now may be called the Nishitani family archive amounts to more than five thousand items; the task of sorting, cataloging, and studying these documents is continuing, and this essay on Nishitani Saku's life as a writer is one outcome of this research.[3]

The Nishitani family was a relative newcomer in the town of Furuichi in Kawachi province (now part of Habikino city in Osaka Prefecture), which had its origins as a country town (*zaigōmachi*) in the fifteenth or sixteenth century. It was in origin a branch family founded in the 1760s by one Heiemon, but when the main Nishitani family line died out the branch line became the main line. The family traded in salt and fertilizers, but it also owned a large amount of land that spread over several neighboring villages. Members of the family gradually added to their property and wealth up to the time of Saku's father, the third head of the family, who also took the name Heiemon; he had the position of *toshiyori* in the village, a post that ranked him directly under the village head. So there are some similarities to the case of Yoshida Ito of Kiryū, for both she and Saku were born not in villages but in country towns and both their families were engaged not in agriculture but in trade. As we shall see, this is suggestive of connections between literacy and social status.

Nishitani Saku's family consisted of her parents, her younger sister Tazu, and herself; there were no sons, so the family headship passed to Tazu's son Tokusaburō, as is shown in figure 25.

---

2. Ibid., pp. 20–34.
3. I have written about Nishitani Saku in Yabuta 1998.

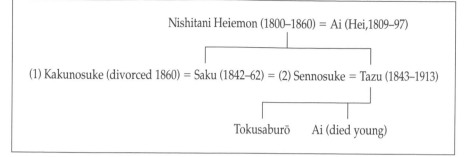

Figure 25. Nishitani Family tree. After Saku's death in 1862, Sennosuke married Tazu, but they were divorced in 1870. Ai later changed her name to Hei, and her granddaughter took the name Ai.

Saku was born on the third day of the second month of 1842; this is clear from a number of documents, preserved by the family to this day, that testify to the perceived value attached to documents pertaining to childhood, even in the case of girls, by this time. Although these documents carry no name, they were probably written by her father. The next piece of evidence that pertains to her is a slim volume that contains the *iroha* syllabary, numbers, an extract from the *Wakan rōeishū* (Japanese and Chinese poems to sing, ca. 1017–21), and other short passages and carries the names of Saku and her sister Tazu; in view of the high quality of the calligraphy, it seems likely that this was given to them for calligraphic practice (fig. 26).

Saku's diary in fact testifies to the existence of *terakoya* schools in the locality, but she does not record the names of the teachers. At the festival of *tanabata*, it was the custom to collect each pupil's calligraphic work and hang it up, and doubtless Saku and Tazu used this volume to practice their calligraphy. The next piece of evidence is a set of documents from the eleventh month of 1853, which seem to be in the hand of their mother, Ai (fig. 27). These record the rents derived from certain agricultural lands, and they seem to be rents that had been set aside for Saku's upbringing. Rather than meeting these expenses from the household budget or business income, land had been set aside for the purpose, an option that would only have been available to households with substantial resources.

For most of the year 1854 Saku was boarding with a certain Kawanabe Tessai in Sakai. This is apparent from a letter written by Tessai to her father. This was probably in order for her to further her education in a larger urban settlement.

The first document in Saku's own hand dates from the second month of 1854, when she was thirteen by Japanese reckoning (fig. 28). It is a letter that Saku and Tazu wrote to their father Heiemon, who was in Kyoto on

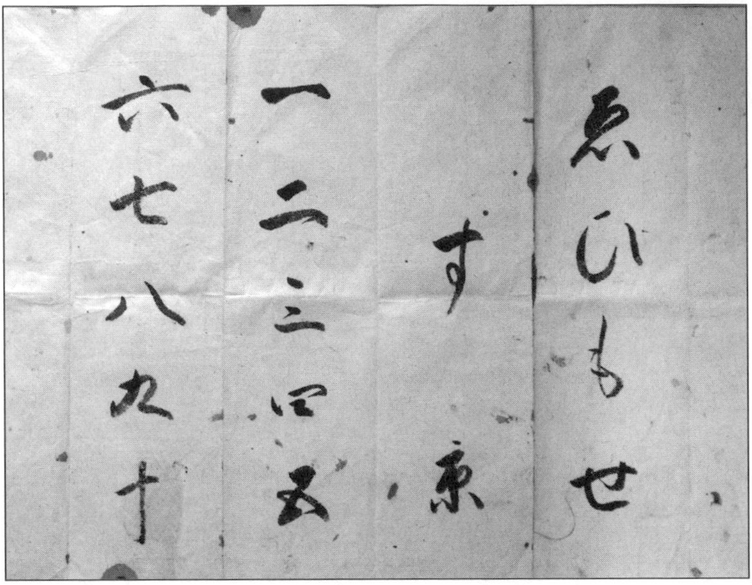

Figure 26. Models for calligraphy practice used by Saku and Tazu.

village business. When the family became separated in this way even for a short while, the practice of writing letters replaced the oral communication of the home. Thus letter writing depended not merely on literacy but on family circumstances as well. Furthermore, Saku's letter fluctuates in style, with some parts written in the formal language used in letter-writing manuals and other parts predominantly in the colloquial; at this stage, it is clear, her education was not yet complete. Nevertheless, the longing of the two girls for their father is only too apparent from their letters, and this is clearly the driving force behind their turn to letter writing as a form of communication.

The year 1854 has left behind a rich trove of documents related to Saku's upbringing. There is, for example, a document listing the titles of tunes for the samisen, which reveals that the two sisters were taking music lessons; in fact, it is clear from their mother's diary of a pilgrimage to Ise and from Saku's own diary that they were both learning how to play the samisen and the koto from a teacher outside the family. There is also a record of expenditures, which bears Saku's name and is, in the author's judgment, in her own hand, entitled "Chichiue-sama ni azukarichō" (Record Kept on Behalf of My Father). As with other documents that have survived, this testifies to the importance of household management skills in the education of girls.

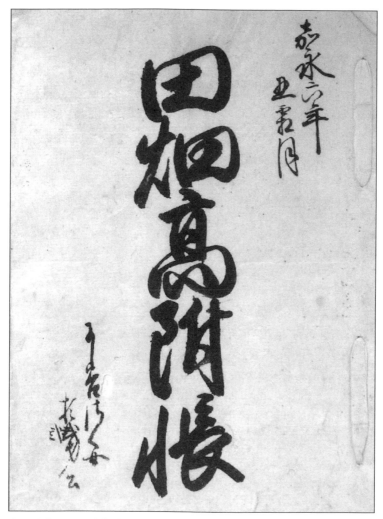

Figure 27. Title page of the list of landholdings used for Saku, whose name and age are in the bottom left.

Horoscopes were drawn up for Saku in 1853 and 1855 when she was twelve and fourteen, respectively, by Japanese reckoning. Those who told her fortune were either local fortune-tellers or specialists from Osaka and Sakai, including Hirasawa Hōgan, a well-known practitioner of divination based on the *Book of Changes* (Ch. *Yi jing*; J. *Ekikyō*). The results include such standard advice as "Not being careless is the way to good fortune," but they also contain more pointed suggestions concerning "an adopted

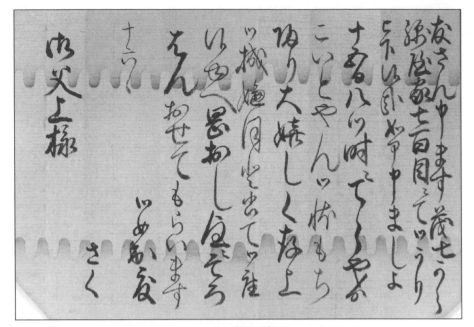

Figure 28.   Concluding portion of Saku's letter to her father in Kyoto.

son-in-law of seventeen or eighteen years of age coming from the north-west," which reflect her status as the elder of two girls and the expectation that she would take a *muko-yōshi*, that is, a husband who would be adopted into the Nishitani family and take the family name.

There is also a document in the hand of Tazu written when she was thirteen years old (fig. 29). This contains an account of dreams seen by Tazu and her mother. They had dreamed, for example, of Mount Fuji or a crane building a nest in a pine tree and had treated themselves to some nice things to eat in celebration of these auspicious dreams. The years, months, and days are duly recorded, and thus the document takes the form of a diary even though it does not go beyond the limited subject matter of dreams. It is written not on scraps of used paper but on fresh paper; given the cost of paper at the time, this is a clear indication that educationally and materially these two girls had a relatively privileged upbringing.

From these and other documents, it is apparent that by the time Saku and Tazu had reached thirteen years of age, by Japanese reckoning, not only had they mastered the mechanics of writing but they were also able to put it to practical use in letter writing and record keeping. The latter implies that they had some experience in use of the *soroban* (abacus); we also know that

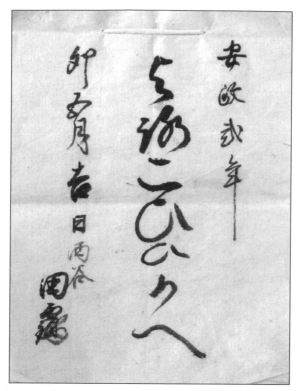

Figure 29.   Title page of Tazu's account of dreams seen by her and her mother.

they were learning the samisen and koto and that the expectation was that Saku would take a *muko-yōshi*.

As a document recording the engagement gifts received shows, the Nishitani family actually took Kakunosuke in as adopted son-in-law in the tenth month of 1857 when Saku was sixteen. The marriage had actually taken place the previous year, on 1856.4.2. As will be discussed later, it may be that the onset of her father's illness hastened matters and persuaded the family of the advisability of speedily concluding the arrangements.

Two documents dating from the first month of 1857 have a bearing on the wedding and are particularly interesting in the light of the fact that in terms of inheritance Saku, as eldest daughter in a family with no sons, could have been considered a "daughter with a house" when it came to looking for a husband for her. The first document is a record of expenditures (fig. 30), and the other is a record of household matters. Both were begun in the first month of 1857; the first ends in 1862 and the second in 1861. By then it was clearly Saku who was effectively running the household. This suggests some reconsideration of Saku's diary, which was the first item to be discovered and begins in the second month of 1860. It is of course the diary of a young woman named Saku, but, given her position in the family, it also has the character of a public record of the Nishitani family. Saku was, after all, keeping separate records of a more private nature at the same time.

Why should Saku, an elder daughter who had just married a man who was to become an adopted son-in-law of the Nishitani family, have needed to begin keeping a more formal record of family matters such as this? Surely it had something to do with a series of unexpected events, beginning with her father's illness, that had begun to impact the family. To throw light on these events there survive two records in the hand of Saku's mother, Ai, which record details of her father's illness and a pilgrimage to Ise undertaken in 1859. It seems, then, that early in 1860, the year of her father's death, Saku and her mother had shared out domestic responsibilities between them, with her mother running the kitchen and Saku taking on overall household management. Thus the diary was begun on 1860.2.7, just a few days after Kakunosuke, the adopted son-in-law, fled the household.[4]

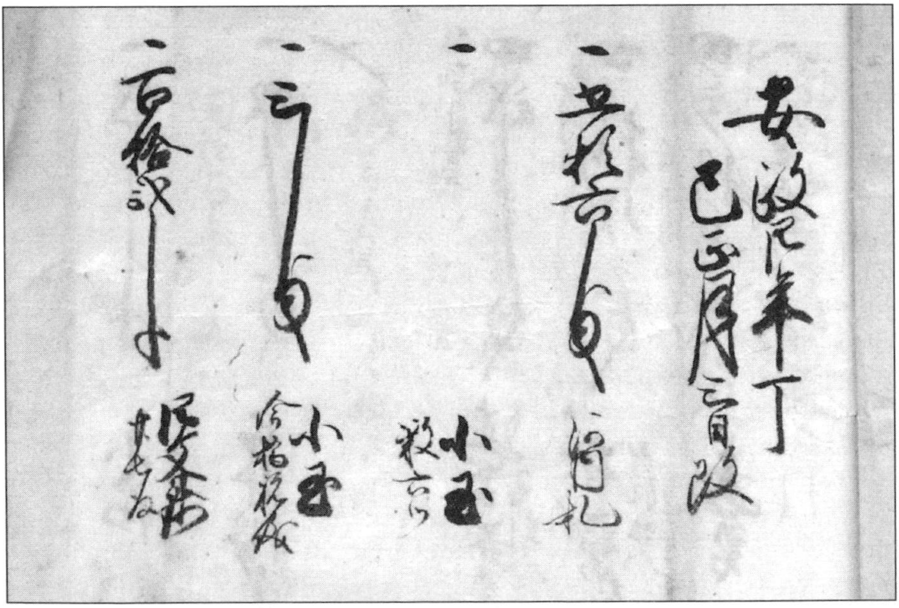

Figure 30.　First page of Saku's record of daily expenditures.

4. For further details, see Yabuta 2006.

In 1862, at age nineteen, Saku was married again to a new adopted son-in-law by the name of Sennosuke. Curiously enough, the records of both her marriages are to be found in a folder labeled "Marriage records of Nishitani Saku," and these are all in the hand of her mother. It was her mother, then, who maintained and preserved the records of Saku's life, including the record of her sudden death in the sixth month of 1862. It is unclear how Saku's mother Ai acquired her literacy, but it is clear that she became the record keeper at the end of Saku's short life and thereafter. A folder dated 1866.6.3 indicating that prayers were said on that day, probably the prayers offered on the anniversary of Saku's death, contains her own recollections and is further evidence of her literacy.

Needless to say, after Saku's death it was her mother who assumed responsibility for household management. In later years she left another record that has the character of a will; this has her handprint at the end but is actually in the hand of her other daughter, Tazu. "Writing," then, is not necessarily something that one carried out oneself but something that others could be asked to carry out on one's behalf. Probably in this case either Tazu was the more literate of the two or her mother was in ill health. Similarly, when Tazu was living in Osaka in 1859 and exchanging letters with her mother, her letters are clearly in her own hand, whereas her mother's were sometimes written for her by Saku.

In conclusion, six points can be made. First, although it is clear that Saku's literacy skills developed in the course of her life and were put to practical use, it is important to stress that the act of writing depended to some extent on chance circumstances such as her father's residence in Kyoto, which brought into play the exchange of letters, or Saku's assumption of responsibility for family management.

Second, the differences in literacy skills between Saku and her mother indubitably reflect differences in educational opportunities, particularly the postelementary education that Saku and Tazu received while boarding with families in Sakai and Osaka. Nevertheless, their writing contains dialect and colloquialisms, and it is clear that in order to write in a more literary way, without dialect and colloquialisms, as, for example, did Arakida Rei and Higuchi Ichiyō, it was necessary to undergo a more extensive education.

Third, names at the end of documents do not necessarily indicate who wrote them, for the act of writing—and especially record keeping—was one that could be asked of others and not necessarily something one undertook oneself.

Fourth, during Heiemon's final illness it was her mother who assumed formal responsibility as head of the household, but in reality it was Saku who kept the records. Although her mother was officially recognized as head of the household, this did not necessarily mean that she kept the records, and it is clear that she parceled out this task to her elder daughter.

Fifth, it is thanks to her mother that so many of the records kept by Saku have survived; doubtless she recognized the contribution to the family that Saku made. Later family headship reverted to a male when Tazu's son, Tokusaburō, took over the function and the records that Saku had kept were put aside. In a patrilineal society there was little space for women as record keepers.

Sixth, while it is possible through surviving documents to trace the writing activities of the Nishitani family women, it is much less easy to grasp how they used their literacy when it came to reading. The family certainly owned a number of books, including the familiar *Onna daigaku takarabako* (Treasure Box of the Greater Learning for Women, 1716), but the only trace of their reading is a brief reference in one of Ai's letters to the value of *Onna daigaku*.

8

The Taming of the Strange:
Arakida Rei Reads and Writes
Stories of the Supernatural

Atsuko Sakaki

It has been acknowledged that language plays an essential role in the formation of subjectivity. Hence, in a recent study of early modern women's literature in English, Jody Greene writes:

> The modern subject is both produced in and created by language . . . and the entry into language is a precondition for intelligibility and agency. Autobiography, then, is a seemingly natural site to which to turn for those wanting to locate the modern subject at the moment of its historical emergence.[1]

How, then, would one come to achieve and comprehend one's own subjectivity by writing something that looks remote from, if not opposite to, autobiography: stories of the archaic, the foreign, and the fantastic, stories that in content are historically, geographically, and ontologically distant from one's own locale?

1. Greene 2006, p. 18.

Ayashi no yogatari (Strange Talks of the Town, 1778), a collection of thirty stories written by Arakida Rei (1732–1806), is usually classified as *giko monogatari* (tales in the pseudoclassical language).[2] But *Ayashi no yogatari* manifests characteristics of many other genres. Given the format of a few poems embedded in prose, each story of the collection—which happens to be the last fictional narrative by this author of prodigious creative output— could be regarded as an *uta monogatari* (tale with poems). Moreover, many of Arakida's sources can be traced to literary Chinese texts whose genres range from *shi* (Chinese verse) to *zhiguai* (accounts of the supernatural) and *chuanqi* (tales of the strange), which is partly why the stories can also be con- sidered *hon'an* (adaptations) or *honmon-dori* (quotations from Chinese). The author's own preface invites a comparison of this work of hers with *Uji shūi monogatari* (Collection of Tales from Uji, early thirteenth century), as I shall explain below, although the absence of didacticism may confute the classifi- cation of Arakida's work as *setsuwa* (didactic tales).

Written at the intersection of several existing genres, then, *Ayashi no yogatari* is anything but a memoir, the genre with which women writers have been most frequently associated. Indeed, considering the impressive range and size of Arakida's literary output, it is noteworthy that memoir is one genre in which she remained mostly silent.[3] She wrote *rekishi monogatari* (his- torical narratives), *kikō* (travelogues), *renga* (linked poetry), *haikai* (nonstan- dard linked poetry), and *kanshi* (Chinese verse). She even annotated *Utsuho monogatari* (The Tale of the Hollow Tree, tenth century), a narrative fiction of substantial length and complexity. However, she did not make her name with *nikki* (memoirs). She does not seem to have been interested in writing of her "self" but devoted herself instead to writing of "others," historical, geo- graphical, and ontological. She wrote of Heian Japan—whether historical events or ostensibly fictional subjects—more extensively and compellingly than she did of Tokugawa Japan, the time in which she lived. She wrote of China, which she never visited. And she wrote of supernatural beings and incidents that were known to her only through literary sources. Her litera- ture, in short, is one of othering, a characteristic that defies the conventional attribution of domesticity and interiority to women's literature.

In light of the unique position that Arakida occupies in the history of Japanese women's literature and of Japanese literature in general, in my previous work I painted a picture of her as an inconvenient figure for liter-

---

2. She is also sometimes referred to as Arakida Reiko or Arakida Reijo in literary history. The title of this work is read *Kaiseidan* by Yosano Akiko (1878–1942). See Yosano 1915.
3. The exception is an autobiographical note that she composed, later given the title "Keitoku Reijo ikō" in Ōkawa 1972.

ary historians, a woman whose unusual orientation cost her a place in the canon.[4] This understanding of the author is corroborated by her infamous dispute with Motoori Norinaga (1730–1801), triggered by his extensive and unsolicited suggestions for stylistic revision of one of her anachronistic and sinophilic stories, "Nonaka no shimizu" (A Pure Stream in the Field, 1772).[5] Even Yosano Akiko, who in 1915 tried to resurrect Arakida from obscurity, did not wholeheartedly approve of her penchant for Heian, Chinese, and fantastic literature or of her seeming aversion to her own empirical experience.

> Reiko's fiction is much indebted to the literature and history of the Heian period, as well as to Chinese literature. It is an imaginary world that she depicts, grounded in an infatuation with the classics with which those works of literature and history had infected her; it reflects nothing of Reiko's direct experience of herself and the world she lived in. In other words, Reiko never managed to grasp the spirit of realism in *The Tale of Genji* but was instead intoxicated by the fantastical motifs of *The Tale of the Hollow Tree*. It is inevitable, therefore, that Reiko's fiction fails to penetrate to the essence and inner workings of human feeling and manners to the extent that Murasaki Shikibu's does.[6]

This quotation makes it clear that Akiko preferred the factual and familiar over the imaginary and unusual.[7] Some of her word choices (to "grasp...realism" over "intoxicated by the fantastical" or "spirit" over "motifs") affirm the hierarchy of significance in which she finds Arakida's work inferior. This comes as little surprise given that Akiko is most renowned for her candidly confessional poetry, which has been read as reflecting the highly publicized biographical facts of her eventful life. In spite of Akiko's own literary orientation (another proclaimed achievement of hers being a modern translation of *The Tale of Genji*), she did not credit Arakida for her distance from the here and now of her life.

When one considers that Arakida's life revolved around reading and writing texts, one wonders if she indeed fulfilled herself by her choice *not* to record quotidian matters of the present but instead to create a space in which unlikely and unusual incidents occur. If reading of the historically

---

4. See Sakaki 2005, pp. 115–21.
5. For Norinaga's corrections, see Ōkubo 1977, pp. 343–86. For brief accounts of the quarrel, see "Kaidai," in Ōkubo, 1977, pp. 23–25; and Kado 1998, pp. 150–57.
6. Yosano 1915, pp. 4–5. Translations are mine unless otherwise noted.
7. Note that Akiko is the pen name of the writer, whose legal name was Yosano Shō.

or geographically distant occupied her time and preoccupied her mind, it seems only "natural" and "true to herself" to write about them. Thus the stories that appear to be least "realistic" may in fact hold the key to her essence, reality, and truth. As we shall see, stories in *Ayashi no yogatari* feature many characters who are avid readers and writers of literature. Their portrayal with both affection and ridicule hints at how Arakida viewed herself and her position in society. She is both self-assertive and self-critical, managing to keep a distance from her alter egos and see herself in perspective.

In this essay, I will examine closely the texts and paratexts of *Ayashi no yogatari* to determine exactly how the author intended to process quoted texts and to what effect, with the ultimate aim of showing how she made her unique mark on literary history. In so doing, I plan to restore Arakida's subjectivity as formed by negotiations with lingual and literary conventions. I will first examine prefaces to the collection to locate her position vis-à-vis her text and its precursors. Next I will take a close look at how literary precedents (and in particular Chinese literary precedents) influence characters' judgments of things beyond their empirical comprehension. I will then discuss women's relation to learning (mainly in Chinese) as it is problematized in some of the stories, for this attests to Arakida's self-reflection as a learned female. The next step will be to look at portrayals of intellectuals in the stories in order to measure the extent to which learning remains valid and valuable in Arakida's view. I will pay particular attention to the narrator's position in relation to characters, both men of letters and those critical of them, in an attempt to identify the author's stance vis-à-vis the limits of the value of learning. To bring us to a denouement of all the issues raised in this study of Arakida, I will explicate "Hitōban" (Head-Flying Savage), a story in the *Ayashi no yogatari* collection, which was inspired by an ancient Chinese legend of a mysterious tribe and yet exceeds what we might expect in a translation or adaptation of a literary precedent. Arakida's reconfiguration of the original legend reveals complex and intense relations between the foreign and the domestic, the supernatural and the ordinary, the female and the male, and the imaginative and the realistic and also offers insight into her negotiation with literary history and formation of subjectivity in it.

Staging Oneself

Needless to say, I never give a thought to serious reading or even the practice of elegant amusements, and so, although the years have piled up, I remain extremely ignorant. My family being in the service of Shinto deities, I observe the taboos in the most traditional manner, but my [neglect] of [Buddhist] devotions for the life to come leaves me uneasy. Once in a great while I will pick up and read one of the few volumes of tales or poems that we have in the house, but . . .[8]

In the "Jijo" (author's preface) to *Ayashi no yogatari*, from which the above passage is taken, Arakida purports not to have read serious texts, not to be skilled in elegant amusements, not to have been devoted to Buddhist practices, and to have read only those poems and tales that happened to be in the family's possession, and only infrequently at that. This pose of ignorance is soon revealed as feigned.

These things that I have scribbled down, as in writing practice, merely to while away the idle hours, are hardly worth taking any notice of whatsoever. Much less do I presume to emulate those of the past, such as that Major Counselor, whatever his name was, who collected all those stories just as they were told to him. These here are a total mess. I've simply recorded what I've chanced to hear from old folks. Some of it concerns China, which, needless to say, I've never seen, and even those stories of ages long past in this country, which I'm told are quite true, I'm unable to determine whether they are true or false. My ears are not sharp, and I've a terrible tendency to mishear what I'm told. Moreover, I've mixed in all manner of unspeakable, unseemly, and unfounded matter. To the outside observer, this nonsense must give the impression that I've taken leave of my senses, but I take comfort in the thought that my abode is too shabby for any stranger to look into it.[9]

The way Arakida describes the process by which *Ayashi no yogatari* took shape seems merely to comply with the convention of apologizing for the audacious attempt to write in spite of one's own deficiencies as a writer. A closer look at her rhetoric, however, reveals many critical issues that are relevant to our shared concern in this volume with literacy such as adaptation of earlier texts within the range of the author's reading knowledge, the relationship between oral and written literature, and the boundaries between private and public practices of writing. Arakida alludes to *Uji shūi*

8. Izuno 1982, p. 1113.
9. Ibid., pp. 1113–14.

monogatari as "all those stories [collected] by that Major Counselor" only to declare that her work is not comparable to his. The negation of a parallel implicitly calls for comparison with the renowned collection of didactic tales. While denying her own work a place in literary history out of staged modesty, the author invites the reader to evaluate her work according to the literary norms established by the precedent. Despite the author's disclaimer that her work does not measure up to the precedent, her own description of the making of her work suggests that she employed a similar method of collecting and jotting down orally transmitted tales, and in the process there emerged a single writer in control of indefinite and anonymous storytellers. When she deems oral transmission of earlier tales potentially erroneous, partly because of her limited aural capacities, she privileges the written accounts over hearsay while ostensibly deprecating the quality of her own writing, which is based on oral literature.

Arakida also states that spatial and temporal distance from the stories (from China and the past, most significantly from Heian Japan, which inspired some of her stories and wherein they are presumably located) prevents her from accurately representing what she has heard. This apology that her work lacks empirical authenticity also serves to prepare the reader for the imaginative flights and digressions from the familiar as they take place in many of the stories in *Ayashi no yogatari*. At the same time, with such self-deprecation Arakida defends herself from the possible criticism that it is idiosyncratic if not eccentric of her to have acquired a vast reading knowledge on which to base her fiction. Instead of obliterating the propensity for the fantastic, which might be perceived as a fault, she admits to it, exposes it to the reader's attention, and joins the imagined chorus of criticism. By doing so, she establishes another self, that of a critic of herself.

Arakida intimates that she does not anticipate public distribution of her work and suggests that she lives in reclusion. This is misleading to say the least, as she is known to have enjoyed social interaction, especially through the practice of linked poetry, which, in its dominant form, requires that a group of poets gather for collective composition. Her remark should be taken primarily as a customary gesture of modesty, an aesthetic preference for the literary minded.[10] Thus, she anoints herself as a woman of letters precisely by disavowing the promise of literary fame.

---

10. At least Arakida does not seem to have been compelled to create what Catherine Gallagher (1994) calls an "author-self" to protect herself from exposure to the public, something that in the wake of print culture seventeenth-century English women writers had to face or risk disgrace.

Women and Literacy

A certain Miss Arakida from Ise, that province blessed by divine winds, was so fond of reading books in the Japanese language that, just for the fun of it, she composed a few fictions of her own. Some of the more interesting of these are collected here as a source of entertainment for readers but also in the hope that they might prove sufficiently edifying to be worthy of the study of young ladies.[11]

In this colophon, the writer Seiasai, who finds *Ayashi no yogatari* useful both for pleasure and for instruction, specifies Arakida's sources as Japanese-language texts and her readers as women motivated to learn to read. This is a delimiting and inaccurate description of the author and her work in question. The intended effect of this belittling of the author's accomplishments and potential might be to protect Arakida from any criticism of the impropriety of her formidable knowledge (especially in Chinese), which far exceeded what was considered the proper range for women at the time. Thus, this colophon promotes women's literacy only conditionally, precluding Chinese-language texts.

The textual segregation of literate women from the circle of literati enjoying *kanshibun* (Chinese writing) and the confinement of them to the domain of *wabun* and *waka* (Japanese writing) is voiced in Arakida's own writing. In the sixth story of *Ayashi no yogatari*, "Nochi no yo no yama" (The Hills of Later Life), a learned courtier proclaims:

Really, women are just hopeless! They can't read the difficult characters, so they've no sense of the profundities of texts written in Chinese/from China.[12]

On the surface, this statement seems an unbridled dismissal of women since they lack learning and intelligence. If we look at the context in which the male courtier issues this statement, however, it becomes evident that his remark is showcased as folly, one of the instances of misconduct for which he is known. This man, while respected for his skills in Chinese composition, is despised for his indiscreet pursuit of amorous affairs and in a subsequent section reveals his incompetence in composing romantic *waka* as

11. Izuno 1982, p. 1287.
12. Ibid., pp. 1140–41.

he approaches a lady-in-waiting. Although some noblemen suggest to the circle of her colleagues that they should be kind to the learned man as he has distinguished himself in *kanshi*, the net effect is that he exposes his deficiencies in social protocol and artistic sensibility. The speech quoted above should thus be read as a sign of his impudence rather than the expression of a widely held understanding of women's intelligence that is endorsed by the narrator.

However, another story reiterates women's inability to attend properly to Chinese-language texts, this time in material terms. In the seventh story, "Yaso no chimata" (Numerous Crossroads), a man and woman are married precisely as their respective parents (who were friends) had predicted years earlier. A significant ramification of this preordained encounter is that eventually the husband comes to possess the inheritance of the woman's late father's books.

> The husband's father, too, was a scholar, and at the time [the two parents] were close friends and had already pledged their children [in marriage] to each other. [The girl's father] was worried that his wife and daughter might, blithely and frivolously, dispose of the treasures that had been handed down in the family, as well as his many books. And so he hid them away, as in the caverns of the two Mounts You, and wrote a detailed will bequeathing them to the husband. As the husband was himself very learned, and earnestly devoted to his studies, it hardly need be stated that he was overjoyed. He tracked down the books, built a library to house them, and moved them there.[13]

The woman's father had not trusted the females in his household to maintain his book collection properly and had hid it in a niche, reminiscent of the Chinese caverns where legend has it that rare books were stored. His intention had been to hand them down to the man he believed his daughter was meant someday to wed. Indeed, this man has grown up to be a man of letters and much appreciates the acquisition of the books through his conjugal connection. In this story, the woman—the daughter of the original scholar—has a limited role in the transmission of the books, merely as their mediator. In contrast to the previously examined story, here there is little criticism implied in the narrator's portrayal of either the father or the husband, and thus the male-male bonding through books seems to be favorably construed at the cost of women, who are deprecated and excluded from the male-oriented intellectual circle.

13. Ibid., pp. 1152–53.

Here, as elsewhere in Arakida's oeuvre, it is difficult to identify her position as both a woman and an intellectual. Biographers tell us that her parents did not approve of her literary education and that her brothers tutored her, providing early support that was continued by her adopted father and husband. Thus, while she embraced the unusual privileges she was afforded by unusually supportive men in her life, she was certainly not oblivious to the bar to education and literary activities that most women of her time had to endure. She was culturally masculine and for that reason might have been alienated from the circle of less educated women to the extent that she became suspicious of other women's intellectual facility. Without further speculating on her ultimate stance on gender and education, I would simply stress the unresolved ambiguity of her identity, which leads her to speak through her work as though she were gender neutral.

China as a Model

TALE NO. 4: "Fireflies above the Stream"
He dimly recalled that, yes, such things had happened in China, and he felt that [his experience] was so unusual that it might well become something that everyone would be talking about.[14]

TALE NO. 19: "Head-Flying Savages"
When the governor consulted Chinese texts, he realized that such things had happened there.[15]

TALE NO. 27: "Clouds at Dawn"
As though to emulate the spirit of the Chinese . . .[16]

"Well, there were examples of this in China," he said with a know-it-all look on his face.[17]

Our next question is exactly which sources the author Arakida was familiar with, and managed to downplay her knowledge of, by transferring the agency of quotation onto her fictional characters. Her practice is in keeping with her stated reading knowledge as far as poems and tales are concerned. Not only quotations of phrases but also the similarity of each story's structure—relatively short prose with poems embedded at important junctures—attest

14. Ibid., p. 1136. For a translation of this story, see Selden 2008.
15. Ibid., p. 1220.
16. Ibid., p. 1264.
17. Ibid., p. 1266.

to the literary lineage to which *Ayashi no yogatari* belongs. Still, Arakida's work reveals a distinct sensibility, as is obvious from the focus on the comical: laughter is ubiquitous in her work, while tears flow abundantly in Heian precursors; and she covers ground other than romantic intrigues, while in *monogatari* romance is a predominant theme. Arakida thus exploits the established format and texture while developing unique thematic dimensions, an approach that speaks to her way of establishing subjectivity as a writer who uses her reading knowledge strategically.

Chinese-language sources that Arakida frequently uses in the text signal departures from the Heian legacy. Quoted texts are not limited to the Middle Tang poets (Bai Juyi, Yuan Weizhi, and others) that were favored by the Heian writers Arakida aspired to assimilate; her sources include High Tang (eighth-century) poetry (for example, by Li Bai and Du Fu), as well as noncanonical if well-known stories of the supernatural such as *zhiguai* from the Six Dynasties and *chuanqi* from the Tang dynasty. The frequent reference to High Tang poetry, which was not fully appreciated in Japan until as late as the early seventeenth century, suggests that Arakida was in tune with the contemporary Japanese reception of classical Chinese poetry. The same goes for her familiarity with *zhiguai* and *chuanqi*. Edo period literati translated stories of the strange, adapted them, and wrote their own stories in a similar mode. Arakida's use of Chinese genres and subgenres other than Middle Tang poetry sets her work apart from its Heian models.

While Chinese poetry typically enters the narratives of *Ayashi no yogatari* as male courtiers recite lines in *kundoku* (Japanese reading), revealing their intellectual level, stories of the strange, the titles of which are not cited, are consulted by characters who face things of which their reason cannot help them to make sense. Unusual incidents that would otherwise remain unaccountable are accepted and registered as true and worthy of record as long as precedents are identified at a great historical or geographical distance. Accounts from China and the Japanese past confer the status of legitimacy as models against which strange occurrences are measured for their recognition in the civilized, orderly world. This insistence on precedents is also by extension a celebration of literacy, as knowledge of the distant land or distant time was available not empirically but only through writing. When we recall the preface in which Arakida expresses her distrust of oral/aural communication, it is understandable that the practice of consulting documentation of the past in Chinese—that is to say, in the language of the establishment—verifies what is real and/or true, though occasionally the practice, if executed improperly, could be criticized as pedantic.

Knowledge of the past or the foreign, however, does not ensure that a character is portrayed in a positive light. The adjective *zaearu*, meaning "learned," especially in Chinese learning, is frequently employed as an indication of the merit of the central character in fourteen out of the thirty stories in *Ayashi no yogatari,* and yet this commendable quality is often (nine times out of fourteen) accompanied with undesirable qualities, leaving the person's overall worthiness questionable. In classical tales male protagonists are often nearly perfect, with gifts and accomplishments that include learning in Chinese, compositional skills, musical talent, an appealing physical appearance, proper behavior, a prestigious family lineage, and high rank. In contrast, Arakida tends to present the learned as deprived of other privileges, especially social position. They are often professional scholars (*hakase*), who ranked relatively low in the Heian period. Not only are these characters socially unimpressive, but they also reveal vulnerabilities as they pursue their objects of affection in rather unseemly ways or are drunk and behave improperly in public. The abundance of men of letters who lack self-discipline and social grace suggests Arakida's ability and propensity to qualify the effects of education and the value of learning and to place in perspective the circle of intellectuals of which she was a part.

As in the case of the second quotation from "Clouds at Dawn," the narrator often caricatures a self-assured scholar who shows off his knowledge of Chinese by employing such deprecating expressions as *shitarigao nite* (knowingly). In addition to criticizing this deficiency in social protocol, the author also manages to elude any possible criticism of pedantry, transferring the agency of quotation to the character while effectively getting across the point of the quotation.

Location of Laughter

TALE NO. 6: "The Hills of Later Life"
He excelled in learning . . . but was strangely foolish and even lustful, which people deplored as unseemly. . . . Since [women] considered him mad and treated him with indifference, he most often slept alone. . . . The court nobles, too, laughed at him. . . . People could not even be bothered to deride him as "appalling" but only laughed at him all the more. . . . They regarded him as foolish . . . and would burst out laughing at him. . . . So nonplussed were they that they even allowed this to be witnessed by the gentlewomen of the court, who were beside themselves with laughter.[18]

18. Ibid., pp. 1140–42.

TALE NO. 10: "Ōmi"

Although his learning could not be faulted, he was by nature such a fool that no one took him at all seriously. . . . He was so full of himself . . . that wherever he went he was the object of uproarious laughter.[19]

TALE NO. 11: "Fire in the Furnace"

Although people laughed at him for the way he became so flustered and panicked over even the slightest of matters, his command of serious scholarship was impressive. . . . His attendants laughed among themselves, saying this was nothing new, but this time his panic was entirely excessive. . . . So shocking yet hilarious was his behavior . . . that people seemed unable to suppress their laughter.[20]

TALE NO. 14: "Katsuragi"

Though exceptionally learned, when it came to matters of the heart he was ridiculously silly . . . so much so that young noblemen would take pleasure in ridiculing him. He became a target of laughter. . . . It was unbearably funny. . . . His facial expression was so foolish that [even he] found it hard to resist the funniness, but [he] tried to pretend to be calm. . . . Noblemen could not suppress laughter. . . . As he sounded serious, even though they came close to bursting into laughter they tried to suppress the impulse. . . . No one could resist his comicality and laughed to their heart's content. . . . Noblemen heard about this and laughed a great deal.[21]

TALE NO. 15: "Fushimi"

He was such a fool that fate had given up on him and no one took him seriously. Still, his learning was respectable. . . . Noblemen took pleasure in ridiculing him. . . . They laughed excessively. . . . The attendants tried to stifle their laughter. . . . The monk and attendants laughed endlessly. People at the elder master's residence also heard about it and laughed even more.[22]

TALE NO. 17: "Yatsuhashi"

His learning was respectable. . . . His attendants said that it was unfortunate that he was intoxicated, which made people laugh. . . . The attendants could not manage to dissuade him [from acting improperly] and let him do as he liked. . . . The servants did not consider his behav-

19. Ibid., pp. 1164–65.
20. Ibid., pp. 1173–76.
21. Ibid., pp. 1188–96.
22. Ibid., pp. 1197–1202.

ior shameful but could not resist laughing in private. . . . Those who followed him could not endure how funny it was [to watch him act so foolishly] . . . . People could not resist the impulse to laugh. . . . [The master] was appalled and displeased with the commotion, but he did not go so far as to punish him.[23]

TALE NO. 21: "Utsusemi"

They were learned, so the people at the office thought it unfortunate. . . . People felt anxious for him. . . . Everyone thought it a trifling flaw, so although they felt embarrassed and worried they could not say anything and stood by and watched. . . . As people looked on, they could not resist his comicality, so they retreated and laughed behind the scenes. . . . Attendants and all who were present could not resist laughing. . . . Attendants did not pronounce "What is this?" and, letting him do as he liked, walked on. . . . The people at the office could not even say as much as "It's embarrassing," laughing their fill. . . . The funniness was irresistible. . . . Thinking it extraordinary, [the master] laughed. The master's sons . . . laughed. The master laughed.[24]

TALE NO. 23: "Pampas Grass"

He was exceptionally learned, but he tended to be a little impulsive and was often laughed at by others. Young noblemen thought him a fool and disliked him. He appeared to be proud of himself. . . . His wife said, "What's the matter with you? How embarrassing you look! People would think you were insane," and tried to stop him. . . . Everyone who saw him laughed. . . . He appeared to be serious, so without questioning him they just laughed in private. . . . People appeared to be laughing as they watched and didn't say a word. . . . People at the master's residence appeared to be laughing as they watched. . . . It was so extraordinarily rare that it was funny.[25]

TALE NO. 26: "Kasatori"

As he was knowledgeable in serious matters, he was taken seriously. Nonetheless, his mind tended to be a little unworldly. Although his appearance was not pleasant, he was promiscuous to the extent that others accused him of behaving beneath his merits. In the palace, servants exchanged gazes and laughed as though he were mad. . . . The master attributed [the man's behavior] to intoxication and assuaged his rage.

23. Ibid., pp. 1207–11.
24. Ibid., pp. 1229–31.
25. Ibid., pp. 1240–42.

There was no severe punishment, and he was pardoned after a while. It must be because he was such a fool [that his misconduct was not taken seriously.][26]

In *Ayashi no yogatari* the narrator does not frame each story with a concluding remark, a lesson to be learned, or a reiteration of the point of the story. This absence of explicit commentary disqualifies the work as a collection of *setsuwa*, as the narrator does not yield to didacticism. If any criticism is issued, it is through characters, often marginal to the core of the story, who typically sniff or laugh at the follies of some of the central characters.

Laughter triggered by anomalous or erroneous conduct is prevalent in many of the stories collected in *Ayashi no yogatari*. The placement of characters who cannot suppress laughter or giggles is effective in framing silly behavior and offering measured criticism without wielding any final moral or ethical judgment on the characters under scrutiny. The typical development of comical incidents in *Ayashi no yogatari* illustrates that those who have flaws (for example, excessive flirtatiousness) get into trouble through their lack of self-discipline. The lapse is often temporary and might be caused, for example, by heavy drinking. They lose control of themselves, or lose the proper perspective from which to view an issue they face, and do things that civilized persons would not normally do (for example, they disguise themselves as ghosts to frighten others who either get on their nerves or stand between them and their object of affection). Laughter breaks out either from the camp of their servants, who are characteristically portrayed as rational and eager to save their master's reputation (with little success), or from the laughable characters' superiors. It is these superiors to whom follies are revealed in the end, where ramifications are inevitable, but, again typically, they do not take these incidents very seriously and are ready to forgive the derailed individuals for their poor judgment.

The stories thus end on a happy note if not without embarrassment on the part of those who have come to their senses. At this point sobering statements from the narrator intended to reinforce the lessons learned would ruin the effect. This consistent structural pattern tells us that Arakida as the author confidently allowed her readers to judge for themselves or trusted her own storytelling skills to articulate the points without expounding on them in the voice of the narrator. Despite the unspoken pact between the author and the reader, both belonging to the intellectual circle, the stories do not affirm the values shared by members of the group as universal.

26. Ibid., pp. 1258–62.

Lack of narratorial intervention in each of the stories not only saves them from didacticism but also locates what I would call discursive accountability within the speeches of characters rather than the framing narrator's statements. References to sources are made not by the narrator but by characters—typically male courtiers—and thus the narrator's erudition is not put to the test. In this case, where the narratorial layer is thin and the reader can easily imagine hearing the author's voice without the narrator's mediation, the placement of quotations effectively releases the author from the responsibility of accounting for them and, perhaps more important, from any uninvited criticism of the inappropriate breadth of her reading knowledge. It is often the case with narratives in the classical Japanese language that a feminine narrator (even if she is not explicitly identified as female) elides quoting Chinese-language poems composed by male courtiers, stating something to the effect that *she* would not do justice to them and is thus inclined to omit them from *her* text. In *Ayashi no yogatari*, the narrator's presence is kept to a minimum, and thus he or she can describe courtiers' compositions with an effect of authenticity without having to apologize for pretentiousness.

Domesticating the Foreign and the Strange: "Head-Flying Savage"

Kado Reiko, a critic who has devoted herself to resurrecting Edo period women writers from relative or overwhelming obscurity, cites a few Chinese sources of supernatural fiction that Arakida used. Among them are the *Soushenji* (early fourth century), which collects *zhiguai* stories of the supernatural; *Taiping guangji* (978), wherein *chuanqi* stories of the strange are found; and *Jiandeng xinhua* (1378), a Ming dynasty collection of stories of the supernatural written in *wenyan* (literary Chinese).[27] As mentioned above, these texts had been translated or adapted into Japanese by Arakida's time, and thus proficiency in Chinese was not a prerequisite for familiarity with them. Nevertheless, their Chinese origin cannot have been lost on readers, and thus quotations from these sources must have evoked fascination with the exotic. In the case of the specific story we are about to examine, "Head-Flying Savage," the foreignness of the woman whose head flies at night is confirmed by a character who consults Chinese sources as quoted earlier. The source that remains uncited within Arakida's story is *Shanhaijing* (Classics of Mountains and Seas), which collects accounts of myths and geography,

27. Kado 1998, pp. 136–42.

flora and fauna, as well as mineral and supernatural phenomena. In order for us to see the extent of modification in the hand of Arakida, let us first consider the original Chinese version of the story of "Head-Flying Savage."

> In Ch'in times, in the south, there lived the Headfall people whose heads were capable of flying about. This particular tribe conducted sacrifices which they named "Insect Fall," and from that ceremony they took their name.
>
> In Wu times, General Chu Huan took a captive maid from there, and each night when he had fallen asleep, her head would suddenly begin to fly about. It would fly in and out of the dog door or the skylight using its ears as wings; toward dawn it would return to its proper place—and this happened many, many times.
>
> Those around General Chu Huan found this very strange, and late one night they came with torches to observe. They found only the body of the girl, the head being missing. Her body was slightly chilled, and her breathing was labored. They covered the body completely with a counterpane, and near dawn the head returned, only to be balked by the bedcovers. Two or three times it attempted to get under the covers with no success; it finally fell to the floor. The sounds it made were piteous indeed, and the body's breathing became agitated. It appeared to be on the brink of death when the men pulled back the covers, and the head rose again to attach itself to the neck. A short while later, her respiration became tranquil.
>
> Chu Huan found their report very strange indeed and, being afraid to keep the girl in his household, released her and returned her to the tribe. Having examined this very carefully, all came to the conclusion that the flying head was a natural attribute of these people.
>
> At that time the commanding general of Yün-nan expeditions frequently came across such tribes. Once someone covered one of the bodies with an inverted copper bowl, and the head being unable to reach its body, both parts perished.[28]

While inheriting the few strange incidents that constitute the center of the story, Arakida domesticated it. As we shall see shortly, the setting is ostensibly in Japan, the characters appear to be Japanese, and the poems inserted are exclusively in classical Japanese.

Unlike Kurahashi Yumiko's parody of the same source, *Kubi no tobu onna* (The Woman with the Flying Head, 1985), a contemporary tale of male

---

28. Translated in DeWoskin and Crump 1996, p. 147, as "The Tribe with Flying Heads."

obsession with a decapitated female body, incestuous desire, and quasi rape or necrophilia, Arakida's story gently relates the lives of ordinary people—who are, while prone to indiscretion, decent in nature—whose otherwise quiet existence is disturbed when one of them, a refined young female servant, is seen to exhibit the extraordinary characteristic of head flying.[29] The first witness is the governor in whose household the woman in question worked as a lady-in-waiting. Secretly in love with her, he had expressed his feelings to her, but when he sneaked into her bedchamber he found that her head was missing.[30] He could not report the "incident" to anyone on the spot for fear that his indiscretion would be revealed and that he might even be suspected of beheading the woman.

> Gathering that she was not as heartless as a rock or lumber, he was intensely tempted to get closer to her. That night he secretly visited her in the quiet after everyone had gone to bed. To his delight, she was not in the quarter with other women but was lying alone in a room on the veranda. Excited, the governor promptly approached her, but his arrival did not seem to stir her. He thought she must have been fast asleep. As he removed the top layer of the bedclothes, she did not utter a sound. In the dim light coming through the screens, although her skin was warm and there was nothing abominable, she did not appear to have a head. "That's strange, it must be my eyes," the governor thought. Uncertain, he raised the curtain a little and took another look—indeed, she had no head. Suddenly feeling repelled and vulnerable, the governor thought of awakening the people around him and letting them know about this horrifying finding. But then his improper conduct would come to be known, which would be bothersome. Given the suspicious circumstances around the woman, he might be wrongly accused of a crime, which would be shameful. So he decided to leave right away, and yet, reminded of having seen this woman's lovely appearance these past days, he could not but turn his head and take another look at her.

> *Ephemeral indeed, morning frost unknowingly waited*
> *   to thaw*
> *Not realizing its color would not endure the sunshine*

29. See Sakaki 2005, pp. 137–38, on the connections between Kurahashi's story and its Chinese Urtext.
30. It is interesting that romantic relationships in *Ayashi no yogatari* are all monogamous or at least predicated on a monogamous social system that is not in keeping with the practice of polygamy in the Heian Japan in which the stories are ostensibly set.

> The governor returned to his chamber as though nothing had happened, but he could not sleep.[31]

The next morning, the governor is shocked to see the woman alive—and with her head, naturally. Soon, however, other members of the household catch sight of her head flying.

> Unbeknownst from where, the woman's head flew in from the sky, like a bird or something, its ears as the wings. All present were frightened and confounded and lay with their faces down, distraught. Then the woman got up innocently. She seemed embarrassed to see so many people around [while she had been asleep]. There was nothing horrifying about her—in fact she looked lovely.[32]

The woman is discharged without being told the true reason (that she is not a normal human being). Distressed by the sudden turn of events, which does not make sense to her, she suspects that the governor's wife has discovered his attraction to her and become enraged with jealousy.

> She did not know what had happened at all and felt ashamed of herself; in the capital, too, she was inexplicably disliked by others and discharged from employment wherever she was hired. Not knowing what to do, she returned home. Then the wife of this governor so intently invited her that she joined her household. In just a short while she was discharged, which was embarrassing. In this household, the mistress appeared to be sincerely welcoming and yet so suddenly dismissed her. Could it be because the mistress had heard of the governor's flirtation and felt distant? The woman was so ashamed that her thoughts were in disarray. As she was about to leave the residence for good, she scribbled on the sliding doors in her quarter:
>
> > *An attendant on Fence Island—even the name sounds alienating.*
> > *The place has presented me a path of separation.*
> > *Cypress pillar, may I rely on you not to forget me?*
>
> Seeing the scribbles, the mistress felt sorry for her in spite of the horror.[33]

31. Izuno 1982, pp. 1218–19.
32. Ibid., p. 1220.
33. Ibid.

Ignorant of her own extraordinary condition, the woman then suffers a fatal accident at the place of her new employment: her flying head fails to reattach itself to the rest of her body, which leads to her death. The narrator uncharacteristically steps in to comment that the woman's parents must have been very distressed by her demise.

> There, too, people witnessed strange incidents, which the governor of Dewa found unusual. As an experiment, they placed a copper basin on the pillow. Without any means to return, the head [of the woman] wandered around until the dawn broke. The woman eventually passed away without her head back. Whichever province she might have gone to, everyone loved her, as she was beautiful, and tried to ignore her horrifying secret. When you think about how her parents and siblings might have felt about her death, I cannot help but feel very sorry.[34]

The unusual narratorial intervention suggests that given the nature of the story the author felt it necessary to defend the woman with the flying head and to lead the reader toward the compassion that she, as a gentle and sensible being, deserved rather than possibly leaving the reader repelled by the horror.

While drawing on the ancient Chinese account of "head-flying savages," this story domesticates the woman with the flying head not only in the sense that she lives in Japan and speaks in Japanese but also in terms of her gentrified, thoughtful, and reserved character, unlikely given her "savage" identity. The male protagonist, her suitor, is also portrayed favorably; his hesitation, regrets, and remorse are described from his own viewpoint, rather than a critic's, as he hides one secret from his wife and another from the head-flying woman. This is not to suggest that the story is a psychological novel but that it offers glimpses into characters' interiors without the narrator passing judgment. Thus, this story draws its reader's attention to humanity rather than savagery and commonality rather than eccentricity and in so doing assimilates the story of the supernatural into the realm of *monogatari* or poetic romance. While the source text *Shanhaijing* attempts to collect and catalog strange stories and thus exoticizes people with flying heads for the benefit of readers assumed to be normal and intellectual, Arakida's text unites humans and super- or subhumans in the cultural practice of good behavior and artistic activities such as *waka* composition.

34. Ibid., p. 1221.

Conclusion

Perhaps it might be well to reconfigure our measures for the identification of authors, shifting the focus from their historical, geographical, and ontological whereabouts (the points they occupy in history, geography, and ontology respectively) to the discursive trajectories in their practices of reading and writing, their own projects/projections vis-à-vis literary norms of scripts, languages, and genres. In other words, identity is not defined by one's place or time of origin, which we can identify geographically or historically, but by the way one departs from it, where one reaches, and by what process, in discursive terms.

In the case of Arakida, her constant disavowal of being one thing or another—a rigorous scholar, a devout Buddhist—may mean more than compliance with the protocol of modesty; it may indicate her desire to be always somewhere else, beyond predictable classifications. Without her reading and writing, she would have been no one. By her engagement with stories of the supernatural and the foreign, she became who she was: a woman with a flying head—whose mind leaves her body to take flight to distant times and places that she found in texts she read, and that she could revisit in texts she wrote.

9

Kishida Toshiko and the Career of a Public-Speaking Woman in Meiji Japan

Sugano Noriko

In an earlier essay I examined the writings of Fukuzawa Yukichi, Hirahara Hokudō and Nakagawa Zennosuke in order to see how *Onna daigaku* (Greater Learning for Women), one of the most widely diffused conduct books for women in the Edo period, fared in the eyes of readers from the beginning of the Meiji period up to the Pacific War.[1] I wanted to understand how it was read by successive generations, whether critically or with approval, and I discussed, among other works, Fukuzawa Yukichi's *Onna daigaku hyōron* (Critique of *Onna daigaku*) and *Shin onna daigaku* (New *Onna daigaku*). Although they were published in 1899, these were actually based on various pieces he had written in the 1880s at the end of the period when the Freedom and Popular Rights Movement (Jiyū minken undō) was at its most active, and it is to this earlier period that I turn my attention here.

Among the many people in that period who were deeply conscious of *Onna daigaku* in their writings was Kishida Toshiko (1863–1901), who was

---

1. Sugano 2006. *Onna daigaku* seems to have been compiled from the section "Joshi o oshiyuru hō" (How to Teach Girls) in Kaibara Ekiken's *Wazoku dōjikun* (published in 1710). The oldest extant edition of *Onna daigaku* dates from 1729.

the eldest daughter of a Kyoto draper. In 1879 she was specially chosen to be a "literary assistant" (*bunji goyōgakari*) at court and lectured to the Meiji empress on *Mencius* and other texts, but after two years she resigned on grounds of ill health and spent some time traveling with her mother. Beginning in 1882 she spent nearly two years touring Japan and speaking on the extension of women's rights, and in 1884 she married Nakajima Nobuyuki (1846–99), vice president of the Liberal Party and president of its sister organization in western Japan, the Japan Constitutional Party. She published a number of essays on educational and social matters in the journal *Jogaku zasshi*, and in 1890, when her husband was elected to the House of Representatives in Japan's first general election and became its first speaker, she assumed the public role of the speaker's wife. When he lost his seat in the 1892 election he was appointed minister to Italy, but they resided only a short while in Rome before returning to Japan; Nobuyuki died in 1899 and Kishida just two years later.

Kishida has been variously described as an activist for people's rights, a critic, and a novelist, but most of the work on her life has hitherto focused on her political activities in connection with the Freedom and Popular Rights Movement.[2] As an advocate of "women's rights," she sought to undermine the familiar notion of *danson johi* (revere men, despise women), which continued to dominate attitudes in her day. To this end she engaged in various activities, but at the heart of her advocacy of women's rights lay her views on women's education.

Kishida as Public Speaker

Kishida was an active public speaker. Between 1882 and 1884 she gave as many as forty speeches in Osaka, Okayama, Shikoku, Kumamoto, Kyoto, and other places in western Japan as she traveled around with her mother. It was one of her speeches, on *hakoiri musume* ("sheltered girls," literally "girls in a box"), that brought her into conflict with the authorities, and it is in this speech that the influence of her thinking on *Onna daigaku* can be detected. Kishida's career as a public speaker seems to have ended soon after the speech on "sheltered girls" in October 1883. The fact that she married in 1884 may also explain the cessation of her speech making. Thereafter she turned to print, writing for *Jogaku zasshi* and other journals.

2. See Suzuki Yūko 1985, 1986; and Ōki 2003. In English, see Copeland 2000; Mackie 2003; and Sievers 1983.

Articulating one's opinions in public in the form of speeches was a new activity that rapidly caught on in the Meiji period and became a particularly effective tool in the hands of the Popular Rights activists. Thus it became essential for such activists to be eloquent in public.[3] Kishida was no exception, and the newspapers reported that her speeches were attracting ever more attention. For example, the *Kumamoto shinbun* reported, "Kishida Toshiko arrived here [in Kumamoto] on the second [of November 1882] and her speech on the evening of the fifth at the Meishin auditorium in Kōya-machi drew such attention that men and women, young and old, thronged the hall and there was hardly any room left."[4] This was also because "speech meetings" in the Meiji period were colored to some extent by elements of "show" or "performance," including fees charged for entry, and it seems that this was a notable feature of Kishida's speeches, especially those delivered in Kyoto. The *Shimei shinpō* reported that, "On the evenings of the fourth and fifth [of November], Kishida Toshiko took part in a speech meeting at the Meishin auditorium in Kōya-machi. On this occasion, too, the audience filled the room and the organizers apparently made a larger profit than expected."[5] At the beginning of her speech on sheltered girls she stated that, as "a woman's mission," she was giving speeches in order to promote women's education, and in response to criticism that "one who used to wear brocade is now coming to small theaters to give performances," she argued that she was acting in the interests of the state.[6] But it is worth recalling that as early as 1877 the *Kinji hyōron* noted that the government was intending to place restrictions on public speeches and that "the object is to prevent excessively young persons or gloomy and discontented persons from using speeches to stir people up and disturb the public peace."[7] If the government saw this as a danger, Kishida, by contrast, saw it as an opportunity and encouraged her youthful audiences to speak their minds, as we shall see.

What were the features of Kishida's two years of public speeches? Not a great deal is known about the actual content of the speeches Kishida delivered before the one on sheltered girls, but the newspaper reports do provide some clues, and it is by using those reports that I analyze her tour of Japan.

---

3. The spread of speech making was noticed in an editorial in *Yūbin hōchi shinbun* on 28 May 1879 (Inada 2000, p. 247).

4. *Kumamoto shinbun*, no. 1392, 8 November 1882.

5. *Shimei shinpō*, no. 48, 9 November 1882.

6. Suzuki Yūko 1985, p. 213. It seems that Kishida did dress theatrically for her speeches and looked like a "princess in a play" (Sōma 1985, p. 49).

7. *Kinji hyōron*, no. 92, 13 November 1877; Inada 2000, p. 258. In fact such a law was passed on 17 July 1878.

In Osaka and Shikoku, most of her speeches were given at political gatherings when she spoke as a member of the Liberal Party and in the company of other members. Regarding a speech she delivered in Shikoku in 1882, the *Futsū shinbun* reported:

> Because she is highly critical of the government, it looked likely, judging by experience, that a dispersal order would be issued, but—surely not because she was a woman—the police in attendance were quite relaxed and seemed to pay little attention. This gave [Kishida] Toshiko greater energy; she spoke fluently and with ever stronger views. She compared the government to heaven: "Listen everybody, the heaven that is above us is about to fall to earth; this is because the pillars that support it are not strong enough. If we continue like this we will all be crushed to death. Our lives may be dispensable, but on what soil could the flag of our empire, which has lasted for three thousand years with a continuous imperial line, rise again? So if heaven is going to fall, let it fall; we will have to stand on top of it, construct firm supports and found a peaceful land afresh."[8]

The political innuendo was unmistakable, and this was responsible for the expectation that the attending police would bring the meeting to a close.

In Okayama she also spoke at political gatherings but without the presence of fellow Liberal Party members. It seems, rather, that her speeches were intended to strengthen women's political activities in the area and to encourage local women activists such as Takeuchi Hisa, Tsuge Kume, and Uemori Misao.[9] According to the *Nihon rikken seitō shinbun* (9 May 1882), when Itagaki Taisuke, the leader of the Liberal Party, was injured in a knife attack, Kishida and her mother nursed him. In this they were aided by Takeuchi Hisa, mother of Liberal Party member Takeuchi Tadashi, and Tsuge Kume, wife of people's rights activist Tsuge Shōgorō. Hisa and Kume accompanied Kishida to Okayama and sought her help in setting up an association for women there.[10]

In Kyushu she gave many speeches in a number of different places, and these were described mostly as "academic" (*gakujutsu enzetsukai*). Unlike lo-

---

8. Speech entitled "Aah, Aah," *Futsū shinbun*, no. 1809, 27 June 1882. She gave fewer speeches in Shikoku than in Osaka.
9. After Kishida finished making speeches in Okayama and returned to Osaka, the *Asahi shinbun*, on 31 May 1882, reported that Uemori Misao had given a speech in which she argued that "Japan, as its ancient history proves, was originally a country in which women had to be respected."
10. *Nihon rikken seitō shinbun*, 9 May 1882.

cal newspapers in Osaka and Okayama, the *Kumamoto shinbun* published detailed reports of her speeches, and it appears from these that her speeches in Kyushu had a considerable impact, that they were attended by many young people, and that they were followed by receptions.[11] Kishida was also quick to respond to male speakers' hesitance to stand on a podium with a woman, bringing more publicity to her already famous name. *Chōya shinbun* reported, "When Kishida Toshiko gave a speech at Hitoyoshi during her tour around Kyushu, since speeches by women were such a rarity, crowds thronged the venue and there were some eight hundred people in the audience. Advertisements had been put up two or three days beforehand, announcing that she would be making speeches with local activists on that day, but some people held that it was unseemly to be giving speeches along with a woman, so the speakers withdrew, complaining of stomachaches, toothaches, and so on. Kishida was aware of this, so when she ascended the rostrum, before launching into her theme, she announced, 'Today several men from the neighborhood were due to give speeches but suddenly developed illness and canceled their speeches, most unfortunately. Now, it might just be my imagination, but I think that this arose from the feeling that it was embarrassing for them to have anything to do with a woman like me. However, if you were to consider the matter carefully, you would find that they are laying themselves open to ridicule for being unable to join a single woman on the platform. I cannot help feeling sorry for these local activists.' After saying this, she turned to her main theme and spoke so well that cries of 'hear, hear!' seemed to well up from the audience."[12]

11. See the following extracts from contemporary newspapers. "Yesterday evening the crowd that attended Kishida Toshiko's speech at the Horikawa auditorium was even larger than that of the previous evening and more or less filled the hall" (*Kumamoto shinbun*, no. 1388, 2 November 1882). "Yesterday evening the scene at Kishida Toshiko's speech at the Fukutomi Theater in Kusaba-machi was just as impressive as that of the previous evening" (*Kumamoto shinbun*, no. 1389, 3 November 1882). "On the twenty-eighth of last month [November] Miss Kishida came to Maeda Kagashi's villa in this village, and the party held for her the same evening was attended by more than five hundred people; there were speeches, and it was a lively occasion" (*Kumamoto shinbun*, no. 1414, 5 December 1882). "It has been bruited about that the woman graduate Kishida Toshiko exploits her skills as a speaker and her gentle appearance to deceive people and foist her views on them; in spite of her poor physical condition, she came all the way up the fast-flowing Kuma River to Hitoyoshi-chō and from the evening of the thirteenth [of November] took part in a speech meeting at the Nakagawara auditorium that lasted three days. This was the first time women gave speeches even in Kumamoto let alone a remote place like this, where it was regarded as most unusual and was apparently a remarkable success, with an audience of seven or eight hundred people thronging in to hear" (*Shimei shinpō*, no. 55, 23 November 1882).
12. *Chōya shinbun*, no. 2741, 6 December 1882.

Kishida's speeches in Kyushu were conducted in pairs. In the first she customarily analyzed the present situation so as to stir the imagination of the audience, pointing out the social shortcomings before their eyes and investigating their historical origins, and in the second she turned her attention to the question of what was to be done to eliminate these shortcomings and urged the women in the audience to bestir themselves, develop their intellects, and put their efforts into education. See, for example, the following articles, printed in *Kumamoto shinbun*, regarding the speeches she gave in late October and early November 1882 in Kumamoto.

> In a speech addressed to "the clever women who have come," Kishida at first argued that there had to be equality of the sexes; referring to the persistence of old customs, she bemoaned the lot of women in East Asia and attributed it to their education. In her next speech, "The Shame of Idle People," she first of all took up the evil of an inactive outlook and spoke about the "sleeping society." She went so far as to argue that, be it for good or for bad, doing something in a fury is better than doing nothing at all. She drew to a close arguing that progress is essential to all aspects of society. It is a shame that her diction employed many Chinese phrases, as a result of which it seems that few people understood.[13]

After these speeches on the situation of women in East Asia and the need for active participation in society, she turned in her next two speeches to the need for girls to take action, discard the old, and embrace the new to accomplish the reform of society.

> In her first speech ["Pliant Willows and Sturdy Pines Share the Same Spirit"], she criticized the lack of energy in the young women of our country, explained that men and women enjoyed the same rights, and argued that there were mistakes in the interpretation of the old texts expounding the morals taught to women hitherto. Women have the physical characteristics of pliant willows but must have the spirit of sturdy pines, she urged. Her next speech, "The Maples on Mount Takao," was long but can be summarized as follows. First, she compared the red of the maples on Mount Takao in Kyoto with the purple of the bush clovers at Kōdaiji. While purple has long been a mark of nobility, red has long been

13. The newspaper went on to observe, "Her speeches, which were very much in favor of liberalism and progressivism, were very skillfully argued, and it was perhaps for that reason that, fortunately, the attending police did not order the meeting to be brought to an end" (*Kumamoto shinbun*, no. 1387, 1 November 1882).

considered to be the color of impropriety and ill-fortune, she said, but now purple is no longer needed by society while red has become [the symbol of] purity and right. She spoke, comparing new and old, to the effect that red now had to be spread throughout society.[14]

In the next two speeches she took up education and intellectual life.

First, in a speech entitled "Customs," she spoke on the harm done by customs, arguing that poor education was at the heart of the problem. Second, in a speech entitled "On Intellectual Ideas," she used the metaphor of the flowers and nightingale to argue that elevated thought sought out freedom while base thought preferred repression, thus covertly speaking of the relationship between the government and the people. Perhaps because the force of her arguments impressed listeners, when she was coming off the platform after her speech and the police in attendance, with stern faces, issued an order for the suspension and dissolution of the meeting on the ground that her speech was harmful to public peace, everybody was astonished, but since the speeches were over neither the speaker nor the audience seemed particularly distressed, and all left the premises peacefully.[15]

The final extract relates to two speeches given a few days later.

The titles of her speeches were "Is It Right That It Should Depend on the Wife Whether a Family Flourishes or Does Not?" and "Difficulties Today and Difficulties Tomorrow." First of all, on the former, the expression "it depends on the wife whether a family flourishes or not" is not of Kishida's invention but comes from the writings of Sima Guang of old; she added the [question] "is it right." Then she cited ancient examples [illustrating] that the fate of a family depends on the woman and said that it was evident from the thirty-five million and more sisters and brothers in our country that the terms *society, people,* and *humanity* do not indicate only men to the exclusion of women. She proceeded to the argument that if women do not progress intellectually such expressions as "the enlightenment of society" (*shakai no kaika*) and "the progress of the people" (*jinmin no shinpo*) cannot be used and that women have the same rights as men. Lamenting that for

14. Ibid., no. 1388, 2 November 1882.
15. Ibid., no. 1389, 3 November 1882.

hundreds of years it has been a custom in our country for women not to be educated, she concluded by comparing the essence of women to flowers, saying, "All of you women gathered here today, more than five hundred of you, instead of putting on lipstick and rouge and hoping that you might be looked upon a little as a [two characters illegible] flower, polish up your skills and abilities and aspire to be looked up to as the flowers of the thirty-five million." In her next speech, she said that ordinary people sought to avoid difficulties, but overcoming them was a source of endless pleasure. Those who limited themselves to what was easy would not experience the greatest happiness. So if you accomplish something difficult today, you should go on and do the same tomorrow. But accomplishing difficult things was not something the foolish could manage, for all over the country they lacked the spirit of independence and self-control, curried favor with the aristocracy and prominent people, and were bound up in things that accrued to their own advantage. When she urged people to reflect on this deeply, for some reason two or three men in the audience, it was noticed, were listening with faces as red as cinnabar. It was a great pity that because both her addresses used somewhat elevated diction they did not seem to get through to the foolish men and women present.[16]

In the first of these two speeches she argued for the inclusiveness of the words *society, people,* and *humanity,* complaining that in Japan they were customarily used to denote only men, a failing she put down to the educational system and the textbooks used.

Kyushu marked a turning point in her speech making, and the explanation probably lies in her experiences in Okayama. After all, although local supporters and Liberal Party members made the preparations for her speeches in Kyushu, there were not large numbers of speakers as had been the case in Osaka and Shikoku; often she was the only speaker, and sometimes she gave two speeches on different topics in one evening. Moreover, the presence of young people in her Kyushu audiences suggests that she had realized that education was the key to changing social consciousness and for this purpose appealing to the young was essential.

Kishida also began referring to her speeches as "academic" rather than "political." This was doubtless partly because of growing government suppression of the expression of political opinions in public, as shown by the strengthening in 1882 of the laws restricting public assembly (Shūkai jōrei)

16. Ibid., no. 1392, 8 November 1882.

so as to put obstacles in the way of public political meetings. But it may also be hypothesized that she had undergone a change in her thinking. When giving speeches in and around Osaka, she had been one of ten or even twenty Liberal Party members speaking, and, given that she always spoke on women's issues, she must have been aware that there was a gulf between the freedoms she was demanding and those demanded by male party members, who were by no means free of *danson johi* thinking themselves. That being so, in all likelihood she came to understand that for women the most urgent priority was education and the best way to foster that issue was to branch out on her own and address younger audiences.

Finally, the speeches in the Kyoto area seem to have been a continuation of those in Kyushu and were by no means confined to the city of Kyoto.[17] Some of them did involve local Liberal Party members, but most took the form of "women's speech meetings" involving not only Kishida but also women who considered themselves her followers, and there was a marked emphasis in the speeches on education for women.

"Sheltered Girls" and *Onna daigaku*

At 6:00 P.M. on 2 October 1883 a major women's speech meeting began in a theater in Kyoto. Kishida spoke on "Sheltered Girls and Incomplete Marriage," Nakamura Tokuko on "Is the Task of Women Light or Heavy?" Tachi Fuji on "Are People Like Blossoms?" and Yanase Namie on "Why Was Hikami County in Tanba Called a Land of Demons in the Past?" Newspapers beforehand noted that this was the first speech meeting to be held in Kyoto, predicted large crowds, and gave a list of the eight places where tickets could be bought.[18] Indeed, such was the crush that part of the audience had to find places on the stage. The first three speeches were heard in silence, but once Kishida began to speak the audience became restless and shouts were heard ridiculing the notion of women giving speeches. Eventually it became impossible for her to continue, but when, after a break, "she returned to the rostrum, she fully expressed her views, giving the crowd great satisfaction and moving them greatly."[19]

Ten days later the same four speakers addressed a meeting at a theater in Ōtsu. It was reported that more than five hundred people turned up in

17. Sōma 1985, p. 47.
18. *Kyōto eiri shinbun*, nos. 182–83, 29–30 September 1883. The "eight places" were mostly bookshops or the homes of supporters.
19. Ibid., no. 186, 4 October 1883. Further reports were carried in the *Jiyū shinbun*, no. 373, 4 October 1883; and *Nihon rikken seitō shinbun*, no. 454, 5 October 1883.

spite of heavy rain and that a detective from the Ōtsu Police Station was in attendance along with three policemen. After the four women had spoken, the police arrested Kishida on the ground that her speech "Sheltered Girls" was a political discourse and detained her at the police station.[20] This was not the first time her speeches had been subject to police intervention, and possibly her speech in Kyoto ten days earlier had attracted police attention, but she had not been imprisoned before. Be that as it may, the police had kept a verbatim record of her speech, and two passages were considered grounds for prosecution.[21] When the case came to trial, this record was read out in court, and Kishida acknowledged its authenticity. Even before she gave the speech, however, Shinshindō of Kyoto had published a book under her name entitled *Hakoiri musume, kon'in no fukanzen* (Sheltered Girls and Incomplete Marriage).[22] Although there are differences of order and expression between the published text and the record of the speech, the overall message is the same; here I shall focus on the record of the speech. Her Ōtsu speech on sheltered girls had also been intended to be paired with a speech on the incompleteness of marriage, but owing to ill health she had been unable to deliver the second. In the second speech, judging by the published version, she had intended to deplore the custom whereby both parties, including the parents, left everything to go-betweens, thus making light of the foundations of their future life together and often leading to marital disharmony.

Hakoiri musume is a common expression in the Osaka-Kyoto area used to refer to upper-class girls, suggesting that they lived in a *hako* (box) created for them by their parents. The box was lovingly made to "instill womanly virtues and lead them along the right path," Kishida said, but she added that "although they have arms, legs, and mouths, their freedom is obstructed so that they cannot move their arms and legs or speak with their mouths." If she were to make a box it would be a box of freedom without any shape so that arms and legs stretched out would encounter no obstacle. People might worry that this would encourage immoral and selfish behavior, but that would not be so, for it would be a box containing proper education and would differ from house to house. There were, she said, three types of boxes in the world: first, boxes that followed the teachings of wise men of old as embodied in books such as *Onna daigaku* and *Onna shōgaku* (Lesser Learning for Women); second, boxes that sought to shut girls off from the world outside by hanging blinds around them; and, third, boxes in which girls were

20. *Nihon rikken seitō shinbun*, nos. 462, 16 October 1883; 467, 23 October 1883.
21. Suzuki Yūko 1985, p. 210.
22. Ibid., pp. 33–35. See pages 213–14 for the record of the trial and the speech.

required to do exactly what their parents said and "the rights of the mother ruled to excess." The second and third were not worth considering, but the first was more "elevated" and was not without merit.

Kishida then turned to ideas of child rearing. The notion that "learning obstructs marriage" was not only a great misunderstanding but, since learning was of benefit to the state, it was "the most important equipment for wives in marriage" and it was essential for girls to acquire it. Learning consisted of economics and moral studies, so that even if widowed a woman could run her household and teach morality to her children. "True parents," she said, should provide their daughters with an education "in keeping with their intellectual development." In the past the old boxes may have sufficed, but "now, since all girls know that the emperor has bestowed freedom upon them, we must surely make boxes in which they can become free." In the new age the old boxes did not "benefit girls but made them suffer." Therefore good parents had to understand the feelings of the girl who was to be put in the box of their making and must "make a box that is as big and free as the world," for "girls put in cramped boxes without freedom" would surely abscond.

The printed text ends at this point, but in her speech Kishida added the following extended metaphor. When flowers are put in cages, she said, they are too confined to open freely. To see beautiful blossoms the cage has to be removed. Daughters are like flowers, and if they are put inside cramped boxes they will want to flee and parents will have to employ servants to restrain them. But if parents give their daughters freedom, they will not have to waste their money on servants.[23]

What caused offense in this speech was this extended metaphor at the end, for it was understood to be an allegory in which daughters represented the people, parents the government, boxes the law, and servants the police. In the indictment brought by the police, the passage about parents making bad boxes was seen as criticism of the government, and that about servants restraining daughters who wanted to run away was taken as an insult to the police. At the trial the second charge was considered unproven, but the first was upheld and Kishida was judged to be in breach of the law on public gatherings and fined five yen. The organizer of the Ōtsu speech meeting was also fined five yen. This was the first time that a punishment had been

---

23. Sōma argues that in the published version "a twenty-one-year-old woman [Kishida] who had not left her girlhood behind her used passion welling from her pure and unsullied heart to ignite the awareness of girls who were still in thrall to old ideas," but in the Ōtsu speech "she veered from this argument to touch upon political matters, hence the problems that ensued" (ibid., 1985, p. 127).

handed down in connection with a woman's speech, and it became known as the Ōtsu Incident; the *Jiyū shinbun* noted that Kishida was "the first to be charged in Japan with breaching freedom of speech."[24]

During the hearings the question of "freedom" became a heated issue between defendant and prosecutor. Kishida stated that she had been talking about "moral freedom, not political freedom. . . . I did no more than argue vigorously about the failings of women's education hitherto and did not take a step outside the topic of women's education, so I deny having made political remarks or having insulted the policemen in attendance."[25] Whether or not Kishida in fact made what could be understood as political remarks in her speech is unclear, but let us look at what she had to say about *Onna daigaku*.

Kishida by no means rejected *Onna daigaku*; on the contrary, she acknowledged that the teachings embodied in books such as *Onna daigaku* and *Onna shōgaku* were "elevated," referring to the moral instruction they provided. Yet at the same time Kishida considered that the *sanjū no michi* ("the way of three obediences," referring to a woman's obedience to father, then to husband, and finally to son) articulated in *Onna daigaku* and other conduct books for women was problematic, arguing that it had been misunderstood and wrongly implemented. It was this issue that she sought to focus on in "Sheltered Girls," and it is no coincidence that it was when she was speaking on this subject in her Kyoto lecture on 2 October that there were the greatest disturbances in the auditorium. This shows how deeply ingrained these ideas were in contemporary society. In Kishida's view, however, they were to be equated with the second and third "boxes" she referred to or, to put it another way, to be repudiated as a system for depriving women of their liberty. To her mind, women's education had hitherto been based on such ideas and was therefore still serving to spread the ideology of *danson johi* throughout Japanese society. It was for this reason that Kishida paid particular attention to the question of female education. Nevertheless, she did not categorically repudiate *Onna daigaku* or the other texts in which these ideas were encapsulated. Instead, she emphasized that there was much to be gained from the moral lessons provided by such texts.[26]

24. *Jiyū shinbun*, no. 411, 20 November 1883.
25. Suzuki Yūko 1985, pp. 113–15.
26. In October 1890, when Iwamoto Yoshiharu's sister, Kameko, married Kimura Shunkichi, Kishida wrote a small book and sent it to her. In it she explained in *Onna daigaku* style what a woman getting married should know in terms of etiquette, household management, and so on (Sōma 1985, p. 175).

What was it that Kishida said about *sanjū no michi* that caused such a disturbance? The police record of her speech gives no clue, but the published text offers more concrete evidence.[27]

> It is my desire to eradicate the mistaken notion of the three obedi-
> ences. It is not the case that [a woman] when she is at home should
> necessarily obey her parents. It is not the case that when she mar-
> ries she should necessarily obey her husband. It is not the case
> that when she is old she should obey her son. If I say no more than
> that, then somebody will surely say, "Women are supposed by
> nature to be compliant but they are not compliant, and when they
> are disobedient to boot then there is nothing more damaging."
> This is a case of knowing the first thing but not knowing what
> follows. For if, as such a critic would suggest, we educate girls
> to be submissive in absolutely everything, how can they possibly
> acquire the knowledge required to distinguish between good and
> evil? This suggestion should be utterly rejected, for it can only
> result in girls becoming idle and ignorant. . . . In order to nurture
> their knowledge there is no better way than to enable them to dis-
> criminate between good and evil and to tell them which way they
> should follow and which they should not. What they should not
> follow is people, and what they should follow is the right way.
> The three obediences I am talking about here consist of following
> the right way as a child while still at home, not of following one's
> parents; of following the way of a wife upon marriage, not of fol-
> lowing one's husband; and of following the way of a parent in old
> age, not of following one's children.

Kishida is emphasizing here that women should not simply obey people as demanded in *Onna daigaku* but should follow (the same verb is used for "obey" and "follow") the Confucian Way, the moral ideal, that is in keeping with their station in life. Kishida was critical of both the bases of education in the Edo period and the ways in which they were interpreted, and here she laid out her own interpretation.

What did she mean by "the Way"? She did not explain what the three paths she referred to consist of in detail, but in various speeches she stated that the way of the child was study and the way of a wife, even after her husband's death, was to manage the family. What she particularly wished to point at, it seems, was that to make "useful and intelligent" girls out of "idle

27. Ibid., pp. 37–40.

and ignorant" girls it was essential to teach them to discriminate between good and evil as their knowledge developed and to guide them to follow not people but the right way. She always insisted that if women married without having gone through such a learning process they would never be able to teach their children and that was the reason girls needed to be properly educated from childhood.

Although Kishida rejected the three obediences of old, that did not mean that she was fundamentally rejecting the *ideology* that lay at the heart of *Onna daigaku*. Rather, she claimed that the teachings embodied in books such as *Onna daigaku* were "elevated" while at the same time reinterpreting them to suit her own purposes. In this she can be compared to earlier Confucian scholars, such as Inooka Gisai, examined in Bettina Gramlich-Oka's essay in this volume, who firmly believed that women, too, could follow the Way.

Kishida and the Young

Kishida as a public speaker benefited from the prolonged succession of speech meetings in which she participated and from the effort she put into developing her strategies as a speaker, trying to arouse the enthusiasm of her audiences and to stir them into taking action. Those who responded to her calls were young girls who had hitherto largely been ignored.[28] The focus of Kishida's speeches in the course of her activities as a public speaker shifted from the extension of women's rights to the question of education, particularly women's education, and she began to insist on the importance of education in early childhood. For those who were too young to have a good grasp of the written language, speeches were potentially an effective means of communicating with the young. They could flock to auditoriums just as if they were going to see a play, and a skillful speech could attract their interest. Newspapers reported that Kishida was indeed a gifted speaker, sometimes almost drunk with excitement, but, as a means of drawing the attention of the young, she also had some of them join her on the platform to support her arguments with their own testimony, and in the following section I consider some such examples.

On 2 October 1883, at a general women's speech meeting held at Shijō in Kyoto, an eight-year-old girl, Yanase Namie, delivered a speech entitled

---

28. Among those who came under Kishida's influence in Okayama were not only the well-known Fukuda Hideko but also followers such as Nakamura Toku of Echizen, Tominaga Raku of Tosa, Tomoi Oto of Harima, Tachi Fuji of Yamato, and Yanase Namie of Tanba.

"Why Was Hikami County in Tanba Called a Land of Demons in the Past?" Her argument was that, although it was close to Kyoto, Tanba was very inadequate in terms of education. It was rural and backward; the people were uncivilized, for they did not educate their children; and such parents were really demons, not humans at all. She had been thinking that she did not want to become like the demons but wanted instead to be an educated woman, and then she met Kishida. "When Miss Kishida came to Tanba this spring," she said, "I had the good fortune to accompany her, so I became one of her followers and began to study, and from now on it is my intention to do all that I should to become a proper human being." Another eight-year-old girl called Tachi Fuji gave a speech entitled, "Are People Like Blossoms?" She introduced herself as a follower of Kishida from Yoshino and started out by saying that Yoshino, which was famous for its blossoms, was in the countryside and so lacked most things, and everything there was inferior to what was found in the cities, beginning with the people. But there was no distinction between the blossoms of the cities and the blossoms of the countryside, and the city people came to Yoshino to admire the blossoms. Just like those blossoms, people in the countryside ought to be able to attract city people. It might appear, she said, that there were all kinds of differences between the two, but those differences in the end came down to nothing more than the difference between wisdom and stupidity; therefore it was important for people to be educated so as to be wise.[29]

Another case was that of Miyakawa Saeko, who, at the age of fifteen was deeply stirred by speeches given by Kishida in Kumamoto on 26 November 1882. She wrote her impressions down and read them out at a subsequent gathering. Since ancient times, she said, Japanese women have been "sunk in degradation and busy only with cooking, cleaning, and needlework without a glimmer of anything more intelligent, while in the countries of Europe and [North] America it is not only men who have been the heroes, for women of similar caliber have come to the fore, too." This difference between Japan and the West she attributed to different methods of education. "Clinging to old customs in Japan hindered the spread of real education, but Miss Kishida had traveled widely, pouring all her energies into education to spread the message of the indispensability of a good education." "Nobody," she said, "not even children three feet high, has not heard her name. . . . She has not neglected even the most backward or remote of places in the provinces, giving speeches, espousing education, and stirring the hearts and minds of people everywhere." Miyakawa would henceforth devote all

29. *Kyōto eiri shinbun*, nos. 186–7, 4–5 October 1883.

her efforts to the pursuit of learning, which would in the future bring benefits one hundredfold. And she concluded by saying that by acquiring some
learning, as Kishida was urging, brilliant young women would certainly
come to the fore, and this was a blessing she had bestowed upon them all.[30]

In addition to these young girls, whose responses have been presented
at some length, many participants at a speech meeting in Kumamoto on
30 November 1882 spoke one after another. These included O-Tsuchi, the
twelve-year-old daughter of Maeda Kagashi (1828–1904), a prominent local
politician and Popular Rights activist, who gave a speech in favor of learning, and Tajiri Kuma, of the same age, whose speech was entitled "Ease Is
the Blossom of Hard Efforts." The contents of their speeches are unknown,
but the newspapers reported that the arguments propounded by O-Tsuchi
in spite of her youth demonstrated the merits of the home education she
had received and Tajiri's speech, too, had been impressive.[31] Finally, it was
reported that before a speech Kishida gave at Hakata in Kyushu speeches
had been given by eight- and nine-year-old girls.[32]

Kishida's insistence that education was essential if women were to escape from backwardness and ignorance and make progress seems to have
struck a chord with these young girls, all of whom commented on the importance of female education. Young girls were employed to attract crowds,
and so they were there as much as a spectacle as because they had a message they wanted to present, but the message they espoused should not be
undervalued. It is important to remember that behind these girls there were
often supportive parents. Miyakawa Saeko's father, for example, was one of
the organizers of a reception for Kishida, and Tachi Fuji's mother accompanied her in 1884 on a trip with Kishida.[33] Clearly, some individuals were
embracing Kishida's position on young women's education and allowing
their daughters to spread that message.

Responses to Kishida's Speeches

Kishida's speeches, the young girls she brought with her onto the stage, and
her message aroused a great deal of comment in the press. Some responses
were very positive. The *Nihon rikken seitō shinbun* wrote, "Her normal state

---

30. *Kumamoto shinbun*, no. 1408, 28 November 1882.
31. Ibid., no. 1414, 5 December 1882.
32. *Tōkyō Yokohama mainichi shinbun*, no. 3601, 21 December 1882.
33. Suzuki Yūko 1986, p. 40. For a similar case of a supportive mother, see Ōki 2003, p. 13.

of mind is courageous and her style of speech lively; seeing the charm of her shining eyes and white teeth, she seems almost to be fluttering her eyelashes at the men; she is truly an astonishing and unusual woman."[34] *Jiji shinpō* reported, "Since childhood she has been known for her intellect, she is widely read in both Chinese and Western literature, and she is a fluent and lively speaker. Thus she never fails to be applauded when she steps onto the rostrum. Hitherto women who have come to hear speeches have been as few as stars in the sky at dawn, but since Toshiko came to the fore their numbers have rapidly increased."[35] After reporting that Kishida had been ordered to break off her speech "Aah, Aah" on account of its topical references, *Jiyū shinbun* stated:

> From this account it might appear that her speech was extreme, but this writer's estimation of her is that she is not only extremely well read as a result of the education she received from her mother but also mild and reticent. She has ambitions that men cannot match, as is clear when she is deploring the fact that women's education is not in a more flourishing state, calling for the establishment of a girls' school in Osaka, encouraging women to take part in speech meetings, or urging the reform of music. Thus there is no sign that she is so foolish as to be seeking momentary fame by making extremist speeches; rather, her speeches embody emotions coming from the heart and so have been mistakenly judged to be extremist. Some newspapers have even held her up to ridicule, but they know nothing of the truth and are no better than dogs barking at the sky.[36]

Some, as this article noted, were somewhat critical of her behavior. Kurita Shintarō stated in 1882, "When it comes to heroic women, there are Queen Elizabeth of England and Empress Jingū of our own country. As for famous women speakers, there are none apart from Kishida Toshiko. Nobody who listens to her speeches fails to be moved. Yet even she has her failings. Her

---

34. *Nihon rikken seitō shinbun*, no. 15, 31 March 1882.
35. *Jiji shinpō*, no. 57, 8 May 1882. See also *San'yō shinpō*, no. 962, 16 May 1882, which observed, "Her manner of speaking was lively and pleasing, and she did not flag. The applause and shouts of approval were such that they could be heard outside." *Nihon rikken seitō shinbun*, no. 59, 23 May 1882, wrote, "She has given political speeches in Okayama, Tsuyama, and elsewhere, and it seems that everywhere people have been stirred by her speeches." A week later the same paper noted, "Kishida Toshiko's speech employed clear arguments and a fluent delivery and had the greatest impact on the audience" (no. 63, 31 May 1882).
36. *Jiyū shinbun*, no. 4, 4 July 1882.

habit of throwing out her words and moving about [during her speeches] are not suitable for a woman and are just what a man might do (women should do things appropriate to their sex). This is her failing."[37] According to the *Nihon rikken seitō shinbun*, several newspapers carried false reports "concerning Kishida Toshiko, who is a member of the Osaka Association of Political Speakers, and in extreme cases have even put it about that she is under secret orders to spy on the internal arrangements of our Constitutional Party. She is not, however, that sort of mean-spirited person, so these are nothing more than fabrications by the sort of miserable people who cannot respond normally."[38] To give one more example, the *Futsū shinbun* wrote:

> Since she has gained a growing reputation as a speaker, people thronged the venue from the very first day in spite of the fact that the rain had turned the roads into mud. Since every evening there were at least two thousand people present, Toshiko became more excited and developed her arguments with fluency and perfect clarity. She mightily impressed all those who packed the auditorium with her incisive analyses of the current situation and the state of the nation; she is truly a remarkably lively speaker. The only regret is that her exposition tends to become so impassioned as to suggest she may be damaging her modesty, and yet this stems naturally from her patriotic impulses, which overflow with eagerness, so there is no reason to be critical of her. Nevertheless, if she were to show a little caution, she would arouse the insatiable interest of intellectuals even if at the expense of gaining less applause from humbler folk.[39]

The various reports, most of which were clearly favorable, though one or two were critical of her gestures or her use of difficult Chinese expressions, show how Kishida's speeches were well attended and well received. Furthermore, the extract from her speech at Hitoyoshi quoted earlier in this essay, where local male speakers apparently did not want to stand on a podium with a woman, reveals in particular how deeply rooted *danson johi* was in Japanese society at the time, justifying the kind of intervention she was attempting to make.

37. Kurita Shintarō, *Jiyū kaishin zenshin hoshu Meiji enzetsu hyōbanki* (1882), quoted in Suzuki Yūko, 1985. On Kurita's work, see Inada 2000, p. 294. Kishida was the only woman included in this critique of the speech making of fifty prominent contemporary speakers.
38. *Nihon rikken seitō shinbun*, no. 53, 16 May 1882.
39. *Futsū shinbun*, no. 1809, 27 June 1882.

Conclusion

The image of women purveyed by *Onna daigaku* was widely disseminated in the Edo period and continued right up to the 1880s in the form of published books, but in the hands of Kishida it was absorbed into the new medium of the public speech. In Kishida's interpretation, ideas such as the "three obediences" were wrongly understood and had become widely accepted in their mistaken form, with the result that "revering men and despising women" had become the norm. Kishida argued that the three obediences were not a matter of obeying a male person—father, husband, or son—but of being true to the moral way appropriate to one's position in life and that it was to eradicate such mistakes that women's education needed to be re-thought. For her, *Onna daigaku* was not beyond the pale; rather, it remained useful for it emphasized that morals were a part of education and education was not the acquisition of knowledge alone. She was only one of a number of Meiji women who sought to recover a version of the Confucian Way and the liberating potential of sinological learning for a new generation. Others longer-lived than Kishida, such as Atomi Kakei (1840–1926) and Miwada Masako (1843–1927), managed to put their views into practice in the form of sinological academies for women.[40]

Kishida was extremely sensitive to time as a feature of the rapidly chang-ing society in which she lived. Old customs were being rejected, new forms of education were becoming ever more necessary, and new responses were called for. Even in the space of the two years in which she traveled making speeches, she changed her approach, moving away from political speeches in the direction of more analytical speeches focusing on contemporary so-ciety. Her slogans changed to match, from declarations of women's rights to advocacy of women's education, and her target audience, too, gradually shifted in favor of the young. These changes surely matched her evolving understanding of the role she could play as a public advocate for women's causes in Meiji Japan.

40. On Miwada, see Anne Walthall's contribution to this volume. See also Mehl 2001.

10

Readers and Writers:
Japanese Women and Magazines
in the Late Nineteenth Century

Mara Patessio

During the last decades of the nineteenth century, Japanese women were participating in public life; were students and teachers in private, government, and missionary schools; and were able to engage government authorities and public society in debates over women's rights and needs, as the work of Sugano Noriko and others has shown.[1] Yet our knowledge of women's participation in the periodical press during the same period remains limited. In this essay, I seek to further our understanding of Meiji women's history by analyzing how women's participation in the print media, and their desire to obtain greater access to public spaces, further their education, and enlarge their social rights were interrelated. The public expression of women's needs and opinions, however, was considered a possible threat to the social order, and therefore women had to be controlled; the most effective ways of doing so were to impose stricter rules on women's education and to limit women's actions in public spaces. As I argue in this essay, restrictions were imposed also by placing in the print media attacks

---

1. See Sugano's contribution to this volume; Copeland 2000; Mackie 2003; and Patessio, forthcoming.

on so-called dangerous reading matter, such as fiction and newspapers, which, it was feared, could lead girls astray by letting them imagine different futures for themselves.

Debates on Meiji Women

Books for women, including educational tracts, collections of poetry, and books about household economy, were published in quantity during the Edo period, and, as Anne Walthall argues in this volume, the Meiji state could not have succeeded in educating men and women had the groundwork not already been laid in the Edo period.[2] Yet during the Meiji period women's roles in society started to be rethought. The topic of women's new roles in Meiji society was discussed in new discursive spaces, especially newspapers and magazines. Soon after the Meiji Restoration the members of the Meirokusha (Meiji Six Society) published their views on the role of Japanese women in their journal *Meiroku zasshi* together with articles on political government and Western philosophical theories. These articles have been widely discussed for the light they shed on the debates concerning women that were taking place within the male elite, but *Meiroku zasshi* was established to explore a variety of issues at a high level of discourse, whereas during the early Meiji period magazines specifically for women began to appear.[3]

The mid-1880s saw a boom in the publication of magazines for women that circulated throughout Japan and brought these debates to a much wider audience. When the craze for Western things started to give way to a reevaluation of Japanese traditions and customs, which male editors and journalists considered should not be seen as uncivilized in comparison to the West, these magazines started to employ nationalistic imagery through increased use of words such as *Japan* and *Great Japan* in their titles.[4] Article 7 of the revised Newspaper Law (Shinbunshi jōrei), promulgated in 1883, ruled that only Japanese men over the age of twenty could become owners, directors,

2. Besides poetry and feminine arts, conduct books for women (*jokunsho*) in the Edo period also provided practical information, including basic medical information: (Saitō 1986).
3. On *Meiroku zasshi* and the discussion of women's role in Japanese society, see Mackie 2003, pp. 16–18; and Sievers 1983, pp. 16–25. Braisted (1976) has translated the entire journal. If not the very first, one of the earliest magazines aimed at a female readership was *Kosodate no sōshi* (Raising Children), which was published in 1877 (Kindai Josei Bunkashi Kenkyūkai 1989, p. 9).
4. See, for example, *Nihon no jogaku* (Japanese Women's Education), founded in 1887; *Nihon shinfujin* (New Japanese Woman, 1888); and *Dai nihon fujin kyōikukai zasshi* (Magazine of the Great Japan Women's Education Society, 1888) (Kindai Josei Bunkashi Kenkyūkai 1989).

editors, or printers of newspapers and other print media; as a consequence, all of these magazines had male writers, publishers, and editors, showing at the same time that a sizable number of well-educated men were interested in the question of women's roles in the development of a new Japan.[5] For example, *Iratsume* (The Maiden, 1887–91), a magazine published in Tokyo, was founded and supported by Nakagawa Kojūrō (1867–1944), later founder of Ritsumeikan University and a member of the House of Peers; Okada Ryōhei (1864–1934), a student at Teikoku University and later a privy councilor; Ichiki Kitokurō (1867–1944), a student at Teikoku University and later chairman of the Privy Council; Masaki Naohiko (1862–1940), later director of the Tokyo School of Arts; Shinpo Banji, who worked at the publishing house Kinkōdō; and Yamada Bimyō (1868–1910), a novelist and the editor of the magazine.[6]

Magazines for women published during the 1880s were largely produced to support the government ideology of *ryōsai kenbo* (good wives and wise mothers), and therefore, generally speaking, they can be considered an extension of the many educational books produced by men for women during the same period.[7] Other publications sought to attract a broader readership by introducing some new features to existing genres. Letter-writing manuals for girls and women had existed in the Edo period as well, but during the Meiji period they provided models for new kinds of letters such as how to order things seen advertised in newspapers or how to subscribe to a magazine.[8] There were also a number of educational tracts written by women during the 1890s, for example, biographies of exemplary women and books on the education of women.[9] These publications indicate the growing visibility of women in the public sphere, for women were participating more and more in the publishing business; however, they do not represent activities that threatened the social order since the underlying ideology espoused was that of *ryōsai kenbo*.

---

5. The legislation can be downloaded from the Kokkai Toshokan Kindai Digital Library, http://kindai.ndl.go.jp. For a discussion of press regulations during the Meiji period, see Huffman 1997.
6. See Yamada 1983, esp. pp. 11–12.
7. On the *ryōsai kenbo* ideology, see Tachi 1984; and Patessio, forthcoming.
8. Tōyama 1896, pp. 63, 66. Others showed how to invite someone to attend a speech meeting organized by a women's group or recommend that someone join a women's study group (Izawa 1894, pp. 113, 146) and how to congratulate someone whose daughter has graduated from a normal school and become a teacher or what to write to the wife of a person who has come home from abroad (Sasaki Nobutsuna 1890, pp. 199–200). Similar manuals were used in private and public girls' schools (Tōkyō-to 1961, p. 158).
9. See, for example, Sakurai 1893; and Miwada 1897. On Miwada Masako see Anne Walthall's contribution to this volume.

During the 1870s and up to the mid-1880s, it was mostly men who discussed women's issues and activities in print, whether in books or articles. From these articles, we know that women read periodicals, participated in women's groups and public speech meetings, graduated from girls' schools, and went on to educate their children or become teachers. What they were not yet doing in significant numbers was playing an active part in opinion formation in the periodical press.

How Accessible Was the Print Media for Women?

Although there were regional differences, as a result of the new postal system and the growing ease of access to information from different parts of the country, even women living in provincial towns could find books and periodicals, and there are a number of examples of girls who decided which school to attend in Tokyo, or found out about women's activities in other areas, from the articles they read in the print media. For example, Yoshioka Yayoi (1871–1959), founder of the Tokyo Women's Medical School (1900), recalled that during her youth, when she was living in a small town in Shizuoka Prefecture, she had been very interested in the reports on political *enzetsu* (public speeches) published in the newspapers her father bought and that reading about the political activist Kishida Toshiko had been inspiring for her and her female friends. Similarly, the educator Hani Motoko (1873–1957) recalled that *Chōya shinbun*, the newspaper her grandfather read in Aomori, her hometown, reported on schools opened in Tokyo, and in that way granddaughter and grandfather could get information about which school was most suitable for her.[10]

In this essay, I focus on women and girl students living in or near relatively large cities, frequenting *fujinkai* (women's groups), and studying at girls' schools. The cases presented below do not tell us about the majority of girls' experiences, but they do show how access to books and newspapers was not necessarily a problem for middle-class women, especially because the circulation of magazines throughout Japan was facilitated by the possibility of subscribing to them and receiving the issues directly at home. For example, around 1895 Ishihara Hatsuko, a girl in her late teens studying at San'yō Girls' School in Okayama, spent her free time reading newspapers,

10. Yoshioka 1998, p. 70; Hani 1928, pp. 43–44. Some years later the same information could be obtained from specialized publications. See, for example, Suzuki Ken'ichi 1901, which included the subjects taught at various schools for girls, their addresses, and their regulations.

books, and magazines. Publications as various as the ninth-century *Tales of Ise*; the journals *Kokumin no tomo*, *Fujin kyōiku zasshi*, *Tsubomi*, *Taiyō*, and *Jogaku zasshi*; Ozaki Kōyō's novel *Iwazu katarazu*; the works of Higuchi Ichiyō; and other novels, including some written by women, are all mentioned in her diary. Some were given or sent to her by friends and relatives, and others were old issues she had acquired somehow, but often they were new issues, and in one entry she mentioned that somebody had come from the San'yō Newspaper Company to collect the monthly subscription.[11] On the other hand, the Dai Nihon Fujin Kyōiku Kai (Great Japan Women's Education Society), which published *Dai nihon fujin kyōikukai zasshi*, reported when issues of various women's magazines were donated to the society so that its members could peruse those magazines at ease without having to buy them.[12] Finally, in a contribution to *Jogaku zasshi* (The Journal of Woman's Education), which began publication in 1885 and was by far the magazine most supportive of women's activities and education, a woman described herself as a person who did not have the money to buy many books but was attracted by new publications partly because of the various advertisements found in newspapers and magazines. She wrote that since libraries were not to be found everywhere and *kashihon'ya* (lending libraries) mostly offered novels and old books, it was difficult to access new publications. Yet ten people she knew had decided to pay ten sen a month to buy new publications, which were circulated among the members of the group. The books were sold to a member after everybody had read them, and the money was added to the pool they paid into monthly. In that way, not only could they afford new books, but they could buy more expensive (and we can suppose more educational or intellectual) publications.[13] Even these few examples show how women were trying to access books and magazines in various ways and how they were devising ways to gain access to *new* publications while periodicals also played a large part in their reading.

Periodicals filled women's free time, but they also became a space in which women could exchange information and discuss issues they considered crucial for themselves and their country, and this development is important for various reasons. When women bought or read books on letter writing, exemplary women, or women in the West, they were broadening their knowledge by educating themselves in matters intended for women's

---

11. Ōta and Takeuchi 2007; see, for example, pages 117, 123, 128, 137, 165, 193, 195, 197, 201, 291, and 293. Ishihara was writing and receiving letters to and from acquaintances all over Japan; she was a fervent Christian.
12. See, for example, *Dai nihon fujin kyōikukai zasshi*, no. 1, 21 December 1888, last page.
13. *Jogaku zasshi*, no. 374, 7 April 1894, pp. 18–9.

consumption, whereas when they read newspapers and magazines the topics and readership were not necessarily gender defined. In the same way, no books seem to have been written by girl students during the nineteenth century, but they could see their letters published in women's magazines, and some newspapers as well, and such letters were sometimes critical of social practices. One need only browse a couple of issues of *Jogaku zasshi* to find many such examples on educational and employment matters. Moreover, although only a relatively small number of books were published during the early Meiji period in which women wrote about political activities, property rights, concubinage, or voting rights, these were all topics that women discussed weekly, if not daily, in the periodical press. Women who became temporary or long-term contributors to magazines and newspapers, provided that such institutions allowed them to express their opinions, could also write without having to worry too much about their reputations since they often avoided using their real names and published under pen names.[14] Furthermore, from *Jogaku zasshi* and *Fujo shinbun*, the only two magazines I have encountered so far that allowed a large number of women to become contributors and express their opinions in print on all sorts of topics, it is clear that, whereas there was no such thing yet as a community of women writers of books or fiction, women writers of articles and their readers did become a community. It is by the late 1880s, in fact, that writers started addressing their female readers not as *dokusha* (readers) anymore but as *aidokusha* (devoted readers), thus implying the development of a community of, and the formation of invisible bonds between, women writers and their (female) readership.[15]

The articles women and men published in *Jogaku zasshi* and other magazines and newspapers during the 1880s and 1890s allow us to understand how women were active in public spaces in those years. They defined their ideal of the family as composed of husband, wife, and children; they protested against the presence of concubines and prostitutes in Japanese society; and they petitioned the central and local authorities for greater educational possibilities, property rights, the right to vote and listen to debates in the Diet; and so on.[16] Throughout this period we also find in the same venues

14. Some articles signed with female names may have been written by men. Ōki, for example, notes that Sakazaki Sakan, a journalist for *Doyō shinbun* and *Jiyū no tomoshibi*, published articles on women's rights in *Jiyū no tomoshibi* in 1884 and 1885 under a female pen name (2003, pp. 127–8). Although there may have been other such examples, I argue that, so far as my research goes, what men such as Sakazaki might have written under female pen names was also or had already been publicly voiced by women.
15. On women novelists in the Meiji period, see Copeland 2000; and Walthall's contribution to this volume.
16. See Patessio, forthcoming.

various novels published in installments, some of them written by women; a large number of articles presenting and evaluating foreign novels; a series of interviews with women novelists; and a plethora of articles suggesting good books that women could read not only to educate themselves but also for personal pleasure.[17]

Dangerous Novels

Amid all this, one series of articles that appeared in 1889 and 1890 dealt with the problem of women reading novels and the danger that novels posed for women. To anticipate my conclusions, I argue that anxiety over what women were reading was not provoked specifically by the content of women's reading so much as the freedoms that girl students and women enjoyed to participate in *fujinkai*, to form a female community, and to read and write for magazines, such as *Jogaku zasshi*, that did not always support government policies. Thus, instead of articles focusing only on good books for women, which continued to be a feature of women's magazines throughout the Meiji period, we find in 1889 and 1890 articles—all but possibly one of them written by men—that discussed the question of dangerous books for women.

Before looking at those articles, a caveat is in order, for rarely were "dangerous novels" identified by their titles. Did readers know what kinds of novels were dangerous or was it that novels in general were the target? The only article I have found that actually named dangerous novels, published a

17. *Iratsume* (no. 23, 15 May 1889, p. 32) included a list of books, apparently in response to a reader's request, that were not harmful and could be bought in Tokyo: *Ernest Maltravers* by Sir Edward Bulwer-Lytton, *The Vicar of Wakefield* by Oliver Goldsmith, *Rip van Winkle* by Washington Irving, and *Ivanhoe* by Sir Walter Scott. In the issue of 15 August 1889 (no. 26, p. 41), again in reply to a reader's request, the author suggested *The Witness of the Sun* by Amelie Rives, *Marriage and Divorce in the United States* by Duncan Convers, *Jerry* by the Duchess (Sarah Barnwell Elliott), and *Guilderoy* by Ouida (Maria Louise Ramée). Titles were given in English. *Jogaku zasshi* also advertized books European and North American women liked to read. Since the titles were in English and the books suggested were not always written by well-known writers, we can suppose that staff members of these magazines wanted to provide their readership with alternative channels of information on what to read. Wakamatsu Shizuko's translation of *Little Lord Fauntleroy* as *Shōkōshi* was published in installments in *Jogaku zasshi* beginning with the issue of 23 August 1890 (no. 227, pp. 21–24) and continued for more than a year. Interviews with women novelists included Koganei Kimiko, Kimura Akebono, Wakamatsu Shizuko, and Tanabe Kaho (*Jogaku zasshi*, no. 205, 22 March 1890, pp. 13–14; no. 206, 29 March 1890, pp. 14–15; no. 207, 5 April 1890, pp. 13–16; no. 209, 19 April 1890, p. 17). I have not found any *books* dealing with what girls should read during the same years, but by 1900 this was a topic discussed in miscellanies, especially those published for a young female readership. See, for example, Toyoda 1901.

few years after the articles to be discussed here, seems to support the second supposition. The article, published in *Fujo zasshi* (Woman's Magazine), is entitled "Young Women and Novels." It stated that by nature young women were susceptible, sentimental, and prone to be carried away by emotion. Thus, *ren'ai shōsetsu* (love novels), in which the story was based on *renjō* (love), were the most dangerous, but *ninjo novels* (melodramatic and romantic stories with a hint of eroticism), such as Kyoku Sanjin's *Musume setsuyō* (Dictionary for Daughters, 1834) and Tamenaga Shunsui's *Shunshoku umegoyomi* (The Love-Tinted Plum Calendar, 1832–33), were to be avoided as well. *The Tale of Genji*, too, though a masterpiece and the quintessence of Japanese literature, was dangerous reading for young women because of its lasciviousness and its central character's temperament. "Sentimental" (*senchimentaru*) novels, for example, Ozaki Kōyō's *Namu amida butsu* (Hail to Amida Buddha, 1889), should not be read because these stirred girls' emotions and provoked useless tears. Domestic tragedies (*sewamono*) were not completely bad, for chaste women were also depicted, but they presented foolish passions and if they were read by emotional women they could be taken as examples of how to behave. Only at the end does the writer give a meager list of what girls should read, implying that the most important thing was to keep women away from fiction. Suitable were educational, historical, and domestic novels (*katei shōsetsu*) that took family life as the subject, and the translation made by Wakamatsu Shizuko of *Little Lord Fauntleroy*. George Eliot's *Silas Marner* could be read by girls who understood English, for her work had not been translated yet.[18]

The earliest article on dangerous novels I have found was printed in *Tsubomi*, a magazine for girl students coedited by various missionary and missionary-supported girls' schools such as Dōshisha Jogakkō in Kyoto, Baika Jogakkō in Osaka, Eiwa Jogakkō in Kobe, San'yō Eiwa Jogakkō in Okayama, Eiwa Jogakkō in Tottori, and Kumamoto Jogakkō in Kumamoto. The article was written by a certain Yamada Toshiko, a student at Dōshisha Jogakkō, and is entitled "Advantages and Disadvantages of Young Women Reading Novels," although she identifies very few advantages.[19] Yamada

18. *Fujo zasshi*, no. 19, 1 October 1894, pp. 3–5. On *katei shōsetsu*, see Ragsdale 1998. On the emergence of the term *shōsetsu* to refer to all forms of fiction, see Zwicker 2006. Zwicker has also analyzed the number of titles published during the early Meiji period for three categories, namely, reprints of Edo fiction, translations, and modern novels. His findings show a steep rise in reprints of Edo fiction during 1886–87, a large number of modern novels published during 1887–88, and a peak in the number of foreign translations, even though there were far fewer compared to the previous two categories, during the same years. Thus, compared to the first twenty years of the Meiji period, these were the years in which, relatively speaking, novels flooded the market (Zwicker 2006, pp. 30–31, 149).

19. *Tsubomi*, no. 4, 21 April 1890, pp. 32–34.

wrote that the bad behavior of girls had become a topic of concern, and she connected such behavior with the reading of novels by arguing that it was better for girls not to read them at all so as to avoid any possible danger. An unsigned article a month later in the same magazine and under the same title explained the point in further detail.[20] First, the author argued, novels such as *Uncle Tom's Cabin* could be considered beneficial because they had the power to enlighten people's hearts, but there were few such works. Others instead were filled with temptations, and young girls who did not have much experience and willpower could easily be carried away by them. Second, as school curricula became better organized life would be busier for students. If novels were important, they would be included in school curricula, but since that was not the case, of course, girls should use their time for more profitable occupations. Third, reading novels trained the mind to think in ways that worked against careful reading and study, so those who read them might lose interest in details and start disliking intellectual reading. Fourth, novels portrayed various states of mind (happiness, sadness, laughter, anger), which, if taken in large doses, would stir students' emotions; because of this they would not realize the passing of time, would forget to eat or to sleep, and would lose their sobriety. This condition even had a medical name: "novel disease" (*shōsetsubyō*). Thus, in the author's opinion, novels should be banned from schools to protect students' well-being.

In fact, some years later the Kōtō Jogakkō and the women's department of Shihan Gakkō in Tokyo did introduce a partial ban on novels. Girls living in the dormitories of the two schools had to obtain permission from the head of the school and the director of the dormitory when subscribing to newspapers and magazines or when reading novels lest they come across material that went against the girls' proper upbringing. Moreover, as a general rule these had to be read in common rooms, where girls could be controlled.[21] However, it was not easy to keep girls away from the wrong kind of novel, for many lending libraries were stocking up on love novels and offering them to upper-class women while at health resorts and hospitals women were reading exactly that kind of novel, perhaps in fact the very women hospitalized because of novel disease.[22]

Novels were not only a waste of time but could also be dangerous. The author of an article entitled "Problems for Girls' Education Created by Novels" argued that women's education had certainly developed but the difference in the quality of learning and mental training between boys and girls

---

20. Ibid., no. 5, 20 May 1890, pp. 1–4.
21. *Fujo shinbun*, no. 26, 5 November 1900, p. 1.
22. *Fujo zasshi*, no. 19, 1 October 1894, p. 5.

was high given that women could only cope with everyday issues. Women readers of novels would lose their will and become the slaves of wild ideas, and even those that were considered good novels were really not good at all, for girl readers could not comprehend the beauty of a literary work and what remained in their brains after reading them was only the concept of "love." They tended to read whatever novels came to hand, concealing themselves from everybody, locking themselves in their rooms, and becoming slaves of their feelings because they did not have the reasoning power to govern their emotions. As a consequence, they would end up not understanding what the main duty of women was and would be lost, and that was something society should fear.[23]

The notion that girls reading novels had a negative influence on society is reflected in what was presented as an American theory in an article published in *Onna shinbun* (Woman's Newspaper) entitled "Growing Number of Divorces Caused by Novels." Novels allowed young women to look at the world with new eyes went the argument, and for this reason readers should not be surprised to hear that the number of divorces was rising. Novels portrayed unreasonable ideas of morality, and girls who read them were approaching marriage with foolish wishes and misguided hopes. They were unhappy because their husbands were not like the male characters in the novels they were reading, and the extreme solution was divorce.[24] If that could happen to American girls, it could happen to Japanese as well, as the writer of another article, entitled "Women and Literature," published in *Yomiuri shinbun*, made clear. The amount of space devoted to *waka* and novels in textbooks, it was argued, was growing. Literature had the virtue of refining people's opinions, but to suppose that this was the aim of girls' education was a mistake. Girls were educated to become "good wives and wise mothers," and for that some literary knowledge could be considered useful, but literature had no value as a topic to be studied at school. On the contrary, girls studying literature would become *namaiki* (conceited) and want to choose their own husbands. They would hate housework, hate raising children, hate their husbands and marriage, and in the end get divorced

---

23. *Shōnen'en*, vol. 2, no. 18, 18 July 1889, reprinted in Hirata 1999, pp. 65–67. According to an article published in *Jogaku zasshi*, some thought it was because of *Jogaku zasshi* that girl students liked literature and idealized writers, and the author of the article considered that *Jogaku zasshi* should be cautious about this. Liking literature, s/he hastened to point out, did not imply disliking or slighting work in the home. If that was so, s/he would be against it, too. George Eliot was a good example of a writer who was a woman in the home and yet could startle the world with her work. Literature, s/he concluded, was a proper and good occupation for women (*Jogaku zasshi*, no. 313, 16 April 1892, pp. 2–3).
24. *Onna shinbun*, no. 94, 15 January 1890, reprinted in Hirata 1999, pp. 68–69.

and live alone. Girl students who loved reading novels often did not have happy marriages because they were not able to get used to their new families.[25] No wonder the author was worried!

That girls were reading love stories and enjoying them is clear from what Sugimoto Etsuko (1873–1950) wrote about her life at Aoyama Jogakuin, a missionary school.

> I think it was my third year in school that a wave of excitement over love stories struck Tokyo. All the schoolgirls were wildly interested. When translations were to be had we passed them from hand to hand through the school; but mostly we had to struggle along in English, picking out love scenes from the novels and poems in our school library. Enoch Arden was our hero. We were familiar with loyalty and sacrifice on the part of a wife, and understood perfectly why [Enoch's wife] Annie should have so long withstood the advances of [Enoch's childhood friend] Phillip, but the unselfishness of the faithful Enoch was so rare as to be much appreciated.[26]

So, rather than rejecting the idea of marrying and raising children, this girl appreciated the qualities of an unselfish and faithful man.

The notion that girls were wasting their lives by putting all their energy into reading novels and would be unable to lead a normal married life is very similar to the argument used by people who opposed women's education during the early Meiji period. Typical was Miyake Kaho, who made one character in her *Yabu no uguisu* (Warbler in the Grove, 1888) state that education made women want to obtain jobs, gain more education, and oppose marriage.[27] Japanese girls, who seemed to some to be so enthusiastic about education that they no longer wanted to have children, were considered a threat to the national project. Thus, criticism of girls reading novels did not take place in a void and was not directed at particular novels. Such

25. *Yomiuri shinbun*, 9 June 1891, reprinted in Hirata 1999, p. 69. Fuess notes that during the last two decades of the nineteenth century statistics reveal one divorce for every three marriages, many more than during the Edo period. He and others contend that those statistics were exaggerated. See Fuess 2004, pp. 120–23.

26. Sugimoto 1990, p. 131. "Enoch Arden" is a long poem by the Victorian poet laureate Alfred, Lord Tennyson (1809–92) first published in 1864. The Japanese translation, entitled "The Story of Enoch Arden," appeared serially in *Jogaku zasshi*, no. 195, 11 January 1890, pp. 16–18; no. 196, 18 January 1890, pp. 19–21; no. 197, 25 January 1890, pp. 19–21; no. 198, 1 February 1890, pp. 21–23; no. 199, 8 February 1890, pp. 20–22; no. 200, 15 February 1890, pp. 20–22; no. 201, 22 February 1890, pp. 20–22; and no. 202, 1 March 1890, pp. 21–24. Copeland notes that the translator was Wakamatsu Shizuko (2000, 129).

27. Copeland 2006b, p. 100.

criticism came to the fore in the print media after girls had become a visible presence, at least in large cities, and had started to ask for more educational and employment opportunities and precisely at a time when they were being portrayed as unruly and unwilling to conform to social expectations about women's position in society. Girl students, who were participating in women's activities and becoming informed about new theories on the social position of women, were seen as particularly at risk of being influenced by the novels they read and their reading habits.

It is not surprising, then, that in the very years in which these articles appeared in the press—1889 and 1890—a series of articles was published in *Yomiuri shinbun* attacking girl students' behavior and morality.[28] These articles also became good material for novelists, and in mid-July 1889 Doi Bansui's (1871–1952) novel *Shitsubō* (Disappointment) was serialized in *Yomiuri shinbun*. It described a suspected scandal at a girls' school, which in the end was shown to be baseless.[29] Only Iwamoto Yoshiharu (1863–1943), the editor of *Jogaku zasshi*, seems to have found the time to check the veracity of the stories published in *Yomiuri shinbun*. He had asked for details about these girls and the schools they frequented but did not succeed in getting them.[30]

Sarah Maza has argued that "the archetypal narrative of a wife's infidelity and insubordination was laden" with "connotations of political chaos and change" while "the most famous stories of female adultery draw their power from the link between sexual transgression and sociopolitical chaos."[31] In other words, disorders in the family are symptomatic of disorders in society. Maza's point helps us to understand that behind the articles lay not so much objective reality as a narrative of anxiety about social change. What girls had done in reality was to overstep the social boundaries of feminine behavior, and because of that they had to be restrained. The blame was attributed to the girls themselves, and the solution, it was thought, lay with educational reform. In 1889 the minister of education, Enomoto Takeaki, was reported to have argued that it was necessary to reform women's education by teaching girls simple subjects such as penmanship, Western and Japanese sewing,

---

28. *Yomiuri shinbun*, 21 (no. 4338, 1), 22 (no. 4339, 1), 29 (no. 4345, 3), 30 (no. 4346, 1) June 1889; no. 4551ff, 20, 21, 22, 23, 24, 26, 28 February 1890, all at page 3; and no. 4561, 02 March 1890, 1. Such stories were quickly taken up by other newspapers as well. See Patessio, forthcoming, for a discussion of this series of scandals.

29. Kornicki 1982, p. 52.

30. Jogaku zasshi, no. 202, 1 March 1890, p. 27; *Jogaku zasshi*, no. 203, 8 March 1890, pp. 25–27; and *Jogaku zasshi*, no. 204, 15 March 1890, back of front cover. An article in *Jogaku zasshi*, no. 283, 19 September 1891, pp. 23–24, also mentioned the criticism in *Yomiuri shinbun* of the ways in which girls spent money and talked but noted that girl students had made much progress, so if people wanted to speak of the use and abuse of money and words they should criticize men.

31. Maza 1993, pp. 264, 283.

and arithmetic and by giving them easy reading from which they would learn moral values. Rather than intellectual training, they should be given moral education so that they would no longer be "conceited."[32]

In spite of the fact that women were now regular contributors to the periodical press, I have found only one article, possibly written by a woman, in which the author ventured to come forward in defense of girl students. The article accused the press of falsehood and argued that all that had been written about the immorality of girl students was intended first to sell newspapers and second to destroy girls' schools and women's education in general. Japanese society still could not do away with the old mentality of looking down on girls and considering them as playthings. This would not support Japan's advancement, and it was incredible that journalists hindered Japan's progress by reporting such scandals.[33]

Iwamoto Yoshiharu tried, soon after the articles mentioned above were published, to give women's opinions more space by putting women in charge of various editorial offices at his magazine, *Jogaku zasshi*, and it is worth quoting at length the reasons for his decision.

> Mr. Iwamoto Zenji [= Yoshiharu] had previously held almost sole charge of the editorial department, but henceforth much of the editorial work will be undertaken by lady writers, eight of whom have been newly engaged. The discussion of current topics will be in the charge of Mrs. Nakajima [Toshiko], wife of the President of the House of Representatives. It will be seen that she has every facility to be well acquainted with the passing questions of the political, no less than of the social and literary world. . . . Mrs. S. [Shizuko] Wakamatsu, and Miss Tanabe [Kaho] will devote themselves to the writing of novels. Mrs. Ogino [Ginko], who is well known as a distinguished graduate of the Female Normal School, and as the first lady physician in Japan, will write on the subjects of hygiene and the nursery. Scientific subjects will be treated of by Mrs. Yoshida, also a well-known graduate of the Female Normal School. Miss Ando, one of the first graduates of the shorthand writing department in the *Meiji Jo Gakko*, will have the charge of the reporters' department. . . . Lastly the editing of the paper will be under the general superintendence and responsibility of Miss T. [Toyoko] Shimizu. . . . The object of the *Jogaku zasshi* has been, ever since the commencement of its existence, to be a reformer and leader among all the periodicals devoted to the interests of the fair sex. It has never sought a large sale by catering

32. *Shinonome shinbun*, no. 429, 19 June 1889, p. 1.
33. *Tsubomi*, no. 3, 20 March 1890, p. 1.

to the prejudices of society. . . . [A] critical moment has arrived in the history of the movement for the elevation of women's position in Japan, and a new responsibility has developed upon the *Jogaku zasshi*. At one time female journals numbered more than ten in the city of Tokyo alone, but they have disappeared one after another until now there remain only three. . . . Simultaneously with this decline of the female cause in the journalistic world, things have been taking a similar course in the sphere of female education. Under these circumstances, the *Jogaku zasshi* thinks it necessary to return to the first days of its existence, and repeat what it then wrote as to the vital importance of promoting female education and elevating the position of women.[34]

Even so, women were not finding many supporters for their cause, as is clear from their reluctance to challenge the allegations made in the press about the effects on young women of reading novels. We must wait a few more years, until the very beginning of the twentieth century, to find further developments in women's use of the print media, especially in the case of *Fujo shinbun*.

FUJO SHINBUN

The magazine *Fujo shinbun* has been almost entirely overlooked in both English and Japanese scholarship on Japanese women's history, but there can be no question that it needs to be seriously considered if we want to understand women's participation in the print media at the beginning of the twentieth century. The fact that the editor of *Fujo shinbun* was a man, as was also true of *Jogaku zasshi*, shows that in 1900 it was still difficult for women to create spaces in which to disseminate their ideas. Nevertheless, *Fujo shinbun* did become a platform for women's ideas, just as *Jogaku zasshi* had been.

The founder of *Fujo shinbun*, Fukushima Shirō (1874–1945), was born in Hyōgo prefecture where his father had been a retainer of the local daimyo. He became a teacher at the prefectural boys' school in Saitama in 1899, the year in which he came upon Fukuzawa Yukichi's (1834–1901) *Onna daigaku hyōron* (Critique of *Onna daigaku*, 1899) in *Jiji shinpō*, the newspaper founded by Fukuzawa.[35] Fukuzawa had written that although men and women were equal in East Asia it was an old custom to despise women. Fukushima understood Fukuzawa's explanation very well, he remembered, for he had

---

34. *Jogaku zasshi*, no. 244, 20 December 1890, inside front cover. The original is in English and is reprinted from the *Tokyo Mail*, 16 December 1890.
35. On the *Onna daigaku hyōron*, see Sugano's contribution to this volume.

experienced just such a situation through the life, and death, of his sister Maki. He wrote that she was married off when he was a young boy but ended up in an old-fashioned household where she had to endure pain and distress. Even when her parents told her to come back to their home, she answered that she had married and her husband's home was where she belonged for she had no other "home." One year after she married, at the age of twenty-one, she died. Fukushima was distressed at the sight of his mother's suffering over his sister's death, and began to question why women like his sister could not return to their families once they had married. He stated that if his sister had known about Fukuzawa's theories on women perhaps her destiny would have been different while there certainly were other women living under the same conditions. His experience and Fukuzawa's writings had helped him to understand the importance of reforming social practices in order to give women and men the possibility of fulfilling their lives and finding personal happiness, and he decided to publish a journal to spread these ideas. He quit his job soon thereafter, moved to Tokyo, found another teaching job to maintain himself, and started planning the launch of *Fujo shinbun*, which was first published on 10 May 1900.[36] The magazine had prominent supporters, and Hozumi Utako (1863–1932), daughter of the Meiji entrepreneur Shibusawa Eiichi and mother of Hozumi Shigetō (1883–1951), a University of Tokyo expert on civil law who supported the revision of the Civil Code of 1898 in relation to women's rights, was one of them, promoting the journal passionately among her female acquaintances.[37]

From the very beginning, *Fujo shinbun* published readers' comments. Of course, one cannot assume that all the letters published in this and other magazines or newspapers were actual submissions, especially when they were either unsigned or signed with a pen name, for they could be written "in-house" to create discussion of a particular topic or to encourage debate. However, two things are clear: women's opinions were given publicity in *Fujo shinbun*, and students' contributions were welcome from the start. One of the first letters that arrived at *Fujo shinbun* in September 1900, for example, was from Hachiya Teiko (1882–1975) giving her opinion, written

36. Fukushima Shirō, *Fujo shinbun no gyōseki* (*Fujo shinbun*'s Achievements), p. 1–3, printed at the end of the volume in Fukushima Shirō 1984. In *Fujo shinbun no gyōseki*, Fukushima also recalled that sales of Fukuzawa's *Shin onna daigaku* (The New *Onna daigaku*) had been prohibited at the Kyoto Furitsu Kōtō Jogakkō (Kyoto Prefectural Higher School for Girls) soon after the first issue of *Fujo shinbun* was published because it was judged to have a negative influence on women's education. Tokyo Furitsu Kōtō Jogakkō instead awarded it as a prize to graduating girl students who had done particularly well (p. 4).

37. Fukushima Shirō 1984, preface written by Hozumi Shigetō, pp. 1–2. On Hozumi Shigetō's criticism of the Civil Code, see Nagy 1991.

under a pen name, of an article written by another woman, the educator Kaetsu Takako (1867–1949). Hachiya had been one of her students; in 1902, after graduating from a girls' school, Hachiya married Fukushima, the editor of the magazine.[38] Fukushima (Hachiya) Teiko gave birth to seven children, helped her husband, wrote for the magazine in her own right, and published at least one book during her lifetime.[39] During the late 1910s, the poet Yosano Akiko (1878–1942), who also gave birth to a number of children, argued that motherhood played only a small part in a woman's life and women should be educated and have occupations in order to participate in public life and support their children. Yosano was criticized by contemporary feminists for proposing an unrealistic ideal for women, for only a few could achieve such goals and independence in the early twentieth century. However, Fukushima Teiko was one such woman, and the way in which she balanced her education, a large family, and active participation in public discourse shows that early Meiji women's struggles to obtain a rewarding private and public life had started to bear fruit.[40]

What were the reasons for the publication of this magazine? An article in the first issue, entitled "Reason for the Publication of *Fujo shinbun*," stated that there were too many theories on the education of women. Should women be educated according to the *Onna daigaku* or according to Fukuzawa's *Shin onna daigaku* (The New *Onna daigaku*, 1899)? Or was there some better way? The second point related to the opening of a women's university in Japan. The magazine would become a space where those in favor and those against university education for women would present their ideas. Actually, Fukushima had originally written that *Fujo shinbun* approved of opening a university for women in Japan. However, Hagino Yoshiyuki (1860–1924), a professor at Tokyo University, had suggested that, given that women's higher education was criticized by many, if *Fujo shinbun* was to be promoted widely it would not be advisable to write such a strong supporting statement. It would be best, instead, to state that the journal would discuss the suitability of such an endeavor. Fukushima also recalled that the definition of "male and female parity of rights" (*danjo dōken*), too, had been erased from the same text by another "adviser," the head of Kazoku Jogakkō, Hosokawa Junjirō (1834–1923), so it is clear that the journal wanted to support all sorts of women's activities and developments in women's lives even if these were not explicitly stated in its pages.[41]

38. *Fujo shinbun* o Yomu Kai 1997, pp. 25–26.
39. Fukushima Teiko 1935.
40. On Yosano's debate with contemporary feminists, see Tsurumi 1998.
41. Fukushima Shirō, *Fujo shinbun no gyōseki* (*Fujo shinbun*'s Achievements), p. 3, printed at the end of the volume in Fukushima Shirō 1984.

Going back to the "Reason for the Publication of *Fujo shinbun*," the next point stated that it was necessary to create proper homes first but then also to reform society, and women had a very important part to play in this task. It was also necessary to form links between various women's groups, publicize the work of charitable institutions, and inform girl students of interesting developments. Readers were asked to help in evaluating new publications, and they would be presented with, and invited to comment on, new works and edifying novels that were being published.[42] Given that Fukuzawa Yukichi had argued in *Shin onna daigaku* that novels, plays, and poems were a waste of time and were responsible for arousing passions, especially in young girls who were susceptible to excessive emotions and tended to put all their energy into reading, Fukushima's emphasis here seems deliberately provocative; clearly, he wanted to discuss the question with his readers.[43]

What, then, is significant about *Fujo shinbun* and how did Fukushima intend to put his aims into practice? First, women could read about, if not directly criticize, other women's magazines in the pages of *Fujo shinbun*. In an article published in 1901, for example, Hōgenshi (a pen name meaning "person writing on random topics") stated that there were plenty of magazines for women but they were antiquated and trite. They carried photographs and paid particular attention to the covers, but their contents were not up to the twentieth century. Girl students were extremely active and bright, but they could not find magazines to suit their lifestyles, for all seemed to lack dynamism and did nothing but seek to flatter their readership. *Jogaku sekai* (The World of Women's Education), published by Hakubunkan, seemed to be the one that sold most copies, and the editor was working particularly hard, but it was a publication that crammed together all sorts of information and did not have a clear agenda. This was also the problem with the majority of women's journals, *Jogaku zasshi* being the only one to be praised.[44] Whereas throughout the Meiji period girl students were supposed to be controlled

---

42. *Fujo shinbun*, no. 1, 10 May 1900, p. 1.
43. "For instance, students of a girls' school, when they learn to read literature or to understand a Western language, begin to put all their energy into composing poems and reading novels, particularly flippant little pieces. For one's cultural accomplishments, classical literature and modern novels are certainly useful, but while one is still young, there must be many other things to study. In the present society, there are many women who excel in poetry composition but who never stop to think or even imagine about their own independence and its meaning, or those who have read dozens or even a hundred novels, but who have never picked up a book on physiology. Moreover, novels and such frivolous works often contain exciting material which is liable to be detrimental to youthful women who are in the spring of their lives" (Fukuzawa 1988, p. 237).
44. *Fujo shinbun*, no. 75, 14 October 1901, p. 6.

and educated according to the government ideology of *ryōsai kenbo*, here was an article stating that instead they should be given fresh food for thought.

Second, *Fujo shinbun* actively began to seek links with its readership. In 1901, for example, one "Wakako" stated that newspapers had no contact with their readers, but *Fujo shinbun* hoped that readers would write in if they had something to say.[45] Wakako also wrote that readers of *Fujo shinbun* should join forces and become guides and instructors for Japanese women. It was the readers who pushed the boundaries forward, she stated, so they should plan what to do together with other contributors.[46] Given that as early as 1900 letters to the magazine had begun to arrive, these short statements were clearly supportive of a strong relationship with the magazine's readers, who for their part seemed to like the idea.

Third, contributors to *Fujo shinbun* debated what they thought was the place of print media in women's lives. In a long unsigned editorial entitled "Women and Newspapers," the author argued that if women's duties were simply to sew and cook, raise children, and lead domestic lives they would have no need for newspapers. But women were members of the Japanese nation (*kokumin*), and they had to have a part in the development of their nation and in the social arena; to read newspapers and learn about what was happening in the world was therefore essential. If it was important that they be able to teach their children about progress achieved in the world, they had to obtain such knowledge from newspapers. Women's education before the Meiji Restoration, the author continued, had deliberately created servile, indecisive women whose place was in the home and who did not know much about the world. If such an educational ideology was right for Meiji women as well, then reading newspapers could actually be dangerous. But they were in the twentieth century, and Japanese women could not be *hakoiri musume* (sheltered daughters, literally "daughters in boxes") anymore. It was impossible to suppose that they could continue living confined to their homes as *okusama* (wives, literally "women whose place is in the interior of the house"). The argument that newspapers were not important for women implied that women did not have to better themselves along with the rest of the world and did not need to know about events in the imperial household, about new prime ministers, about the opening of the Diet, about international wars, about the spread of the Black Death, or about naval technological development. Some people did argue that it would be sufficient if women were like dolls, without knowledge, wearing kimonos and sitting

---

45. Ibid., no. 37, 21 January 1901, p. 7.
46. Ibid., no. 40, 11 February 1901, p. 7.

modestly, others that it was dangerous for women to read newspapers. In the world there were those who demanded certain services and those who, in response to the demand, offered those services. So newspapers that published indecent, vulgar, or scandalous pieces would not survive if there were no demand. If there were a large demand for decent newspapers, somebody would certainly satisfy it.[47]

The author of this article supported the notion that women should be educated for their own good and the progress of their nation, and in this respect he or she thought twentieth-century women differed considerably from previous generations of women. Women did not have the political right to vote or be elected, but the author argued that they ought to be politically educated, and this point is even more important if we remember that the Public Peace Police Law, Chian keisatsu hō, was implemented in 1900, reinforcing the 1890 Public Meeting and Political Association Law's ban on women joining political associations or attending political meetings, and that the notion of "parity of male and female rights" was erased from the first issue because of its "dangerous meaning."[48] Moreover, whereas during the 1870s and 1880s women's behavior and reading were attacked in newspapers and magazines, by 1900 women had a different tool with which to defend their education, namely, the argument that newspapers were not dangerous for women and if part of Japanese society liked reading indecent and vulgar articles the solution was to reform those publications (and that part of society), not to prohibit women from reading them.

I turn finally to two additional articles published in *Fujo shinbun* that stressed this last point. We have seen how girl students were implicated in a scandal that was used to discredit women's education. Subsequently, as far as I have been able to ascertain, no newspapers carried news of similar scandals until 1901, coincidentally the year in which the Nihon Joshi Daigakkō (Japan Women's College) was established. In 1901 four newspapers described a certain Kudō Mitsu, an eighteen-year-old student of the Japan Women's College who had been exchanging letters with a man as an *inpon musume* (indecent daughter) and *daraku jogakusei* (degenerate girl student). An unsigned editorial in *Fujo shinbun* commented that in *Jinmin* (one of the newspapers) "the facts" were reported in installments, as though they were a novel. The editorial was entitled "Newspaper Journalists' Responsibilities," and in it the author(s) (*warera*) stated that when journalists took up their pens they had to take responsibility for what they wrote. Since four

---

47. Ibid., no. 48, 8 April 1901, p. 1.
48. See Garon 1997, pp. 118–19.

journals had published the same news on the same day, the author(s) continued, it was clear that not much effort had been put into searching for the truth. Those newspapers had not had the time to check the validity of their information, and so:

> They got a piece of unchecked information that was like a bone, covered it with blood and skin, clothed it, decorated it in various ways and disguised the truth, and with that they spiritually killed an innocent girl. In so doing, they reached the nadir of violence. An innocent girl, yes, we are calling Kudō Mitsu an innocent girl.

This was already a *j'accuse*, but the author(s) went even further, stating that they had discovered the real story, which was as follows. Kudō had lived all her life with her family in the countryside and had graduated in 1901 from Morioka Shiritsu Jogakkō. As she was just eighteen, her parents had been afraid to let her go to Tokyo to study by herself, and even the idea of putting her in the dormitory of the school did not seem right, so her mother accompanied her to Tokyo and the two of them rented a house there. However, two months after they had arrived in Tokyo news came that the girl's grandmother was ill, and there was nothing else they could do but go back home. Of course in just two months Kudō had not become accustomed to Tokyo or life there. Since she was under the close supervision of her mother, the writer argued, however bad a girl she might have been, could two months have been long enough to become somebody's lover? True, a man had written her a letter, which was now in the hands of Naruse Jinzō (1858–1919), the head of the school, the main purpose of which was to apologize for having used coarse language and to invite her to join a newly formed literary association. Kudō herself had not known what the first part of the message referred to, and, not having answered the first letter, she received a second one. But she did not answer this second letter either and went back home with her mother. The writer(s) stated that three precious columns on the first page of *Fujo shinbun* were being used "to defend the college and one individual girl" because the problem concerned not only journalists' responsibilities but also women's well-being. It was to be hoped that such awful words as "indecent daughter" and "degenerate girl student" would not be used again to refer to women. Men could restore their honor, but what about women insulted by newspapers? It was as bad as a capital sentence in front of the whole of society, for it was impossible to show one's face in public again. If there was a punishment for denuding a person and exposing her in front of everybody so that passersby could laugh at her, this would be the perfect case for such punishment to be applied.[49]

The tone of the article was very angry, visceral even, and if not by a female contributor it was probably written by more than one person including at least one woman. One person who might have contributed to, if not written, the editorial was someone from Kobe signing herself with the pen name Jiyūko (Miss Freedom) who wrote a long article congratulating *Fujo shinbun* on having reached its one-hundredth issue. The style of the two articles is similar, and the choice of terms, linked so much to the body and blood, is similar, too. *Fujo shinbun*, she wrote, was born to give voice to women's problems and had started raising its voice in a sleeping world. This voice had become louder in Japan since its publication and louder and louder with its growth. The magazine's development went hand in hand with the development of a strong voice on women's problems in Japanese society, and it would lower its voice only when all women's problems had been addressed. But this would take time, and therefore the magazine could not afford to lower its voice; *Fujo shinbun*'s work would be long and difficult. The work that it had hitherto done, shouting at the top of its voice so much that it had spat blood (*aran kagiri no koe o agete sakebi, konnichi made chi o haite sakebi kita koto haya*), was really important. Nevertheless, its goal was still far ahead; it was important that it maintain its energy and continue voicing women's problems until it was hoarse (literally "until its throat cracked") in order to save those women who found themselves in sad circumstances. The world did not belong to men or women, the author continued; it was a place in which men and women should live happily together. *Fujo shinbun* had a long future ahead, and so long as it had a life (literally "so long as it had blood," *chi no aru kagiri*) it must strain its throat (*nodo o shibotte*) and raise its voice for women. For the magazine to have reached its one-hundredth issue was not something to feel complacent about; so long as it had a tongue (*shita no aru kagiri*) it must raise its voice and exert itself for the creation of a world in which men and women could live properly together. "I (*watashi wa*) do not think that the magazine's hundredth issue is a reason to rejoice," she concluded, "for it is still not enough. It is necessary to arrive at its one-thousandth or ten-thousandth issue" before women would be able to celebrate. "Your destination is far ahead, and your baggage is heavy, but given that your mission is to raise women's voices until [their desires are met and] they fall quiet, I urge you

49. *Fujo shinbun*, no. 62, 15 July 1901, p. 1.

to be ready to use your strength until your throat has dried up and you spit blood."[50]

Conclusion

During the late 1880s and 1890s newspaper articles were discussing what women should read because intellectuals and writers were trying to control their education and prevent women from gaining access to publications that they believed would give women an unsuitable understanding of Japanese society and their position in it. The fact that young women's public behavior created anxiety among male writers and at the government level is clear when we look at the debates over women's education that took place between male writers and the minister of education. In the same period, some argued that novels discouraged girls' intellectual growth, whereas others maintained that girls' education should be based on simple subjects and easy reading from which moral values could be learned. It was not novels as such that were dangerous but the way in which girls seemed to be reading them, looking for examples of women who were not exclusively supporting the governmental ideology of "good wives and wise mothers." This, together with the fact that many of those girls were attending girls' schools and obtaining an education, created social tensions that some attempted to diffuse by prohibiting girl students from reading certain kinds of books or obtaining a certain kind of education.

During the same period, there was also an identifiable female readership of women's magazines published by men. Despite the small number of female authors of novels, and although it was the male editors of women's magazines that caught the attention of the media because of their high profile, women were active contributors to the print media not only through their articles and (in the case of *Jogaku zasshi*) their official roles within the publishing companies but also through the letters they sent. Women were becoming active participants in a dialogue with intellectuals and the government. At the same time, they had also begun to form an imagined community of readers, a community that was used to share and discuss ideas.

By 1900 a further step had been taken when the press was criticized for false representations of women's activities and lifestyles. True, I cannot state for certain that the last two articles discussed above were written by

---

50. Ibid., no. 102, 21 April 1902, 4. According to *Fujo shinbun* o Yomu Kai 1997, p. 91, Jiyūko signed this name in the magazine at least twenty-four times, although it is not clear in which years.

women, but the anger they convey strongly supports my suggestion that they were at least partly written by a female hand. At the very least, it is possible to say that women read these angry replies to another scandal involving girl students. Meiji journalism was a commercial enterprise, and sales were often driven by (imaginary) juicy scandals, so it is not difficult to understand why immoral girls were an interesting and lucrative topic and why not much substance lay behind the allegations. More scandals about "degenerate girl students" were still to come, but what is important is that they no longer had the same effect. The "scandal" of 1901 met with a vigorous response and an informed rebuttal of the charges. The difference, then, lay in the fact that women were by then participating much more actively in the periodical press and were therefore better placed to use the print media as a public tool with which to defend themselves.

11

Women and Literacy
from Edo to Meiji

Anne Walthall

Comparing board games (*sugoroku*) produced in the Edo and Meiji periods not only dramatizes the differences in women's experiences and expectations but also points to the changing social context for literacy. A game designed for young women by Hiroshige in the early 1840s starts with a solitary pupil seated at her desk.[1] A game published for the 1910 January issue of the magazine *Fujin sekai* has four starting points: female workers, young ladies (*reijō*), a maid, and two schoolgirls greeting their teacher.[2] The first game depicts the pupil learning performing arts such as tea ceremony, stringed musical instruments, dancing and drumming, martial arts, visual arts (including tray painting), flower arranging, calligraphy, literary arts such as poetry, and the bodily training imparted by etiquette. Embedded in this game is the notion that literacy is fundamental to a constellation of disciplines, all essential for a young woman to make her way in the world

---

1. For examples of early-nineteenth-century *sugoroku* for women, see Katō and Matsumura 2002; and Namiki 2007.
2. The 1910 *sugoroku* can be seen at http://showcase.meijitaisho.net/entry/litho_fujinsugoroku .php.

(*risshin shusse*). The 1910 game celebrates the appearance of the professional working woman: hairdresser, laundress, nurse, telephone operator, accountant, cook, doctor, and teacher. Only one box, labeled *keigo*, refers to the polite arts of the earlier age by showing a girl learning flower arranging while a young woman practices the koto. The goal of the first game is to attain a high-ranking position secluded in the shogun's great interior (*ōoku*); the goal of the second is to create a happy home for a three-generational family.[3]

Comparing these two games dramatizes the transformation in public space brought about through the modernizing policies of the Meiji state. No longer did women study reading and writing valued for the performance of cultivated femininity in the privacy of home and neighborhood; instead they learned skills useful to society at large in institutional settings. The state's involvement in the education of children meant that all women were supposed to have access to literacy, although they did not always use this knowledge for ends approved by the state. Another consequence of state-sponsored education was that women enjoyed considerably less flexibility in what they studied than in the past. Along with standardization in content came new divisions; divorced from the polite arts, literacy gained a much more stringent patriotic and moral imperative than it had ever had before.

So much of what we know about female literacy can also be applied to male literacy that any study of women reading and writing risks bringing nothing more than a supplement to the history of education. Furthermore, women have always written within the context of their relations with men, but men often write in a homosocial context that has nothing to do with women at all. The goals for board games aimed at women incorporate men; board games for men often ignore women completely or posit them only as an object of diversion (as a prostitute or courtesan) on the way to loftier achievement. Male writers are read as individuals; female writers are all too often read as representing something more than themselves.[4] Bashō stands for himself alone; his female disciples are known for their social backgrounds as much as for their poems. In dealing with early modern Japan in particular, we have to remember that this was an androcentric world, that adult men dominated cultural production, and that the male gaze was never absent.[5] Does this mean, then, that examining women simply adds to what we have learned through the study of men? One answer comes through the work of

---

3. Many Edo period *sugoroku* also had marriage as their goal, but even so the path was different, leading through the private pitfalls of jealousy and care for a mother-in-law rather than employment in public.
4. Wender makes this point regarding Resident Koreans, or indeed any minority, but it applies equally well to women (2005, pp. 37, 48).
5. Pflugfelder 2000.

Joan Scott, who argues that women's history challenges the notion that any history can claim completeness. Simply requesting that history include information about women suggests that it is already incomplete and partial.[6] Bringing women into the equation does not just complicate it; instead, such a move opens a new avenue for approaching historical transformations.

My analysis of the transformations wrought in female literacy between the Edo and Meiji periods is structured around the following topics. The first concerns the features that distinguished Edo period literacy for both men and women and men versus women. Edo is often called Japan's early modern period, implying that it provided the foundation for modern Japan. If such was the case, then to what extent did patterns of literacy for men and women carry forward? In order to disrupt a sense of linear progression from Edo to Meiji, an even more important question, particularly for women, is not only what changes but what gets lost. To develop this contrast, I posit a shift from the private patriarchy of family control to the public patriarchy of state control. Drawing on Judith Bennett's notion of the patriarchal equilibrium, I weigh the advantages and disadvantages of both for women before concluding with an assessment of what a focus on the female subject can teach us about the Edo-Meiji divide.[7]

Female Literacy in the Edo Period

A focus on either female or male literacy obscures the characteristics they shared in common. Even though authors might address their writings specifically to either men or women, literate members of both sexes read or could read the same texts and wrote in the same genres. Without denying the possibility of setting up distinctions between feminine versus masculine lore, it is better to see the range of reading and writing as spanning a continuum. For that reason, many of the features that characterized female literacy during the Edo period characterized male literacy as well.

First let us consider what this continuum might include. Both men and women were encouraged to read didactic literature aimed at inculcating moral standards and ethical behavior, although the specific content varied. Much attention has focused on *Onna daigaku* (Greater Learning for Women) and similar texts whose titles proclaim their designated audience (including *onna* in such titles marks their contents as partial in contrast to books for men, which demonstrate their universality by not specifying a readership),

6. Scott 1992.
7. Bennett 1997.

but boys, too, learned correct behavior from books. Men and women studied etiquette books.[8] They attended Kabuki and contributed to *surimono* (privately commissioned one-page prints combining images and poetry) lauding their favorite actors.[9] They read popular fiction. We might assume that women would be more likely to read *Nise Murasaki Inaka Genji* (The Fake Murasaki's Rustic Genji), set as it was in the shogun's great interior and the pleasure quarters, both deemed worlds of women, whereas men read Takizawa Bakin's *Nansō Satomi hakkenden* (The Biographies of Eight Dogs), a didactic multivolume work about the adventures of eight stalwart warriors. Bakin insisted that his books were not for women and children, but two prints found by Itasaka Noriko for this volume show women reading his work. Men and women read and copied sutras, although here again the content could differ, as with various iterations of *Ketsubon kyō* (Blood Bowl Sutra), which promised women eternal damnation in a pool of blood for the crime of having shed blood during menses and childbirth.[10] Although men were more likely to read and write *kanshi* (Chinese poetry) and *haikai*, women were not excluded. Both wrote *waka*, though always greater numbers of men than women. In short, it is better to speak of Edo period literacies than literacy.[11] Few men or women had an interest in or the opportunity to master them all.

Distinctions that can be made between male and female literacies have to be carefully qualified. Although a few women wrote Chinese poetry, with the exception of a few abbesses from the imperial family they did not write Chinese prose.[12] On the other hand, only the most highly educated sinophilic men wrote in Chinese; for ease of communication, most preferred Japanese. Tadano Makuzu's challenge to Bakin came as much in how she expressed herself as in what she said. Although she utilized an essay format in archaic Japanese much in the style of the celebrated tenth-century writer Sei Shōnagon, she used it to discuss politically sensitive issues. She had such difficulty in being heard that her writings remained unpublished until the modern period. The sole woman famous for her prose is Arakida Rei, who wrote novels and travelogues that contained large doses of poetry. Late in life Kutsukake Nakako (1749–1829) from a village headman family in Shinano also wrote a treatise in prose on poetry, but her writings remained

---

8. For a detailed study of etiquette books for men, see Ikegami 2005.
9. Gerstle, Clark, and Yano 2005, pp. 102–3, 134, 153, 172.
10. See Williams 2004, especially the appendix.
11. This is a point made in Kornicki 1998, p. 30.
12. Yabuta makes the point that women read literature and men read philosophy (1995, p. 245). The writings by abbesses consist of inscriptions on portraits; see Medieval Japanese Studies Institute 2009, pp. 41, 57, 72.

unknown outside her locality.[13] These exceptions suggest that while women could read prose they were discouraged from writing it lest they run the risk of appearing unfeminine.

Although people in the Edo period distinguished between appropriate texts for girls and boys, between what was suitably masculine and suitably feminine, they often had to make do with whatever was available. As late as 1841, after Hirata Atsutane had been exiled to Akita, his wife Orise wrote her son-in-law Kanetane asking him to send some books for her husband's niece, then twelve years old, preferably selections from *The Tale of Genji* or *Miyakoji*, observing, "She likes to learn and writes well, but here there are no instruction books for girls, only for boys."[14] The girl was a member of the samurai class living in a castle town. If her family could not find female-specific texts, how much more difficult would it have been for peasants?

As Orise's letter suggests, for both men and women in the Edo period what kind of literacy and whether they acquired it was largely a matter of chance. The learning experience depended on whatever happened to be available in terms of texts and teachers, circumstances that could change at any time during a person's life. Sugano Noriko has documented the extreme regional variation, often ascribable to individual difference, in types of textbooks used and to what extent basic literacy skills were supplemented by the polite arts.[15] Economic conditions also played a part. In manufacturing centers such as Kiryū, expanded opportunities for women to work also meant that households could afford to send daughters to school in a self-reinforcing virtuous circle.[16] In his recent study of popular literacy, Richard Rubinger demonstrates that while literacy rates climbed in urban areas and central Japan they remained low in the southwest and northeast. He concludes that in providing opportunities to learn reading, writing, and arithmetic, geography trumped gender.[17]

Both men and women faced obstacles to acquiring literacy, although generally speaking those for women were greater. Men had more mobility than women, especially at a young age, which allowed them to travel in search of education. When daimyos established domain schools starting in the late eighteenth century, they restricted access to men, as did the famous merchant school Kaitokudō and other private academies.[18] Women were

---

13. Maeda 1998, pp. 160–73.
14. Watanabe 1942, p. 388.
15. Sugano 1998, p. 146.
16. Nishigaki 1997, pp. 248–49.
17. Rubinger 2007, pp. 133–34.
18. Yamanashi Shigako's (1738–1814) sons attended private academies in Edo; her education came through correspondence and familial practice (Maeda 1998, pp. 196–206).

much more dependent on chance encounters with teachers; in many cases they pursued whatever path had already been trod by a close relative, usually, though not always, male. Economic and social factors also matter; some types of acquired techniques cost much more to master in terms of time and money, leading Rubinger to posit the existence of two cultures within villages, one for the cultivated elite and one for the unlettered poor.[19] Historical factors, especially changing attitudes toward what constituted meaningful writing counted as well.

Let me give an example of how happenstance functioned in the acquisition of literacy. A seventeenth-century marital connection between the Hori daimyo of Iida and the Nijō aristocratic family of Kyoto first brought a knowledge of *waka* to the Ina Valley where it was confined to Buddhist priests, male retainers, the lord, and the lord's birth mother. In the early eighteenth century, one teacher set up shop in Iida where he taught four women and many men. A few teachers passed through the valley, holding one or two poetry meetings before moving on. People who wanted more advanced study, for example, Sakurai Chie (1724–1813), had to travel to Kyoto and Edo.[20] Her great-granddaughter, Matsuo Taseko (1811–94), was more fortunate in that by the time she started to pursue the way of poetry, a castle town pharmacist had set up a poetry-writing circle. Although latter-day critics have denigrated his skill, he promoted the study of the imperial anthology, *Shinkokinshū*, and Taseko dutifully memorized poems from it. After he died in 1848, his circle dispersed. Taseko tried for a time to study through correspondence with a teacher living near Hamamatsu. The thick texture of allusion and quotation that characterizes her poems shows that she received conventional training in Heian period literature, including *The Tale of Genji* and *Tales of Ise*. Having studied poetry with Iwasaki Nagayo (1807–81), a disciple of Hirata Atsutane who settled in the Ina Valley in the 1850s, she then wrote poetry that drew on the *Man'yōshū*. In no case did she study any of these texts in their entirety.[21] Her education in the classics was haphazard at best, haphazardness being a necessary corollary of happenstance.

A focus on what women might study and produce also has to highlight changing attitudes toward meaningful expression. Over twenty-five years ago, Seki Tamiko pointed to transformations in *kanshi* aesthetics initiated by Ogyū Sorai (1666–1728) to explain how women acquired the opportunity to write in Chinese. The Sorai School made *kanshi* into a vehicle through

---

19. Rubinger 2007, pp. 7, 132.
20. Murasawa 1936, pp. 29–31, 285–87. See also Ichimura 1929. Another example of a woman whose father promoted her education through travel is Hoashi Misako from Kumamoto, who went to Matsuzaka at age fourteen (Maeda 1998, pp. 9, 121).
21. See Walthall 1998.

which to express a correct understanding of the classics. Later Ichikawa Kansai (1749–1820) argued for the importance of using poetry to express natural emotions in simple language by pointing out that half the poems in the *Book of Odes* were written by "working men and thinking women." No longer forced into an archaistic style about morality or political matters, nineteenth-century commoner men and women wrote about everyday life and private emotions.[22]

Seki's account of historical transformations in the aesthetics of *kanshi* requires some modification. Tetsuo Najita has pointed out that Sorai himself insisted on preserving a personal space eminently suitable for the production of *kanshi* in which to express private emotion apart from the realm of public duties.[23] A survey of women writers of *kanshi* shows that not all of them waited for Kansai or even Sorai before embarking on their enterprise. As early as the 1660s, Ayabe Shichi (1649–1711), the wife of a Confucian scholar, is known to have written *kanshi*, as did three women in the Genroku era (1688–1704). All were of high status, as was Tachibana Gyokuran, daughter of the Yanagawa domain lord, who wrote *kanshi* in the 1750s. In the late eighteenth century, Hoashi Misato (1787–1817), daughter of a shrine priest from Kumamoto, took advantage of her father's tutelage to study *kanshi*.[24] These individuals aside, Seki is right that the early nineteenth century saw commoner women from wealthy families and the lower-ranking nobility discovering the opportunity to learn *kanshi*, a trend that continued across the Edo-Meiji divide.

Since *kanshi* required a higher level of erudition than other forms of poetry and thus attracted fewer adherents, it provides an excellent example of regional variation in patterns of literacy. Before the early nineteenth century brought increased educational opportunities, female writers of *kanshi* tended to be of high status and from western Japan. Notable were imperial abbesses whose wealth and family background allowed them to achieve an extraordinarily high level of artistic achievement in addition to *kanshi*, including painting, calligraphy, *waka*, tea ceremony, and flower arranging. As early as the Muromachi period, abbesses hosted literary salons, a trend that continued in the Edo period.[25] An exhibition of artifacts related to women's culture in Tottori included evidence that the daimyo's women learned Chinese-style calligraphy and poetry beginning in the eighteenth century.[26] Maeda

22. Seki 1980, pp. 167–90.
23. Najita 1998, pp. xxxi, xxxvi.
24. Maeda 1998, pp. 17–18; 1999, pp. 223–336.
25. See the catalog for the exhibition titled "Amamonzeki jiin no sekai" (Medieval Japanese Studies Institute 2009).
26. Tottori Kenritsu Hakubutsukan 2006. 22. Seki 1980, pp. 167–90.

Yoshi's study of female poets shows that before 1800 they all came from western Honshu, Shikoku, or Kyushu. Even women who published in Edo, such as Yanagawa Kōran (1804–79), Ema Saikō (1787–1861), or Hara Saihin (1798–1859), received their education elsewhere. It is possible that for purely fortuitous reasons we know about more female *kanshi* writers in western Japan because that is where historians today have done the most painstaking archival work. Besides, given how easily writings by women disappear, we can never be certain that they did not exist in the first place. These caveats aside, I suspect that through the eighteenth century western Japan, with its cultural centers of Kyoto and Osaka, simply maintained a higher level of personal cultivation than did eastern Japan. Insofar as writing in Chinese continued to be valued as the epitome of literary accomplishment, it marked a cultural divide between east and west, a divide accentuated by points of origin for women writers.

Although the most famous female poets of the Edo period wrote *haikai*, the field proved almost as unwelcoming to them as *kanshi*. Following the age of Matsunaga Teitoku (1571–1653) and his more famous successor Matsuo Bashō (1644–94), during a fifty-year hiatus between 1726 and 1774 women disappeared from *haikai* anthologies. Some have argued that *haidan* as the settings for social networks were viewed as unsuitable venues for respectable women. Yet women participated in *waka* poetry meetings in which gender and status distinctions mattered less than the ability to write a good poem. Instead I speculate that the reason needs to be sought within the history of differing poetic traditions. *Haikai*'s origins can be found in the linked verse (*renga*) circles spawned during the Muromachi period. During this misogynist era, many practitioners were Buddhist priests notably unfriendly to women. There may have been women who participated in writing *renga*, but neither they nor a definably feminine sensibility marked the genre. Thus a woman who wished to write *haikai* during the Edo period did not have noteworthy models to cast a cloak of hoary tradition over her efforts. Furthermore, *haikai*'s brevity lent itself more to wit and cleverness than the layering of poetic allusion, making it popular with courtesans in the Genroku era and later, who entertained their customers with word games. To the extent that *haikai* poets followed the example of Karai Senryū (1718–90) in making poetry out of ordinary speech by incorporating vulgarities and allusions to bodily functions, *haikai* became even less appealing to women wishing to use poetry as a means of self-cultivation.

There was little agreement on what kinds of literacy in early modern Japan promoted self-cultivation. Nakano Setsuko has argued that before the appearance of texts such as *Greater Learning for Women*, the purpose of seventeenth-century erotic books was to teach women how to conform to men's desires.[27] Yokota Fuyuhiko has argued that the expansion in different types of work performed by women at the turn of the eighteenth century necessitated the establishment of codes of behavior in didactic texts to enable women to conform to conventional norms of respectability, and Sugano Noriko has demonstrated that they circulated widely.[28] Not all women read them. In her autobiography, Etsu Sugimoto recounted how her father, a member of the samurai class, had her learn the Confucian classics from books intended for boys.[29] In her memoir–cum–literary treatise, Kutsukake Nakako described how her grandmother had her memorize *Hyakunin isshu* and the "spring" section of *Kokinshū* before she learned to write. As a matter of course, she also learned that she must subjugate herself to her father, her husband, and then her son.[30] The famous *kanshi* poet Yanagawa Kōran referred to maxims for women in her poetry as well.[31] Yet when Orise requested books for her husband's niece, she made no mention of didactic literature, asking, as we have seen, for classical texts even though Atsutane saw the way of poetry as frivolous. Male educators of women disagreed about whether the Japanese literary tradition or Chinese didactic texts provided the best teaching tools, but, depending on happenstance, women might study one or the other or both.

When I did a close reading of Matsuo Taseko's poems, what struck me was how little they had to do with didactic literature. She wrote many poems on conventional subjects: seasonal change, landscape, and love. She knew the appropriate salutations for letter writing, she gave specimens of her calligraphy on poem cards to her acquaintances, and she studied tea ceremony. In other words, she worked at cultivating a self apart from her everyday work of raising silkworms and managing a household. A married woman with seven living children, she wrote letters enticing men to come and visit her by incorporating the type of poems exchanged between lovers. In poetry meetings, she wrote poems about thwarted love affairs, the morning after, and committing adultery. At least in her heart she abrogated the dictates for women found in *Greater Learning for Women*.[32]

Most women did not specialize in just one form of poetry; they acquired literacy for utilitarian purposes, and their pursuit of self-cultivation went beyond learning to read and write. Writing *haikai* did not preclude writing *waka* or even *kanshi*. Shopkeepers' wives needed to be literate in order to

27. Nakano 1997, p. 300.
28. Yokota 1999; Sugano 1998.
29. Sugimoto 1990, pp. 19–20.
30. Maeda 1998, pp. 163–70.
31. Seki 1980, pp. 188–89.
32. See Walthall 1997, pp. 196–206.

assist in the family business, but other kinds of work also required knowledge of letters and figures. As William Lindsey has said, "[L]iteracy among courtesans indicates that while not all women could read and write . . . [at least some individuals in] all categories of women could do so. Typically this literacy was functionally appropriate to their professional and personal aspirations."[33] Mary Elizabeth Berry highlights the variety of household encyclopedias for both men and women. In her view, the most fundamental of the polite arts were calligraphy, letter writing, gift giving, poetry, and tea ceremony.[34] Playing a musical instrument, especially the koto, was another way to cultivate femininity. In a status system designed to lock families in place, one arena in which competition took place was the aesthetic sphere; hence a highly cultivated woman could rebound with credit on her family's reputation. In other words, it is important to embed the reading and writing done by women in the context of all the qualities that informed the cultivated self.

Women could always claim that cultivating femininity rebounded to their family's credit, but the process also contained shades of ambiguity. The board game that shows a young girl polishing her skills at poetry, calligraphy, painting, music, and tea ceremony in order to rise in the world suggests by implication that the proper place for her performance was the inner quarters of the ruling class, where, at least in popular opinion, women led lives of idleness in a world devoid of men. Illustrations presume that they must have whiled away their time reading novels and looking at pictures. A particular favorite was said to have been *Nise Murasaki Inaka Genji*, written by Ryūtei Tanehiko between 1829 and 1842. Mitamura Engyo's grandmother served in the shogun's great interior in the late 1830s, and according to her every woman there was reading the book. It was so popular that she procured her own copy.[35] Set in the rarified world of the Muromachi shogun Yoshimasa, *Inaka Genji* appealed to women who saw themselves living a similar if less dramatic existence. Andrew Markus points out that Tanehiko had a difficult time reconciling Genji's amoral pursuit of every woman who crossed his path with the stricter moral standards of his own time. The text is filled with plots typical of Kabuki—mistaken identity, the search for stolen heirlooms—and it is, of course, heavily illustrated. As Itasaka indicates in this volume, by the time it became a best seller, women reading for pleasure appeared less cultivated than self-absorbed.

33. Lindsey 2006, pp. 10–11.
34. Berry 2006, p. 205.
35. Markus 1992, p. 147.

Although men and women learned many of the same polite arts, there were differences in the processes of their self-cultivation. Even as a child, Kutsukake Nakako had wanted to devote herself to the way of poetry and become a woman of letters, but first she had to marry, raise six children, and restore the family fortunes when her husband, a sake brewer and money-lender, died when she was forty. Only at the end of her life was she finally freed to find self-expression in her writings and her own identity as a seeker of truth in the Zen tradition. Men such as Suzuki Bokushi (1770–1842) polished their identities in the course of their work; for women, especially rural women, becoming the kind of woman they wanted to be had little practical application. For that reason, it had to be done after the serious business of being a woman—marriage, childbirth, and running a household—was finished.[36]

Men and women also differed in their access to public space. Noguchi Takehiko has argued that the women writers of this time do not stand out because they were unable to ride the wave of commercial publishing, nor were they allowed to participate in new genres of prose.[37] Yosa Buson (1716–83) encouraged women to publish *haikai* anthologies because he wished to restore *haikai* to the position of respectable refinement it had enjoyed under Bashō, but they offered little competition to male-centered *senryū* anthologies. Maeda Yoshi has examined a number of poetry anthologies compiled by women in northern Kyushu under the leadership of the shrine priest Itō Tsunetaru (1774–1858), but these remain either in manuscript or in local publications.[38] Women publicized their calligraphy and poetry by producing pieces suitable for hanging or wrote poetry cards to give to friends and relatives. They did not aim at the publication of their poetry the way men did. (Suzuki Bokushi's twenty-year search for a publisher for *Snow Country Tales* suggests that provincial men also lacked access to commercial publishers.)[39] Although it was excerpted in *Tokugawa jikki*, Ōgimachi Machiko's (?–1724) homage to Yanagisawa Yoshiyasu (1658–1714) circulated only in manuscript during the Edo period (see the essay by G. G. Rowley in this volume). Various reasons can be adduced to explain why writings by women stayed out of print, including the supposition on the part of publishers that they would not sell or, given that male authors often offered their publishers sizable subventions, a lack of capital. In the case of *Matsukage nikki*, since it named the political leaders of the day, it could have run afoul of censorship. But

---

36. The clearest statement of differences in male and female life courses can be found in Nagashima 1986.
37. Noguchi 1985, p. 109.
38. Maeda 1999, pp. 169–220.
39. Walthall 1986.

I think the ultimate reason why it and other works by women remained unpublished was because, given that the writings by women of the Heian period also circulated in manuscript, for female authors to have their work published would have branded them as unfeminine.

Female Literacies in Meiji Japan

It is well known that the promulgation of a nationwide educational system in 1872 transformed the relationship between state and people, but what did it mean for women as opposed to men? Although it took decades for the promise of universal literacy to be achieved, the notion that the state took the responsibility for imposing education on everyone, male and female, marked a radical break with the laissez-faire attitude of the Tokugawa military regime. Substituting public supervision for what had previously been a private family affair forecast the development of the modern intrusive state; women both gained and lost in the process.

The Meiji state could not have succeeded in educating the populace had the groundwork not already been laid in the Tokugawa period. It is easy to trace an expansion in literacy rates from Tokugawa to Meiji and on into the twentieth century, but it is also important not to overlook what gets lost. Harootunian has pointed out that "modernism was so powerful a force that it managed to show how all preceding history was nothing more than its antecedent."[40] To challenge its force, we need to recall historical dead ends. Men such as Fukuzawa Yukichi complained that much of what characterized the literacy of their day was not just useless but also counterproductive, suggesting that the Tokugawa legacy was ambivalent, nowhere more so than in the case of women. Men and women who debated women's education invoked new notions of class; they praised some texts while denigrating others, and they turned women into symbols for both modernist transformation and tradition.[41]

One of the ways in which early modern Japan served as a prototype for the modern is in the establishment of gender-differentiated learning. Sugano's detailed study of schools with female teachers shows that, for commoners at least, boys and girls both studied reading and numbers, the difference being that girls also studied sewing.[42] On his visit to a primary school in Kyoto in 1869, Fukuzawa Yukichi noted that boys and girls be-

40. Harootunian 2000, p. ix.
41. Kamp (2006) raises the possibility of women figuring in both modernist and traditionalist rhetoric.
42. Sugano 1998, p. 146.

tween the ages of seven and fourteen sat side by side in the same classroom for the study of reading and arithmetic but were separated to learn penmanship. Girls learned sewing taught by a female instructor.[43] In other words, sex segregation was based on aesthetic values regarding what constituted appropriately feminine and masculine behavior, not on morality. Textbooks designed for girls from 1892 on show that twenty years after the inauguration of compulsory coeducation, the Ministry of Education still authorized separate instruction in calligraphy.[44] Not until higher school did those few boys and girls who attended them face sex segregation not just in specified subjects but school by school.

Just as women had been shut out of private and domain academies, the modern educational system imposed by the Meiji state discriminated against them at higher levels. Although the first middle schools established in Kyoto included both girls and boys, they were soon replaced with public schools mandated by the national government that segregated educational opportunities above the age of compulsory education. The first normal schools established in 1871 were for men only; teacher-training schools for women came three years later. At the founding in 1877 of the first public university, [Tokyo] Imperial University, one woman tried to take the entrance exam. She was refused because even if she had passed she would not have been allowed to attend classes. When Ogino Gin (1851–1913) first applied to sit for the medical examination, she, too, was refused. Only after a number of prominent men came to her defense was she allowed to obtain her license.[45] Most women with an interest in medicine received training as midwives.[46] Ogino remained an exception, not the rule.

Caught between old standards of knowledge and the state-driven requirements for the modern age were women professionals. Kusumoto Ine (1827–1903), daughter of Philipp Franz von Siebold, received an advanced medical education for her day and practiced obstetrics. Even during the 1870s, she continued to see patients in Shikoku, where she was living at the time. But when Tokyo handed down new standards for medical practice, no one in her locality had the stature to stand up for her as had been done for Ogino Gin. Lacking the training required of new midwives, she was relegated to the category of "old midwife."[47] Educated by her father in Kyoto,

43. Fukuzawa 1985, pp. 74, 76.
44. Ono 1892–93.
45. One of these men was Inoue Yorikuni, who took credit for challenging the bureaucracy based on the argument that there had been female doctors in Japan's past. See Tanabe 1921, p. 146.
46. For an outline of changes in the regulations governing midwives, see Ochiai 1999, p. 242.
47. Nakamura 2007.

Miwada Masako (1843–1927) was twelve years old when she first taught male students of all ages. After the death of her husband, in 1879, she supported her family by opening a school for boys in Matsuyama, Shikoku. Despite her early experience in the education of men, in 1883 Ehime Prefecture appointed her to a position in charge of women's education. In 1887 she returned to Tokyo where she opened a school providing training in English, Chinese, and mathematics with two sections, one for boys and one for girls. The girls' electives included etiquette, sewing, knitting, music, singing, and Japanese literature. The boys' section soon disappeared, and in 1902 she opened a high school for girls, which still stands in Tokyo today.[48]

It could be argued that the literacies Kusumoto and Miwada acquired in the Edo period (one in Western medicine, the other Chinese) provide examples showing how education in early modern Japan laid the foundation for modern Japan. Yet much was also lost. Kusumoto's skills quickly became obsolete under the impact of late-nineteenth-century advances in medical knowledge. While men, too, discovered that hard-won knowledge in a number of fields had become useless (the Dutch language for one), she faced an additional disability in competing for recognition of her talents by virtue of being a woman in a medical field then dominated by men. Miwada's history shows that there was enough flexibility in early modern education for women to teach men (a situation borne out by the female instructors analyzed in Sugano's work), even in subjects deemed a male preserve such as Chinese. When the Meiji state took over teacher training and certification, it relegated women to areas of knowledge deemed suitable for their lesser capabilities. As exceptional women, Kusumoto and Miwada both benefited from the lack of structure enjoyed by individuals under the Tokugawa military regime. The institution of sharper gendered distinctions between masculine and feminine subjects driven by the intrusive modernizing state opened opportunities for all men and women to gain at least a basic literacy, but by imposing uniform standards the state allowed less leeway for people, male and female, who did not fit the mold. Women whose claims to competence rested on outmoded but high levels of education were thus left with an ambivalent heritage and uncertainty about how to represent their achievements.[49]

Sharper gender distinctions also had an impact on writing styles. Although highly educated Meiji men displayed their erudition in Chinese by larding their texts with obscure characters and compounds, women such as

---

48. Miwada Masako Sensei Gojūnensai Kinen Shuppankai 1977.
49. Kamp (2006) makes this argument for all women who start in traditional schools and then have to switch to modern.

Miwada Masako did not. She continued to use more characters than women educated primarily in the Japanese classical tradition even when she wrote for the new women's magazines that appeared in the late nineteenth century on topics related to women's education and roles in society, but she tended to adhere to those that were easily comprehensible. Besides, as became the case generally with writings aimed at the masses, she included *furigana* to help the less educated ascertain her meaning. Turning her attention from education for boys to education for girls had a major impact on what she wrote and how she wrote it.

The polite arts provide another example of how developments in early modern Japan laid the foundation for modern Japan but only by decoupling them from their previous context. Morgan Pitelka has called "cultivated femininity" a key social category of modernity, and, as we have seen, that aim already existed in the Tokugawa period.[50] Although some women had practiced tea ceremony even then, notable in the Meiji period is the way they emerged en masse, transforming what had been an art identified with masculine self-cultivation into a space for women. The same is true for flower arranging (ikebana). The board game by Hiroshige demonstrates that young women (and young men) learned literacy in the context of the training in the polite arts that they needed to become useful members of society. In many cases they received their education twenty-four hours a day either at their parents' home or as a live-in pupil or apprentice. For the parents and employers of unmarried teenagers, work was seen as a process of acculturation, not just as the exploitation of cheap labor. A holdover is the promise by textile mills to provide education but only at night after the workers were exhausted by the day's work. Education through labor has continued to define apprenticeships, at least in crafts deemed traditional, but the apprentice came to be defined as male.[51] When schools replaced apprenticeship for women, the Meiji government placed education at the service of training and substituted moral instruction for lived experience. Rather than encouraging young women to read *The Tale of Genji*, it promoted *Greater Learning for Women* and home economics.

The Meiji state homogenized what had been piecemeal and diverse. Literacies created by happenstance disappeared to be replaced by standards set by the Ministry of Education. When learning came to be associated with schools, men and women alike assumed that basic knowledge was to be acquired by children, not at any stage of life. New Western-style accomplishments such as piano playing had to be developed while young under

50. Pitelka 2005, p. 158.
51. Kondo 1990 makes this point most elegantly.

the supervision of teachers with certificates proving their credentials. Even women past their child-rearing years who practiced the polite arts relied less on chance circumstance for instruction than on nationwide networks of private academies. And what a boon this proved for teachers, many of them female, who, rather than depending on whatever their pupils had to offer, could now charge set fees for instruction.[52]

Reading practices also changed in the Meiji period. Especially for the vast majority of the population that lived a day's or a week's walk away from cities, it had been difficult to obtain any books during the Edo period, gender specific or not, despite the boom in publishing. Matsuo Taseko's letters indicate that when she had borrowed a book from her cousin she read it repeatedly and copied large sections. Like readers in early modern Europe, her reading was intensive rather than extensive.[53] What mattered was not how many books had been consumed but how deeply they had been absorbed. Composing *waka* required the memorization of hundreds if not thousands of poems taken from classical anthologies that had long since been divided into independently bound chapters, meaning that familiarity with one section of a particular collection did not necessarily mean a knowledge of the whole. Inventories of books kept in farmhouses suggest that the same was true for other complex works, from Kabuki librettos to military tales to records of peasant uprisings.[54] Thus reading in fragmented texts went hand in hand with deep reading, to be replaced in modern times with wider reading in readily forgettable newspapers and magazines.

The transformation of the Japanese publishing industry through the introduction of cheap paper and Western-style typesetting opened the way for publications targeted at specific audiences. While the Edo period had originated what can be called "niche literature"—texts designed for specific audiences—publishers could ill afford to be too selective, especially when it came to texts for a marginal group such as women. Didactic literature aimed at establishing normative behavior, for example, had not differentiated between classes or status groups. The continuation of this trend into the Meiji

52. In letters to her stepdaughter and son-in-law, Hirata Atsutane's wife Orise complained that when Atsutane offered instruction during his exile in Akita he was most often paid in goods, especially food, not cash (Watanabe 1942, p. 384).

53. Darnton 1991, p. 148.

54. I had the good fortune to visit Aoki village near Matsumoto in the early 1980s while graduate students were preparing catalogs of family documents. In the Kutsukake family library were selections from *Amakusa gunryakuki* about the 1637 Shimabara rebellion along with selections of other texts. Historians who surveyed village collections have emphasized the range of materials rather than whether texts were complete and have given little indication of whether the texts were aimed at women or men or both. See Kimura 1983; and Nagatomo 1977.

period need not obscure the creation of discrete markets that began by its end. Particularly noteworthy is the 1885 inauguration of *Jogaku zasshi*, Japan's first widely read woman's magazine, by the Christian Iwamoto Yoshiharu. It took a progressive stance that contradicted the tenets in texts such as *Greater Learning for Women* by promoting monogamy, the abolition of prostitution, and equality of men and women in the home. Like magazines designed for men, it tried to attract and hold a readership by publishing serialized novels. Soon other magazines targeting women developed the genre of *katei shosetsu* (novels about family life) that, as the name suggests, focused on domestic dramas.[55]

Men still wrote most of the domestic dramas published in women's magazines, but they no longer dominated literary production the way they had in the Tokugawa period. Then men had written about women in texts from Ihara Saikaku's *Life of an Amorous Woman* to Tanehiko's *Inaka Genji*, and their writings had constituted the majority of what women read. The only chance women had to read what women wrote was in classical texts such as *The Tale of Genji*. And, as is widely known, although the writer of that text was a woman, she took a man's perspective. Far less frequently did Tokugawa period women read texts that took a more female-centered perspective such as *The Pillow Book of Sei Shōnagon* or *Izumi Shikibu Diary*. Although Higuchi Ichiyō is the most famous of Meiji period women writers, Rebecca Copeland and others have shown that she was by no means an exception. Almost universal access to basic education, a greater supply of reading material for women, and a greater demand for reading material by women opened new avenues for women to appear in print and be read by other women.[56]

Yet, despite the new opportunities afforded women writers, they faced a daunting array of challenges. Because almost without exception Tokugawa period women had not appeared in print, Meiji women, indeed Meiji intellectuals, remained ignorant of their achievements. For this reason, "[W]omen had to reinvent themselves as writers . . . as if they were the first to arrive on the scene."[57] More so than in the Tokugawa period, they had to conform to rigid standards that valued literature only in terms of its service to the state while at the same time writers of fiction in particular were expected to remain amateurs, engaging in literary production only as a pastime not a profession. But perhaps the greatest obstacle that confronted

---

55. See Ragsdale 1998, pp. 229–55.
56. See Copeland 2000.
57. Copeland applies this statement to twentieth-century female writers, but it applies just as well to their late-nineteenth-century counterparts (ibid., p. 229).

women writers was their limited access to public networks and organizations capable of providing them with outlets for their work. For this reason, Iwamoto's decision to open the pages of *Jogaku zasshi* to a small, carefully selected group of women editors has special significance. And, as Mara Patessio demonstrates in this volume, by soliciting readers' comments, journals such as *Jogaku zasshi* and *Fujo shinbun* provided a public platform for women's ideas. But even these writers had to conform to male expectations because the press regulations instituted by the Meiji state did not permit women to publish journals, another example of how even in modern times women's participation in the public sphere remained restricted.[58]

In the Edo period women had occasionally noted in private writings what literacy meant for them, but they had left public statements on this topic to men. In the first phase of rapid Westernization during the early Meiji period, debates in *Meiroku zasshi* on the woman question did not engage women's voices at all, even though most male writers agreed that a strong nation required educated women. As William Rowe has pointed out in the case of China, "[C]ivilization was something elite men did to subordinates."[59] One crucial question centered on *Greater Learning for Women*. The notion that women should focus their study on this text sank deep roots into Meiji Japan, but Fukuzawa Yukichi, for example, opposed this trend, waxing polemical on all the reasons why it contradicted everything modern, particularly in its teaching that women should subordinate themselves to men. Although Fukuzawa denigrated the women of his day, calling them ignorant and lacking in intelligence, he claimed that the remedy was simple: a basic education in practical matters such as science, bookkeeping, and general affairs. On the other hand, he promoted education for women in order for them to fulfill their "natural duties," raising children and running a household.[60]

Toward the end of the nineteenth century, women joined the debate on the purpose of literacy and the ability of women to benefit from it. In contrast to Fukuzawa's emphasis on female education for the purpose of managing the household, Miwada Masako took a more expansive view. First serialized in the journal *Jokan* starting in 1891, her most representative work, *Joshi no honbun* (The Chief Function of a Woman) had prefaces by Fukuzawa Yukichi and Nishimura Shigeki, crucial testaments if her work were to be taken seriously. She believed that men and women were equal but not that they were the same. Each had her or his own portion in life, and the woman's portion

58. Ibid., pp. 28–36.
59. Quoted in Schneewind 2006, p. 39.
60. Fukuzawa 1988, pp. 67, 201, 222, 233, 241, 243.

was different from that of men. She reserved her fiercest condemnation for the contemporary trend of respecting men and despising women (*danson johi*), a trend she blamed on Western education and customs. In terms of practical education for women, the West was more advanced but Japan was better in terms of teaching ethics and moral values. Although Miwada is often lumped together with conservatives owing to her views on the importance of morality, she took the side of progressives in advocating education for the purpose of women's work outside the home, including medicine, teaching, and the arts. [61]

Women, like men, soon learned to use literacy for purposes other than those intended by the state. Though educated in didactic texts that promoted patriotism and the *ryōsai kenbo* (good wife, wise mother) ideal, at least for members of the middle class, many of these same women used their education and the public space that opened up in journals and appropriately female-centered organizations to debate state policy regarding women. Kishida Toshiko and Fukuda Hideko most famously gave public lectures at which they demanded rights, liberty, education, and equality for women, but, as Mara Patessio has demonstrated, less renowned women developed networks based on common interests that did not always intersect with those of the state. The most prominent was the Nihon Fujin Kyōfūkai (Japan Women's Temperance League), which advocated not only prohibition but also monogamy at a time when Meiji statesmen and even the Meiji Emperor continued to keep concubines.[62] These activists associated in public only by advocating changes in spheres deemed appropriate to women. As with women writers, they, too, had to veil themselves with norms of femininity established by men lest they, not the promiscuous men they targeted for criticism, become the subjects of scandal.

What does a focus on the female subject teach us about the transformation from the Tokugawa period to Meiji Japan? From the perspective of female writers and readers, what stands out is change in the forms of male dominance. Before the 1880s, women had scant opportunity to read the writings of other contemporary women except in private poetry circles or through the exchange of letters; they played a marginal role in the creation and dissemination of literacies. Thereafter, women founded educational institutions and published their work, but they did so under the auspices of men and subject to a state that offered them new outlets for their talents on the one hand while constraining what they might do with them on the

61. Miwada Masako Sensei Gojūnensai Kinen Shuppankai 1977, pp. 122, 193–98.
62. Patessio 2006, pp. 155–82.

other. Women had new opportunities to appear in print but only if they conformed to male desires. As Copeland has pointed out, those who went beyond the boundaries of appropriately feminine themes defined by men were reviled as loose women. While we can say that the education of women is a key component of modernity because, more than any other single measure, it threatens male dominance in the private sphere, it necessarily takes place under the impersonal domination of state.

Conclusion

What did women gain and lose in the transition to modernity? In contrast to men, who became subject to state control through the legal system, registration for conscription, and compulsory education, women were subjected only to laws and the education system, an example of how the state's intrusion into the lives of its subjects differed according to gender. Leaving aside the issue of to what extent the poor and people in remote areas actually sent their daughters to school, the promise of compulsory education opened a window to a wider world through books and articles in journals, some of them written by women. The imposition of a common literacy did away with the literacies of the past; now women would read books designed for them. By the end of the nineteenth century, a range of occupations had opened up for women, from telephone operators to ticket takers to teachers, as demonstrated in the board game from 1910. But what women gained from expanded educational opportunities they lost in the message inculcated through standardized texts, a message that limited their autonomy by discouraging any challenge to their subordination to men. This type of indoctrination into normative roles was reinforced in another register by the 1898 Civil Code, which rebalanced the patriarchal equilibrium by enforcing the private patriarchy of the family with the public patriarchy of the state.

In rapidly modernizing societies such as that of as Japan, women are often relegated to becoming the repositories of tradition, an objective that compromises both what is meant by modernity and what is meant by tradition. Given that no society can become modern if half its members are excluded, women become willy-nilly participants, as they did in Japan through the education system and new forms of work. But denying that women ought to be or can become as modern as men creates the type of uneven development in gendered relations that Harootunian decried as one symptom of the crisis of modernity, writing, "In this world women are forced to remain as reminders of the old and traditional, even though modern life has made it possible for them to live more autonomously, while men are always permitted to live the new as if it was natural to them."[63] Or, as David Howell has put it, in modern times it was easier for men to assert their individuality.[64] I would like to complicate this understanding of unevenness by questioning the possibility that anyone or any group of people can hang on to the practices of the past once they have to engage with a modern world. Making such an effort requires transforming these practices to enable them to fit into new types of leisure spaces created by modern modes of living. Turning traditional arts over to women results in the creation of new traditions of female participation in what had once been dominated by men. Furthermore, by participating in poetic forms now called *tanka* and *haiku* or the polite arts of tea ceremony and flower arranging, women gained access to the types of social networks once the purview of men. In this way, they prefigured the new women of the twentieth century and became symbols of modernist transformation.

63. Harootunian 2000, p. xxiv.
64. Howell 2005, p. 165.

Bibliography

❀

Unless otherwise stated, Japanese books were published in Tokyo. Articles in newspapers and magazines cited in the notes are not included in this bibliography since on each occurrence they come with a full citation.

Abbreviations

HJAS	*Harvard Journal of Asiatic Studies*
MN	*Monumenta Nipponica*
NKBZ	*Nihon Koten Bungaku Zenshū*. 1970–76. 51 vols. Shōgakukan.
SNKBT	*Shin Nihon Koten Bungaku Taikei*. 1989–. 100 vols. Iwanami Shoten.
ZGR	*Zoku Gunsho Ruijū*. 1959–60. 37 vols. plus 3 supplementary vols. Zoku Gunsho Ruijū Kanseikai.

Abe Yoshio 阿部吉雄. 1965. *Nihon shushigaku to chōsen* 日本朱子学と朝鮮 (Japanese neo-Confucianism and Korea). Tōkyō Daigaku Shuppankai.

Amano Haruko 天野晴子. 1998. *Joshi shōsokugata ōrai ni kansuru kenkyū* 女子消息型往来に関する研究 (A study of primers for women in the form of letters). Kazama Shobō.

Aoki Michio 青木美智男. 2003. *Fukayomi Ukiyoburo* 深読み浮世風呂 (A deep reading of *Ukiyoburo*). Shōgakukan.

Aoyama Nao 青山なを. 1970. *Meiji jogakkō no kenkyū* 明治女学校の研究 (A study of girls' schools in the Meiji period). Keiō Tsūshin.

Aoyama Tadakazu 青山忠一. 1982. *Kanazōshi jokun bungei no kenkyū* 仮名草子女訓文芸の 研究 (A study of seventeenth-century conduct books for women). Ōfūsha.

Ariyoshi Tamotsu 有吉保, Inukai Kiyoshi 犬養廉, and Hashimoto Fumio 橋本不美男, eds. 1994. *(Ei'in-bon) Hyakunin isshu taisei* 影印本百人一首大成 (A collection of facsimiles of *Hyakunin isshu*). Shintensha.

Asakura Haruhiko 朝倉治彦. 2006. "Kokatsujiban *Jokunshū* ni tsuite" 古活字版『女訓集』について (On the movable type edition of *Jokunshū*). *(Kokugakuin Daigaku) Kinsei bungakukai kaihō* 国学院大学近世文学会会報 12: 10–16.

———. 1985. *Kanazōshi shūsei* 仮名草子集成 (Collected *kanazōshi*). Vol. 6. Tōkyōdō Shuppan.

Asano Shūgō 浅野秀剛 and Timothy Clark. 1995. *Kitagawa Utamaro* 喜多川歌麿. Chiba: Chiba City Art Museum.

Aston, W. G. 1899. *A History of Japanese Literature*. London: Heinemann.

Atomi. 1995. *Hyakunin isshu kankei shiryō mokuroku* 百人一首関係資料目録 (Catalog of materials related to *Hyakunin isshu*). Atomi Gakuen Tanki Daigaku Toshokan.

Atsuta Kō 熱田公. 2000. "Kaidai" (Introduction to *Renchūshō*). In *Renchūshō, chūsei jiten, nendaiki* 簾中抄・中世事典・年代記. Vol. 48 of *Reizei-ke Shiguretei sōsho* 冷泉家時雨亭叢書 (Collected works from the Reizei family's Shiguretei), pp. 3–18. Asahi Shinbunsha.

Azuma Shōko 東聖子. 2001. "Baishi no bunji" 梅颸の文事 (The writing of Baishi). In *Rai Baishi nikki no kenkyū* 頼梅颸日記の研究 (A study of the diary of Rai Baishi), ed. Ōguchi Yūjirō 大口勇次郎, pp. 51–69. Ochanomizu Joshi Daigaku Jendaa Kenkyū Sentaa.

Baishi ko nikki 梅颸古日記 (The old diary of Baishi). Manuscript in the Rai San'yō Museum (Rai San'yō Shiseki Shiryōkan 頼山陽史跡資料館) in Hiroshima.

Baishi nikki 梅颸日記 (The diary of Baishi). 1983. In *Rai San'yō zensho* 頼山陽全書 (Complete works of Rai San'yō), ed. Kizaki Aikichi 木崎愛吉 and Rai Seiichi 頼成一, vol. 6. Kokusho Kankōkai. Reprint of the 1931 edition.

Barney, Stephen A., ed. 1991. *Annotation and Its Texts*. New York: Oxford University Press.

Beerens, Anna. 2006. *Friends, Acquaintances, Pupils, and Patrons: Japanese Intellectual Life in the Late Eighteenth Century, a Prosopographical Approach*. Leiden: Leiden University Press.

Bennett, Judith M. 1997. "Confronting Continuity." *Journal of Women's History* 9.1: 73–94.

Berry, Mary Elizabeth. 2006. *Japan in Print: Information and Nation in the Early Modern Period*. Berkeley: University of California Press.

Bodart-Bailey, Beatrice M. 2006. *The Dog Shogun: The Personality and Policies of Tokugawa Tsunayoshi*. Honolulu: University of Hawai`i Press.

———. 1979. "Councillor Defended: *Matsukage Nikki* and Yanagisawa Yoshiyasu." *MN* 34.4: 467–78.

Bodart-Bailey, Beatrice M., ed. and trans. 1999. *Kaempfer's Japan: Tokugawa Culture Observed*. Honolulu: University of Hawai`i Press.

Bollmann, Stefan. 2006. *Reading Women*. Trans. Christine Shuttleworth. London: Merrell. The original edition, *Frauen, die lesen, sind gefährlich*, was published in Munich by Elisabeth Sandmann Verlag in 2005.

Bornstein, Diane, ed. 1978. *Distaves and Dames: Renaissance Treatises for and about Women*. New York: Scholars' Facsimiles and Reprints.

Bousquet, Georges. 1877. *Le Japon de nos jours et les échelles de l'Extrême Orient*. Paris: Hachette.

Bowring, Richard. 1996. *The Diary of Lady Murasaki*. New York: Penguin Classics.

———. 1992. "The *Ise monogatari*: A Short Cultural History." *HJAS* 52.2: 401–80.

———. 1988. *Murasaki Shikibu: The Tale of Genji*. Cambridge: Cambridge University Press.

Braisted, William, trans. 1976. *Meiroku Zasshi: Journal of the Japanese Enlightenment*. Cambridge: Harvard University Press.

Brokaw, Cynthia J. 2007. *Commerce in Culture: The Sibao Book Trade in the Qing and Republican Periods*. Cambridge: Harvard University Asia Center.

Bryson, Norman. 2003. "Westernizing Bodies: Women, Art, and Power in Meiji *Yōga*." In *Gender and Power in the Japanese Visual Field*, ed. Joshua S. Mostow, Norman Bryson, and Maribeth Graybill, pp. 89–118. Honolulu: University of Hawai`i Press.

Butler, Judith. 1997. *The Psychic Life of Power: Theories in Subjection*. Stanford: Stanford University Press.

Butler, Lee. 2002. *Emperor and Aristocracy in Japan, 1467–1680: Resilience and Renewal*. Cambridge: Harvard University Asia Center.

Carlitz, Katherine. 1991. "The Social Uses of Female Virtue in Late Ming Editions of *Lienü zhuan*." *Late Imperial China* 12.2: 117–48.

Carrothers, Julia D. 1879. *The Sunrise Kingdom; or, Life and Scenes in Japan and Woman's Work for Woman There*. Philadelphia: Presbyterian Board of Education.

Carter, Steven D. 2007. *Householders: The Reizei Family in Japanese History*. Cambridge: Harvard University Asia Center.

Chance, Frank. 2003. "In the Studio of Painting Study: Transmission Practices of Tani Bunchō." In *Copying the Master and Stealing His Secrets: Talent and Training in Japanese Painting*, ed. Brenda G. Jordan and Victoria Weston, pp. 60–85. Honolulu: University of Hawai`i Press.

Chang, Kang-i Sun, and Haun Saussy. 1999. *Women Writers of Traditional China: An Anthology of Poetry and Criticism*. Stanford: Stanford University Press.

Chikaishi Yasuaki 近石泰秋. 1973. "Inoue Tsū-jo shōden narabi ni nenpu" 井上通女小伝並に年譜 (The life of Inoue Tsū with a chronology). In *Inoue Tsūjo zenshū* 井上通女全集 (Complete works of Inoue Tsū), pp. 371–91. Marugame: Kagawa Kenritsu Marugame Kōtō Gakkō Dōsōkai.

Childs, Margaret [Magaretto Chairusu]. 1981. "Supensaa korekushon zō *Genji monogatari emaki*: E to kotoba no sōgo sayō" スペンサーコレクション蔵「源氏物語絵巻」— 絵と詞の相互作用 (The relation between picture and text in the Spencer Collection *Genji monogatari emaki*). *Kokugo kokubun* 国語国文 50.7: 32–37.

Chino Kaori 千野香織. 1991a. *Emaki: Ise monogatari emaki* 絵巻—伊勢物語絵巻 (The *Ise monogatari* picture scroll). *Nihon no bijutsu* 日本の美術, no. 301. Shibundō.

———. 1991b. "Kasugano no meisho-e" 春日野の名所絵 (The celebrated view of Kasugano). In *Bijutsushi ronbunshū* 美術史論文集 (Essays on art history), ed. Akiyama Terukazu Hakase Koki-kinen Ronbunshū Kankōkai 秋山光和博士古希記念論文集刊行会, pp. 421–61. Benridō.

Clark, Timothy. 1992. *Ukiyo-e Paintings in the British Museum*. London: British Museum Press.

Cook, Lewis. 2008. "Genre Trouble: Medieval Commentaries and Canonization of *The Tale of Genji*." In *Envisioning* The Tale of Genji: *Media, Gender, and Cultural Production*, ed. Haruo Shirane, pp. 129–53. New York: Columbia University Press.

Copeland, Rebecca L. 2006a. "Fashioning the Feminine: Images of the Modern Girl Student in Meiji Japan." *U.S.-Japan Women's Journal* 30–31.1: 13–35.

———. 2000. *Lost Leaves: Women Writers of Meiji Japan*. Honolulu: University of Hawai`i Press.

Copeland, Rebecca L., trans. 2006b. "Warbler in the Grove." In *The Modern Murasaki: Writing by Women of Meiji Japan*, ed. Rebecca Copeland and Melek Ortabasi, pp. 80–125. New York: Columbia University Press.

Cornwallis, Kinahan. 1859. *Two Journeys to Japan*. 2 vols. London: Thomas Cautley Newby.

Darnton, Robert. 1991. "History of Reading." In *New Perspectives on Historical Writing*, ed. Peter Burke, pp. 140–67. Cambridge: Polity Press.

Dekker, Rudolf. 2002. "Introduction." In *Egodocuments and History: Autobiographical Writing and Its Social Context since the Middle Ages*, ed. Rudolf Dekker, pp. 7–20. Hilversum: Verloren.

Deuchler, Martina. 2003. "Propagating Female Virtues in Chosŏn Korea." In *Women and Confucian Cultures in Premodern China, Korea, and Japan*, ed. Dorothy Ko, Jahyun Kim Haboush, and Joan Piggott, pp. 142–69. Berkeley: University of California Press.

Devitt, Jane. 1979. "Santō Kyōden and the *yomihon*." *HJAS* 39.2: 253–74.

DeWoskin, Kenneth J., and J. I. Crump, trans. 1996. *In Search of the Supernatural: The Written Record*. Stanford: Stanford University Press.

Dore, Ronald P. 1992. *Education in Tokugawa Japan*. Ann Arbor: Center for Japanese Studies, The University of Michigan. Reprint of the 1965 edition.

Edo jidai joryū bungaku zenshū 江戸時代女流文学全集 (Collected works of women's literature of the Edo period). 2001. 4 vols. Nihon Tosho Sentaa. Facsimile of 1918 edition published by Bungei Shoin.

Edo jidai josei bunko 江戸時代女性文庫 (Edo period library for women). 1994–98. 100 vols. Ōzorasha.

Eger, Elizabeth, Charlotte Grant, Clíona Ó Gallchoir, and Penny Warburton. 2001. *Women, Writing, and the Public Sphere, 1700–1830*. Cambridge: Cambridge University Press.

Emori Ichirō 江森一郎, ed. 1993–94. *(Edo jidai) Josei seikatsu ezu daijiten* 江戸時代女性生活絵図大事典 (Illustrated dictionary of the life of women in the Edo period). 10 vols. Ōzorasha.

Erdmann, Axel. 1999. *My Gracious Silence: Women in the Mirror of Sixteenth-Century Printing in Western Europe.* Lucerne: Gilhofer and Ranschburg.

Ferrante, Joan M. 1980. "The Education of Women in the Middle Ages in Theory, Fact, and Fantasy." In *Beyond Their Sex: Learned Women of the European Past*, ed. Patricia H. Labalme, pp. 9–42. New York: New York University Press.

Fister, Patricia. 1991. "Female Bunjin: The Life of Poet-Painter Ema Saikō." In *Recreating Japanese Women, 1600–1945*, ed. Gail Lee Bernstein, pp. 108–30. Berkeley: University of California Press.

———. 1988. *Japanese Women Artists, 1600–1900.* Lawrence: Spencer Museum of Art, University of Kansas.

Flanagan, Sabina. 1989. *Hildegard of Bingen, 1098–1179: A Visionary Life.* London: Routledge.

Flint, Kate. 1993. *The Woman Reader, 1837–1914.* Oxford: Clarendon Press.

French, Calvin L. 1974. *The Poet-Painters: Buson and His Followers.* Ann Arbor: University of Michigan Museum of Art.

Fuess, Harald. 2004. *Divorce in Japan: Family, Gender, and the State, 1600–2000.* Stanford: Stanford University Press.

Fujisawa. 1995. *Fujisawa shishi shiryō shozai mokuroku kō* 藤沢市史資料所在目録稿 (Draft catalog of material related to the history of Fujisawa City). Vol. 24. Fujisawa-shi.

Fujita Yoshimi 藤田美実. 1984. *Meiji jogakkō no sekai* 明治女学校の世界 (The world of schools for girls in the Meiji period). Seieisha.

Fujo shinbun o Yomu Kai. 1997. *"Fujo shinbun" to josei no kindai* 『婦女新聞』と女性の近代 (*Fujo shinbun* and women in the modern age). Fuji Shuppan.

Fukai Jinzō 深井甚三. 1995. *Kinsei josei tabi to kaido kōtsū* 近世女性旅と街道交通 (Women's traveling in the early modern period and communications on the highways). Toyama: Katsura Shobō.

Fukazawa Akio 深沢秋男. 2004. *Iseki Takako no kenkyū* 井関隆子の研究 (A study of Iseki Takako). Osaka: Izumi Shoin.

———. 1978–81. *Iseki Takako nikki* 井関隆子日記 (The diary of Iseki Takako). 3 vols. Benseisha.

Fukuma chōshi 福間町史 (History of Fukuma town). Shiryōhen 4 vols. Fukuma-chō: 1997.

Fukushima Riko 福島理子. 1995. *Edo kanshisen* 江戸漢詩選 (Selected Edo period Chinese verse). Vol. 3, *Joryū* 女流 (Women poets). Iwanami Shoten.

Fukushima Shirō 福島四郎. 1984. *Fujinkai sanjūgo nen* 婦人界三十五年 (Thirty-five years of the Fujinkai). Fuji Shuppan.

Fukushima Teiko 福島貞子. 1935. *Nichiro sensō hishichū no Kawahara Misako* 日露戰争秘史中の河原操子 (Kawahara Misako and the secret history of the Russo-Japanese War). Fujo Shinbunsha.

Fukuzawa Yukichi. 1988. *Fukuzawa Yukichi on Japanese Women: Selected Works*. Ed. and trans. Eiichi Kiyooka. Tokyo: University of Tokyo Press.

———. 1985. *Fukuzawa Yukichi on Education: Selected Works*. Ed. and trans. Eiichi Kiyooka. Tokyo: University of Tokyo Press.

Gallagher, Catherine. 1994. *Nobody's Story: The Vanishing Acts of Women Writers in the Marketplace, 1670–1820*. Berkeley: University of California Press.

Garon, Sheldon. 1997. *Molding Japanese Minds. The State in Everyday Life*. Princeton: Princeton University Press.

Gatten, Aileen. 1977. "The Secluded Forest: Textual Problems in the *Genji monogatari*." PhD diss., University of Michigan.

Genji monogatari. 1970–76. Abe Akio 阿部秋生, Akiyama Ken 秋山虔, and Imai Gen'e 今井源衛, eds., *Genji monogatari* 源氏物語 (The Tale of Genji). 6 vols. *NKBZ* 12–17. Shōgakukan.

Gerstle, C. Andrew, with Timothy Clark and Akiko Yano. 2005. *Kabuki Heroes on the Osaka Stage, 1780–1830*. Honolulu: University of Hawai`i Press.

Goodwin, Janet R. 2007. *Selling Songs and Smiles: The Sex Trade in Heian and Kamakura Japan*. Honolulu: University of Hawai`i Press.

Goodwin, Janet R., Bettina Gramlich-Oka, Elizabeth A. Leicester, Yuki Terazawa, and Anne Walthall. 2001. "Solitary Thoughts: A Translation of Tadano Makuzu's *Hitori kangae*." *MN* 56.1: 21–38, 56.2:173–95.

Gramlich-Oka, Bettina. 2009. "From Education to Cultivation: Rai Shizuko and Her Father Inooka Gisai." In *Ekkyō suru Nihon bungaku kenkyū: Kanon keisei, jendaa, media* 越境する日本文学研究—カノン形成・ジェンダー・メディア (New horizons in Japanese literary studies: Canon formation, gender, and media), ed. Haruo Shirane, pp. 71–76. Bensei Shuppan.

———. 2006a. "Tokugawa Women and Spacing the Self." *Early Modern Japan: An Interdisciplinary Journal* 14.1: 51–67.

———. 2006b. *Thinking Like a Man: Tadano Makuzu (1763–1825)*. Leiden: Brill.

———. 2001. "Tadano Makuzu and Her *Hitori kangae*." *MN* 56.1: 1–20.

Greene, Jody. 2006. "Francis Kirkman's Counterfeit Authority: Autobiography, Subjectivity, Print." *Proceedings of the Modern Language Association* 121.1: 17–32.

Groner, Paul. 2002. *Ryōgen and Mount Hiei: Japanese Tendai in the Tenth Century*. Honolulu: University of Hawai`i Press.

Gyokueishū. 1969. Ii Haruki 伊井春樹, ed. *Gyokueishū* 玉栄集 (Gyokuei's collection). In *Gengo kenkyū shiryōshū* 源語研究資料集 (Collection of materials related to the study of *The Tale of Genji*), vol. 87 of *Hekichūdō sōsho* 碧冲洞叢書, pp. 121–62. Ōbuchō, Aichi-ken: Yanase Kazuo.

Gyokuyoki 玉輿記 (Records of jeweled palanquins). 1917. In *Ryūei fujo densō* 柳営婦女伝叢 (Collected biographies of women who worked for the shogunate), ed. Saitō Matsutarō 斎藤松太郎 and Inoue Naohiro 井上直弘, pp. 1–54. Kokusho Kankōkai.

Hackel, Heidi Brayman. 2003. "'Boasting of Silence': Women Readers in a Patriarchal State." In *Reading, Society, and Politics in Early Modern England*, ed. Kevin Sharpe and Steven N. Zwicker, pp. 101–21. Cambridge: Cambridge University Press.

Haga Noboru 芳賀登, Nakajima Kuni 中嶌 邦, Ichibangase Yasuko 一番ヶ瀬 康子, and Soda Kōichi 祖田 浩一, eds. 1993. *Nihon josei jinmei jiten* 日本女性人名辞典 (Dictionary of Japanese women). Nihon Tosho Sentaa.

Handford, S. A., trans. 1963. *Sallust, The Jugurthine War, The Conspiracy of Catiline*. Harmondsworth: Penguin.

Handlin, Joanna F. 1975. "Lü K'un's New Audience: The Influence of Women's Literacy on Sixteenth-Century Thought." In *Women in Chinese Society*, ed. Margery Wolf and Roxane Witke, pp. 13–38. Stanford: Stanford University Press.

Hani Motoko 羽仁もと子. 1928. *Hansei o kataru* 半生を語る (Telling my life). Fujin no Tomosha.

Harootunian, Harry D. 2000. *Overcome by Modernity: History, Culture, and Community in Interwar Japan*. Princeton: Princeton University Press.

Harper, Thomas J. 1989. "*The Tale of Genji* in the Eighteenth Century: Keichū, Mabuchi, and Norinaga." In *Eighteenth-Century Japan: Culture and Society*, ed. C. Andrew Gerstle, pp. 106–23. Sydney: Allen and Unwin. Reprinted in London by Routledge in 2000.

Hashimoto Masanobu 橋本政宣. 2002. "Kanpaku Konoe Sakihisa no Kyōto shuppon" 関白近衛前久の京都出奔 (Chancellor Konoe Sakihisa's flight from Kyoto). In *Kinsei kuge shakai no kenkyū* 近世公家社会の研究 (Studies of aristocratic society in the early modern period), pp. 6–45. Yoshikawa Kōbunkan.

Hashimoto Shinkichi 橋本進吉. 1972. "*Renchūshō* no ichi ihon *Hakuzōshi* ni tsuite" 簾中鈔の一異本白造紙について (On the *Hakuzōshi*, a variant version of *Renchūshō*). In *Denki, tenseki kenkyū* 伝記・典籍研究 (Biographical and textual studies). Vol. 12 of *Hashimoto Shinkichi hakase chosaku shū* 橋本進吉博士著作集 (Collected works of Dr. Hashimoto Shinkichi), pp. 317–38. Iwanami Shoten.

Hastings, Sally A. 2002. "Hatoyama Haruko: Ambitious Woman." In *The Human Tradition in Modern Japan* ed. Anne Walthall, pp. 81–98. Lanham, Md.: Rowman and Littlefield.

Hatoyama Haruko 鳩山春子. 1981. *Jijoden* 自叙伝 (Autobiography). *Nihonjin no jiden* 日本人の自伝 (Autobiographies of Japanese), vol. 7. Heibonsha.

Hayashi Yoshikazu 林美一 and Richard Lane. 1995–2000. *Teihon ukiyoe shunga meihin shūsei* 定本浮世絵春画名品集成 (Collection of masterworks of ukiyo-e erotica). 24 plus 2 vols. Kawade Shobō Shinsha.

Hirao Michio 平尾道雄. 1973. *Anritei monjo: Nonaka En no tegami* 安履亭文書: 野中婉の手紙 (Letters of Nonaka En). Kōchi: Kōchi Shimin Toshokan.

Hirata Yumi 平田由美. 1999. *Josei hyōgen no Meiji shi: Higuchi Ichiyō izen* 女性表現の明治史: 樋口一葉以前 (A history of women's articulations in the Meiji period: Before Higuchi Ichiyō). Iwanami Shoten.

Hla-Dorge, Gilberte. 1936. *Une poétesse japonaise au XVIIIe siècle, Kaga no Tchiyo-jo*. Paris: G.-P. Maisonneuve.

Horiuchi Hideaki 堀内秀晃 and Akiyama Ken 秋山虔. 1997. *Taketori monogatari Ise monogatari* 竹取物語・伊勢物語 (The Bamboo Cutter's Tale, Tales of Ise). *SNKBT* 17. Iwanami Shoten.

Hōsa Bunko 蓬左文庫. 1988. *Kinsei jōryū fujin no kyōyō* 近世上流婦人の教養 (The education of upper-class women in the early modern period). Nagoya: Hōsa Bunko. Exhibition catalog.

Howell, David L. 2005. *Geographies of Identity in Nineteenth-Century Japan*. Berkeley: University of California Press.

Huffman, James L. 1997. *Creating a Public. People and Press in Meiji Japan*. Honolulu: University of Hawai`i Press.

Hull, Suzanne W. 1982. *Chaste, Silent, and Obedient: English Books for Women, 1475–1640*. San Marino, Calif: Huntington Library.

Ichikawa Seigaku 市川青岳. 1991. *Kinsei joryū shodō meika shiden* 近世女流書道名家史伝 (Biographies of early modern women calligraphers). Nihon Tosho Sentaa. Facsimile of the 1935 edition published by Kyōiku Shuppansha.

Ichiko Natsuo 市古夏生. 1996. "Kinsei ni okeru jūhan, ruihan" 近世における重版・類版 (Copyright infringements in the early modern period). *Edo bungaku* 江戸文学 16: 26–39.

Ichiko Natsuo and Kan Satoko 菅聡子, eds. 2006. *Nihon josei bungaku daijiten* 日本女性文学大事典 (Dictionary of women's writing in Japan). Nihon Tosho Sentaa.

Ichiko Teiji 市古貞次 et al., eds. 1993–99. *Kokusho jinmei jiten* 国書人名辞典 (Dictionary of Japanese authors). 5 vols. Iwanami Shoten.

Ichimura Minato 市村咸人. 1929. *Ina sonnō shisō shi* 伊那尊王思想史 (History of imperial loyalism in Ina). Iida: Shimo-Ina Gun Kokumin Seishin Sakkōkai.

Idema, Wilt, and Beata Grant. 2004. *The Red Brush: Writing Women of Imperial China*. Cambridge: Harvard University Press.

Ii Haruki 伊井春樹. 2008. "Didactic Readings of *The Tale of Genji*: Politics and Women's Education," trans. Saeko Shibayama. In *Envisioning* The Tale of Genji: *Media, Gender, and Cultural Production*, ed. Haruo Shirane, pp. 157–70. New York: Columbia University Press.

———. 2002. "Kaoku Gyokuei ei '*Genji monogatari* kanmei waka' ni tsuite" 花屋玉栄詠『源氏物語巻名和歌』について (On Kaoku Gyokuei's "Poems on the Chapters of *The Tale of Genji*"). In *Genji monogatari to sono kenkyū sekai* 源氏物語とその研究世界 (*The Tale of Genji* and the world of its study), pp. 1055–60. Kazama Shobō.

———. 2001. *Genji monogatari chūshakusho, kyōjushi jiten* 源氏物語注釈書・享受史事典 (Dictionary of commentaries on, and the reception of, *The Tale of Genji*). Tōkyōdō.

———. 1969. "Kaidai" (Introduction to *Gyokueishū*). In *Gengo kenkyū shiryōshū* 源語研究資料集 (Collection of materials related to the study of *The Tale of Genji*). Vol. 87 of *Hekichūdō sōsho* 碧冲洞叢書, pp. 12–28. Ōbuchō, Aichi-ken: Yanase Kazuo.

Ikebe Yoshikata 池辺義象. 1914. "Kaidai" (Introduction to *Matsukage nikki*). In vol. 11 of *Kokubun sōsho* 国文叢書, pp. 6–8. Hakubunkan.

Ikegami, Eiko. 2005. *Bonds of Civility: Aesthetic Networks and the Political Origins of Japanese Culture*. Cambridge: Cambridge University Press.

Imanishi Yūichirō 今西祐一郎. 1991. *Tsūzoku Ise monogatari* 通俗伊勢物語 (Popular versions of *Tales of Ise*). Heibonsha.

Inada Masahiro 稲田雅洋. 2000. *Jiyū minken no bunkashi: Atarashii seiji bunka no tanjō* 自由民権の文化史—新しい政治文化の誕生 (A cultural history of the Freedom and Popular Rights Movement). Chikuma Shobō.

Inaga Keiji 稲賀敬二. 1967. *Genji monogatari no kenkyū: Seiritsu to denryū* 源氏物語の研究—成立と伝流 (A study of *The Tale of Genji*: Formation and transmission). Kasama Shoin.

Inooka Gisai 飯岡義斎. 2001a. "Bōgosō" 耄語草 (Notes of a foolish old man). In *Rai Baishi nikki no kenkyū* 頼梅颸日記の研究, ed. Ōguchi Yūjirō 大口勇次郎, pp. 130–32. Ochanomizu Joshi Daigaku Jendaa Kenkyū Sentaa.

———. 2001b. "Yakakusō" 夜鶴草 (A sentinel's notes). In *Rai Baishi nikki no kenkyū*, ed. Ōguchi Yūjirō, pp. 121–26. Ochanomizu Joshi Daigaku Jendaa Kenkyū Sentaa.

Ise monogatari zuroku. 1992. *(Tesshinsai Bunko shozo) Ise monogatari zuroku* 鉄心斎文庫所蔵伊勢物語図録 (Illustration of the copies of *Tales of Ise* held in the Tesshinsai Bunko). 20 vols. Odawara: Tesshinsai Bunko Ise Monogatari Bunkakan.

Ishikawa Matsutarō 石川松太郎. 1973. *Nihon kyōkasho taikei ōraihen* 日本教科書大系往来編 (Japanese textbook series: Popular texts of the Edo period). Vol. 15, *Joshiyō* 女子用. Kōdansha.

Itasaka Noriko 板坂則子. 2006. "Kusazōshi no dokusha – hyōzō to shite no dokusho suru josei" 草双紙の読者—表象としての読書する女性 (The readers of popular fiction: Women as readers). *Kokugo to kokubungaku* 国語と国文学 83.5: 1–13.

———. 2003. "Shinsaku iroha tanka kō" 『しんさくいろはたんか』考 (On *Shinsaku iroha tanka*). *Ilbonhaku yǔngu* 日本學研究 13: 3–13.

Itō Toshiko 伊藤敏子. 1984. *Ise monogatari-e* 伊勢物語絵 (Illustrations to *Tales of Ise*). Kadokawa Shoten.

Itō Tsuneashi 伊藤常足. 1915. *Oka no agata shū* 岡県集. Fukuoka-ken Kurosaki-chō: Hayashi Shigeki.

Itsuō Bijutsukan 逸翁美術館. 1982. *Goshun* 呉春. Osaka: Itsuō Bijutsukan.

Iwai Shigeki 岩井茂樹. 2005. "Koi-uta no shōmetsu—*Hyakunin isshu* no kindai-teki tokuchō" 恋歌の消滅—百人一首の近代的特徴 (The disappearance of love poems: The modern qualities of the *Hyakunin isshu*). In *Hyakunin isshu mangekyō* 百人一首万華鏡, ed. Shirahata Yōzaburō 白幡洋三郎, pp. 33–54. Kyoto: Shibunkaku.

Iwakuni. 2001. *Iwakuni shishi* 岩国市史 (History of Iwakuni city). Shiryōhen vol. 2 "Kinsei." Iwakuni-shi.

Izawa Takao 伊沢孝雄. 1894. *Joshi nichiyō shintaibun no shiori* 女子日用新体文の栞 (Guide to the new everyday style of writing for women). Osaka: Sansōkan.

Izuno Tatsu 伊豆野タツ, ed. 1982. *Arakida Reijo monogatari shūsei* 荒木田麗女物語集成 (Collected fiction of Arakida Rei). Ōfūsha.

Joshi Gakushūin 女子学習院. 1939. *Joryū chosaku kaidai* 女流著作解題 (Dictionary of literary works by women). Joshi Gakushūin.

Kado Reiko 門玲子. 2006. *Waga Makuzu monogatari: Edo no joryū shisakusha tanbō* わが真葛物語—江戸の女流思索者探訪 (My Makuzu monogatari: An exploration of a women thinker of the Edo period). Fujiwara Shoten.

————. 1998. *Edo joryū bungaku no hakken* 江戸女流文学の発見 (The discovery of Edo period women's literature). Fujiwara Shoten.

Kagami. 1985. *Kagami chōshi* 香我美町史 (History of Kagami town). Vol. 1. Kōchi-ken, Kagami-chō.

Kajiwara Chikuken 梶原竹軒. 1917. *Wakae Nioko to sono icho* 若江薫子と其遺著 (Wakae Nioko and her posthumous works). Takamatsu: Kagawa Shinpōsha.

Kakehi Kumiko 筧久美子. 1982. "Chūgoku no jokun to Nihon no jokun" 中国の女訓と日本の女訓 (Chinese and Japanese conduct books for women). In *Nihon joseishi* 日本女性史, vol. 3, pp. 289–324. Tōkyō Daigaku Shuppankai.

Kamens, Edward. 1988. *The Three Jewels: A Study and Translation of Minamoto Tamenori's Sanbōe*. Michigan Monograph Series in Japanese Studies, no. 2. Ann Arbor: Center for Japanese Studies, University of Michigan.

Kamp, Marianne. 2006. *The New Woman in Uzbekistan: Islam, Modernity, and Unveiling under Communism*. Seattle: University of Washington Press.

Kaokushō. 1936. *Kaokushō* 花屋抄 (Kaoku's gleanings), ed. Yoshizawa Yoshinori 吉沢義則. Vol. 11 of *Mikan kokubun kochūshaku taikei* 未刊国文古註釈大系 (Collected unpublished old literary commentaries), pp. 384–448. Teikoku Kyōikukai Shuppanbu.

Kasaoka. 2001. *Kasaoka shishi* 笠岡市史 (History of Kasaoka city). Shiryōhen vol. 2. Kasaoka-shi.

Katagiri Yayoi 片桐弥生. 1989. "Hakubyō Genji monogatari emaki ni okeru e to kotoba: Supensaa-bon o chūshin ni" 白描源氏物語絵巻における絵と詞—スペンサー本を中心に (Text and pictures in the monochrome *Tale of Genji* scrolls with special reference to the Spencer Collection manuscript). *Philokalia* フィロカリア 6: 88–114.

Katagiri Yōichi 片桐洋一, ed. 1981. *Ise monogatari: Keichō jūsan nenkan Saga-bon dai isshu* 伊勢物語：慶長十三年刊嵯峨本第一種 (The 1608 Sagabon edition of *Tales of Ise*). Osaka: Izumi Shoin.

Katō Yasuko 加藤康子 and Matsumura Noriko 松村倫子, eds. 2002. *Bakumatsu Meiji no esugoroku* 幕末・明治の絵双六 (Illustrated board games of nineteenth-century Japan). Kokusho Kankōkai.

Kawase Kazuma 川瀬一馬. 1967. *Zōho kokatsujiban no kenkyū* 増補古活字版之研究 (A study of movable type editions). 3 vols. Antiquarian Booksellers Association of Japan.

Kendenmeimeiroku. 1938. Masamune Atsuo 正宗敦夫, ed. *Kendenmeimeiroku* 顕伝明名録 (Record of illustrious biographies). 2 vols. Nihon Koten Zenshū Kankōkai.

Keyes, Roger S. 2006. *Ehon: The Artist and the Book in Japan*. Seattle: University of Washington Press.

Kimura Motoi 木村礎. 1983. *Mura no kataru Nihon no rekishi* 村の語る日本の歴史 (History of Japan as told by villages). Soshiete Kabushiki Kaisha.

Kindai Josei Bunkashi Kenkyūkai 近代女性文化史研究会, ed. 1989. *Fujin zasshi no yoake* 婦人雑誌の夜明け (The dawn of magazines for women). Ōzorasha.

Kinsei joshi kyōiku shisō 近世女子教育思想 (Ideas on women's education in early modern Japan). 2001. 3 vols. Nihon Tosho Sentaa.

Kiryū. 1988. *Kiryūshi kyōikushi* 桐生市教育史 (A history of education in Kiryū city). Vol. 1. Kiryū: Kiryū-shi Kyōiku Iinkai.

Kiryū hataya no ichihime nitarō 桐生機屋の一姫二太郎 (The families of the Kiryū weavers). 1998. Gunma Kenritsu Monjokan. Catalog of an exhibition in Maebashi.

Ko, Dorothy. 1994. *Teachers of the Inner Chambers: Women and Culture in Seventeenth-Century China.* Stanford: Stanford University Press.

Kobayashi Tadashi 小林忠, ed. 2002. *Suzuki Harunobu, seishun no ukiyoeshi: Edo no kararisuto no tōjō* 鈴木春信、青春の浮世絵師—江戸のカラリストの登場 (The rise of Edo colorists: Suzuki Harunobu). Chiba: Chiba City Museum of Art. Exhibition catalog.

Kōchi-han. 1986. *Kōchihan kyōiku enkaku torishirabe* 高知藩教育沿革取調 (Investigation into the history of education in Kōchi domain). Kōchi: Tosa Shidankai. Facsimile of the 1884 edition.

Koizumi Yoshinaga 小泉吉永. 2005. "Joshi-yō ōrai to *Hyakunin isshu*" 女子用往来と百人一首 (Primers for women and the *Hyakunin isshu*). In *Hyakunin isshu mangekyō* 百人一首万華鏡 (*Hyakunin isshu* kaleidoscope), ed. Shirahata Yōzaburō 白幡洋三郎, pp. 55–70. Kyoto: Shibunkaku.

———. 1998. *Nyohitsu tehon kaidai* 女筆手本解題 (Bibliography of calligraphy manuals for women). Musashi-murayama: Seishōdō Shoten.

———. 1997. "Isome Tsuna no joyō bunshō" 居初津奈の女用文章 (Texts for women by Isome Tsuna). In *Edo-ki onna kō: shiryō to jinbutsu* 江戸期おんな考：資料と人物 (On the women of the Edo period—sources and individuals), vol. 8, pp. 48–74. Kashiwa Shobō.

Koizumi Yoshinaga 小泉吉永, ed. 2003–6. *Onna daigaku shiryō shūsei* 女大学資料集成 (Collection of materials on *Onna daigaku*). 21 vols. Ōzorasha.

Kokushi daijiten 国史大辞典 (Great dictionary of Japanese history). 1979–97. Ed. Kokushi Daijiten Henshū Iinkai. 17 vols. Yoshikawa Kōbunkan.

Kokusho Kankōkai 国書刊行会, eds. 1969. *Ueda Akinari zenshū* 上田秋成全集 (Complete works of Ueda Akinari). Vol. 1. Kokusho Kankōkai.

Kōkyō dōjikun 孝経童児訓 (Lessons for children from the *Classic of Filial Piety*). 1781. Kyoto: Yamamoto Chōbei and Ōmiya Jirōkichi.

Komono. 1987. *Komono chōshi* 菰野町史 (History of Komono town). Vol. 1. Komonochō Kyōiku Iinkai.

Kondo, Dorinne. 1990. *Crafting Selves: Power, Gender, and Discourses of Identity in a Japanese Workplace.* Chicago: University of Chicago Press.

Kornicki, P. F. 2006. "Manuscript, Not Print: Scribal Culture in the Edo Period." *Journal of Japanese Studies* 32.1: 23–52.

———. 2005. "Unsuitable Books for Women? *Genji monogatari* and *Ise monogatari* in Late Seventeenth-Century Japan." *MN* 60.2: 147–93.

———. 1998. *The Book in Japan: A Cultural History from the Beginnings to the Nineteenth Century.* Leiden: Brill.

———. 1982. *The Reform of Fiction in Meiji Japan.* London: Ithaca Press.

Kornicki, P. F., and Nguyen Thi Oanh. 2009. "The *Lesser Learning for Women* and Other Texts for Vietnamese Women: A Bibliographical and Comparative Study." *International Journal of Asian Studies* 6.2: 147–69.

Kōshoku. 1988. *Kōshoku shishi* 更埴市史 (History of Kōshoku city). Vol. 2. Kōshoku-shi.

Koyama Toshihiko 小山利彦. 2010. "Senshū Daigaku toshokan zō den Hideyoshi hitsu *Genji no monogatari no okori* shiron: Taikō Hideyoshi to Konoe-ke" 専修大学図書館蔵伝秀吉筆『源氏の物語のおこり』試論—太閤秀吉と近衛家 (Toyotomi Hideyoshi and the Konoe house: An essay on the manuscript of "The Origins of *The Tale of Genji*" attributed to Hideyoshi in the collection of the Senshū University Library). In *Genji monogatari honmon no saikentō to shinteigen* 源氏物語本文の再検討と新提言 (The Reexaminations and the New Proposals of the Texts of *The Tale of Genji* [sic]), no. 3, pp. 29-50. Edited by Toyoshima Hidenori 豊島秀範. Kokugakuin Daigaku Bungakubu Nihon Bungakuka.

Kubo Takako 久保貴子. 1993. "Buke shakai ni ikita kuge josei" 武家社会に生きた公家女性 (Aristocratic women in samurai society). In *Josei no kinsei* 女性の近世 (Women in the early modern period), ed. Hayashi Reiko 林玲子, pp. 71–96. Vol. 15 of *Nihon no kinsei* 日本の近世. Chūō Kōronsha.

Kumagaya Keitarō 熊谷敬太郎. 1913. *Nihon retsujoden* 日本列女傳 (Biographies of Japanese women). Meiji Shuppansha.

Kurokawa Yōichi 黒川洋一, ed. 1990. *Edo shijin senshū* 江戸詩人選集 (Collected works of Edo *kanshi* poets). Vol. 4. Iwanami Shoten.

Kurushima, Noriko. 2004. "Marriage and Female Inheritance in Medieval Japan." Trans. Michiko Okubo. *International Journal of Asian Studies* 1.2: 223–45.

Kyokutei Bakin 曲亭馬琴. 1850. *Ominaeshi goshiki no sekidai* 女郎花五色石台. Part 4.

Laffin, Christina. 2009. "Grappling with Women's Education: Gender and Sociality in Nun Abutsu's *Menoto no fumi*." In *Ekkyō suru Nihon bungaku kenkyū: Kanon keisei, jendaa, media* 越境する日本文学研究—カノン形成・ジェンダー・メディア (New horizons in Japanese literary studies: Canon formation, gender, and media), ed. Haruo Shirane, pp. 62–66. Bensei Shuppan.

Lebra, Joyce Chapman. 1991. "Women in an All-Male Industry: The Case of Sake Brewer Tatsu'uma Kiyo." In *Recreating Japanese Women, 1600–1945*, ed. Gail Lee Bernstein, pp. 131–48. Berkeley: University of California Press.

Leupp, Gary P. 1992. *Servants, Shophands, and Laborers in the Cities of Tokugawa Japan*. Princeton: Princeton University Press.

Lindsey, William R. 2007. *Fertility and Pleasure: Ritual and Sexual Values in Tokugawa Japan*. Honolulu: University of Hawai`i Press.

Link, Howard A. 1980. *Primitive Ukiyo-e from the James A. Michener Collection in the Honolulu Academy of Arts*. Honolulu: University of Hawai`i Press.

Lynch, Deirdre Shauna. 2004. "Introduction." In Jane Austen, *Persuasion*, pp. vii–xxxiii. New ed. Oxford: Oxford University Press.

Mackie, Vera. 2003. *Feminism in Modern Japan*. Cambridge: Cambridge University Press.

Maeda Yoshi 前田淑. 2001. *Kinsei Fukuoka chihō joryū bungei shū* 近世福岡地方女流文芸集 (Literary works by early modern women in the Fukuoka region). Fukuoka: Ashi Shobō.

_____. 1999. *Edo jidai joryū bungeishi: Chihō o chūshin ni—haikai, waka, kanshi hen.* 江戸時代女流文芸史—地方を中心に—俳諧和歌漢詩篇 (History of women's writing in the Edo period with a focus on the provinces: Poetry). Kasama Shoin.

_____. 1998. *Edo jidai joryū bungeishi: Chihō o chūshin ni* 江戸時代女流文芸史: 地方を中心に (History of women's writing in the Edo period with a focus on the provinces). Kasama Shoin.

Mann, Susan. 1997. *Precious Records: Women in China's Long Eighteenth Century.* Stanford: Stanford University Press.

Markus, Andrew Lawrence. 1992. *The Willow in Autumn: Ryūtei Tanehiko, 1783–1842.* Cambridge: Council on East Asian Studies, Harvard University.

_____. 1982. "Representations of *Genji monogatari* in Edo Period Fiction." Paper presented at the eighth conference on Oriental-Western Literary Cultural Relations, Bloomington, Indiana, August.

Matsudaira Sadanobu 松平定信. 1893. *Rakuōkō isho* 楽翁公遺書 (The writings left by Matsudaira Sadanobu). Yao Shoten.

Maza, Sarah. 1993. *Private Lives and Public Affairs: The Causes Célèbres of Prerevolutionary France.* Berkeley: University of California Press.

McCormick, Melissa. 2008. "Monochromatic *Genji*: The *Hakubyō* Tradition and Female Commentarial Culture." In *Envisioning* The Tale of Genji: *Media, Gender, and Cultural Production*, ed. Haruo Shirane, pp. 101–28. New York: Columbia University Press.

_____. [Merissa Makōmikku]. 2006. "Genji no ma o nozoku: Hakubyō *Genji monogatari* emaki to nyōbō no shiza" 源氏の間を覗く—白描源氏物語絵巻と女房の視座 (Glimpsing the *Genji* room: The gentlewomen's gaze in *hakubyō* illustrated scrolls of *The Tale of Genji*). In *Egakareta Genji monogatari* 描かれた源氏物語 (*The Tale of Genji* illustrated), ed. Mitamura Masako 三田村雅子 and Kawazoe Fusae 河添房江, pp. 101–29. Vol. 1 of *Genji monogatari o ima yomitoku* 源氏物語をいま読み解く (Understanding *The Tale of Genji* today). Kanrin Shobō.

Medieval Japanese Studies Institute, ed. 2009. *A Hidden Heritage: Treasures of the Japanese Imperial Convents (Kōjotachi no shinkō to gosho bunka: amamonzeki jiin no sekai).* Sankei Shinbun.

Mehl, Margaret. 2001. "Women Educators and the Confucian Tradition in Meiji Japan (1868–1912): Miwada Masako and Atomi Kakei." *Women's History Review* 10.4: 579–602.

Meiji Nyūsu Jiten Hensan Iinkai. 1983–86. *Meiji nyūsu jiten* 明治ニュース事典 (Dictionary of Meiji news). Mainichi Communications.

Meikanshō 明翰抄 (Directory of calligraphers). 1958. *ZGR* 927. Zoku Gunsho Ruijū Kanseikai.

Mencius. 1970. *The Works of Mencius.* Trans. James Legge. New York: Dover.

Meng Ch'iu: Famous Episodes from Chinese History and Legend, by Li Han and Hsü Tzu-Kuang. 1979. Trans. Burton Watson. Tokyo: Kodansha International.

Merritt, Helen, and Nanako Yamada. 2000. *Woodblock kuchi-e Prints: Reflections of Meiji Culture.* Honolulu: University of Hawai`i Press.

Mie. 1994. *Mie-ken shi* 三重県史 (History of Mie Prefecture). Shiryōhen kinsei 5. Tsu: Mie-ken.

Minakawa Mieko 皆川美恵子. 1997. *Rai Shizuko no shufu seikatsu: "Baishi nikki" ni miru jukyō katei* 頼静子の主婦生活—「梅颸日記」に見る儒教家庭 (Rai Shizuko's life as a housewife: The Confucian family as seen in *Baishi nikki*). Kirara Shobō.

Minobe Noriko 見延典子. 2000. *Supporapon no pon: Rai San'yō no haha* すっぽらぽんのぽん — 頼山陽の母 (Rai San'yō's mother). Hiroshima: Nannansha.

Miwada Masako 三輪田真佐子. 1897. *Joshi kyōiku yōgen* 女子教育要言 (Words on the education of women). Kokkosha.

Miwada Masako Sensei Gojūnensai Kinen Shuppankai, ed. 1977. *Baika no fu: Miwada Masako den* 梅花の賦 — 三輪田真佐子伝 (The life of Miwada Masako). Miwada Masako Sensei Gojūnensai Kinen Shuppankai.

Miyakawa Yōko 宮川葉子. 2007. *Yanagisawa-ke no kotengaku* 柳沢家の古典学 (The classical studies of the Yanagisawa family). Vol. 1: *Matsukage nikki* 松陰日記 (The *Matsukage nikki*). Shintensha.

———. 2005. "Ōgimachi Machiko no jippu" 正親町町子の実父 (Ōgimachi Machiko's true father). *Gunsho* ぐんしょ 18.2: 7–13.

———. 2002. "Ōgimachi Machiko no seibo" 正親町町子の生母 (Ōgimachi Machiko's birth mother). *Gunsho* ぐんしょ 15.1: 1–5.

———. 1999. *Sanjōnishi Sanetaka to kotengaku* 三条西実隆と古典学 (Sanjōnishi Sanetaka and the study of the classics). Kazama Shobō.

———. 1990. "Rakushidō to *Genji monogatari*: Ōgimachi Machiko to *Matsukage nikki* o chūshin ni" 楽只堂と『源氏物語』—正親町町子と松蔭日記を中心に (Rakushidō [Yanagisawa Yoshiyasu] and *The Tale of Genji*). In vol. 15 of *Genji monogatari no tankyū* 源氏物語の探究 (Research on *The Tale of Genji*), pp. 405–42. Kazama Shobō.

Miyazaki Yoshikuni 宮崎嘉国. 1879. *Seiyō retsujoden* 西洋列女伝 (Biographies of Western women). Kinshindō. Translation of *Noble Deeds of Women* by Elizabeth Stirling.

Miyoshi Teiji 三善貞司, ed. 2000. *Ōsaka jinbutsu jiten* 大阪人物辞典 (Osaka biographical dictionary). Osaka: Seibundō.

Mori Senzō 森銑三. 1988–89. *Mori Senzō chosakushū* 著作集 (Collected works of Mori Senzō). 13 vols. Chūō Kōronsha.

Mori Shigeo 森繁夫. 1928. *Den Sute-jo* 田捨女. Osaka: Seiunsha.

Mostow, Joshua S. 2009a. "*Onna daigaku takara-bako* ni miru *Genji monogatari* kyōju" 『女大學宝箱』にみる『源氏物語』享受 (The reception of *The Tale of Genji* as seen in *The Treasure Box of the The Greater Learning for women*). In (*Genji monogatari sennen-ki kinen) Genji monogatari kokusai fōramu shūsei* 『 (源氏物語千年記念) 源氏物語国際フォーラム集成 (*Genji millennium commemoration*: The Tale of Genji *international forum*), ed. Ii Haruki, pp. 217–27. Kadokawa Gakugei Shuppan.

————. 2009b. *"The Tale of Light Snow*: Pastiche, Epistolary Fiction, and Narrativity Verbal and Visual." *Japan Forum* 21.3: 363–87.

————. 2008. *"Genji monogatari* to jokunsho" 『源氏物語』と女訓書 (*The Tale of Genji* and conduct books for women). In *Genji monogatari to Edo bunka* 『源氏物語』と江戸文化 (*The Tale of Genji* and Edo culture), ed. Komine Kazuaki 小峰和明, Kojima Naoko 小嶋菜温子, and Watanabe Kenji 渡辺憲司, pp. 337–46. Shinwasha.

————. 2004. "Inventing a New 'Classical' Theme: Tan'yū and the *One Hundred Poets.*" In *Critical Perspectives on Classicism in Japanese Painting, 1600–1700*, ed. Elizabeth Lillehoj, pp. 133–67. Honolulu: University of Hawai`i Press.

————. 2003a. "The Gender of *Wakashu* and the Grammar of Desire." In *Gender and Power in the Japanese Visual Field*, ed. Joshua S. Mostow, Norman Bryson, and Maribeth Graybill, pp. 49–70. Honolulu: University of Hawai`i Press.

————. 2003b. *"Ise monogatari-e: Sōzō-teki na mohō to seiji-teki na tōyō"* (*Tales of Ise* pictures: Creative copying and political stealing"). In *Plagiarism, Imitation, Originality: Questioning the Imagination of Japanese Literature*, pp. 1–20. Proceedings of the twenty-seventh International Conference on Japanese Literature, National Institute of Japanese Literature, Tokyo, 2003. National Institute of Japanese Literature.

————. 2002. "Court Classics and Popular Prints: Poetry and Parody in Ukiyo-e." In *Masterful Illusions: Japanese Prints in the Anne van Biema Collection*, ed. Ann Yonemura, pp. 36–51. Washington, D.C.: Arthur M. Sackler Gallery, Smithsonian Institution.

————. 2000a. "Modern Constructions of *Tales of Ise*: Gender and Courtliness." In *Inventing the Classics: Modernity, National Identity, and Japanese Literature*, ed. Haruo Shirane and Tomi Suzuki, pp. 96–119. Stanford: Stanford University Press.

————. 2000b. "Canonization and Commodification: Illustrations to the *Tales of Ise* in the Modern Era." In *Issues of Canonicity and Canon Formation in Japanese Literary Studies*, ed. Stephen D. Miller, vol. 1, pp. 89–119. Proceedings of the Association for Japanese Literary Studies, Denver, Colorado, 1999. West Lafayette, Ind.: Association for Japanese Literary Studies, 2000.

————. 1997. "Shisen no poritikusu: Heian jidai josei no monogatari-e no yomikata" 視線のポリティクス—平安時代女性の物語絵の読み方 (The politics of the gaze: Feminine reading of illustrated romances in the Heian period). Trans. Ikeda Shinobu. In *Bijutsu to jendaa: Hi-taishō no shisen* 美術とジェンダー: 非対称の視線 (Art and gender: The asymmetrical regard), ed. Suzuki Tokiko 鈴木杜幾子, Chino Kaori 千野香織, and Mabuchi Akiko 馬淵明子, pp. 61–84. Brücke.

————. 1996. *Pictures of the Heart: The Hyakunin Isshu in Word and Image.* Honolulu: University of Hawai`i Press.

Mostow, Joshua S., with Mitamura Masako 三田村雅子 and Kawazoe Fusae 河添房江. 2004. "(Intabyū) *Genji monogatari* no shikaku-teki kyōju-shi o megutte" (インタビュー) 源氏物語の視覚的享受史をめぐって (On the visual reception of *The Tale of Genji*). *Genji kenkyū* 源氏研究 9: 155–76.

Mou, Sherry J. 2002. *Gentlemen's Prescriptions for Women's Lives: A Thousand Years of Biographies of Chinese Women.* Armonk, N.Y.: M. E. Sharpe.

Murasawa Takeo 村澤武雄. 1936. *Ina kadōshi* 伊那歌道史 (History of poetry in Ina). Iida-machi: Yamamura Shoin.

Murase, Miyeko. 1986. *Tales of Japan: Scrolls and Prints from the New York Public Library.* New York: Oxford University Press.

Muroki Hideyuki 室城秀之. 2003. "Arakida Reijo no giko monogatari no sekai" 荒木田麗女の擬古物語の世界 (The world of Arakida Rei's pseudoclassical tales). *Bungaku* 4.4: 51–60.

Nagano. 1984. *Nagano kenshi* 長野県史 (History of Nagano Prefecture). Kinsei shiryōhen vol. 9. Nagano-ken.

Nagashima Atsuko 長島淳子. 1986. "Bakumatsu nōson josei no kōdō no jiyū to kaji rōdō – Bushū Tachibana-gun Namamugi-mura *Sekiguchi nikki* o sozai to shite" 幕末農村女性の行動の自由と家事労働—武州橘樹郡生麦村『関口日記』を素材として (The domestic work and freedom of movement of women in mid-nineteenth-century farming villages). In *Ronshū kinsei joseishi* 論集近世女性史 (Essays on early modern women's history), pp. 139–73. Yoshikawa Kōbunkan.

Nagatomo Chiyoji 長友千代治. 1977. "Edo jidai shomin no dokusho" 江戸時代庶民の読書 (The reading of commoners in the Edo period). *Bungaku* 文学 45.9: 99–109.

Nagy, Margit. 1991. "Educating Prewar Japanese Women in Their Legal Rights: The Role of Male Mentors." *Intercultural Communication Studies* 1.1: 295–308.

Najita, Tetsuo. 1998. *Tokugawa Political Writings.* Cambridge: Cambridge University Press.

Nakaba Yoshiko 中葉芳子. 2000. "*Kaokushō* no chūshaku taido: 'Osanaki hito, onnadochi' no tame ni" 『花屋抄』の注釈態度—「おさなき人・女達」のために (For "young people and women": The commentarial stance of *Kaokushō*). *Kokubungaku* 國文學 80.1: 17–30.

———. 1999. "*Kaokushō* no honmon ishiki: Kandai toshokanbon no shōkai o kanete" 『花屋抄』の本文意識—関大図書館本の紹介を兼ねて (The sense of the original in *Kaokushō* with an introduction to the Kansai Daigaku Library manuscript). *Kokubungaku* 國文學 79.1: 35–43.

Nakaizumi Tetsutoshi 中泉哲俊. 1966. *Nihon kinsei kyōiku shisō no kenkyū* 日本近世教育思想の研究 (Educational thought in the early modern period). Yoshikawa Kōbunkan.

Nakajima Masukichi 中鳥益吉. 1907. *Meien no gakusei jidai* 名媛の学生時代 (The student days of famous women). Yomiuri Shinbunsha.

Nakama Shishi Hensan Iinkai, ed. 1992. *Nakama shishi* 中間市史 (History of Nakama city). Vol. 2. Nakama-shi.

Nakamura, Ellen. 2007. "In Her Father's Footsteps: Nakamura Ine (1827–1903) and Medical Networks in Nineteenth-Century Japan." Paper presented at the annual meetings of the Association for Asian Studies, Boston.

Nakamura Yukihiko. 1982. "Hayashi Razan no hon'yaku bungaku" 林羅山の翻訳文学 (Literature translated by Hayashi Razan). In *Nakamura Yukihiko chojutsushū*

中村幸彦著述集 (The writings of Nakamura Yukihiko), vol. 6, pp. 7–29. Chūō Kōronsha.

Nakano Setsuko 中野節子. 1997. *Kangaeru onnatachi: Kanazōshi kara Onna daigaku* 考える女たち―仮名草子から『女大学』(Thinking women: From *kanazōshi* to *Onna daigaku*). Ōzorasha.

Namiki Seishi 並木誠士. 2007. *Edo no yūgi – kaiawase karuta sugoroku* 江戸の遊戯―買合せ・かるた・すごろく (The amusements of Edo: Shell matching, cards, and board games). Kyoto: Seigensha.

Nenzi, Laura. 2008. *Excursions in Identity: Travel and the Intersection of Place, Gender, and Status in Edo Japan*. Honolulu: University of Hawai`i Press.

———. 2004a. "Intersections: The Place of Recreational Travel in Edo Culture and Society." PhD diss., University of California, Santa Barbara.

———. 2004b. "Women's Travel Narratives in Early Modern Japan: Genre Imperatives, Gender Consciousness, and Status Questioning." *Journeys: The International Journal of Travel and Travel Writing* 5.1: 47–72.

Newhard, Jamie Lynn. 2005. "Genre, Secrecy, and the Book: A History of Late Medieval and Early Modern Literary Scholarship on *Ise monogatari*." PhD diss., Columbia University.

Nihon fūzoku zue. 1914. Kurokawa Mamichi 黒川真道. *Nihon fūzoku zue* 日本風俗図絵 (Genre paintings of Japan). Vol. 6. Nihon Fūzoku Zue Kankōkai.

Nihon kokugo daijiten. 1974. Nihon daijiten kankōkai 日本大辞典刊行会, ed. *Nihon kokugo daijiten* 日本国語大辞典 (Great dictionary of the Japanese language). Shogakukan.

Nihon koten bungaku daijiten 日本古典文学大辞典 (Great dictionary of Japanese classical literature). 1983–85. 6 vols. Iwanami Shoten.

Niimi Akihiko 新美哲彦. 2009. "Kaoku Gyokuei to 'Chaa': den Hideyoshi hitsu *Genji monogatari no okori* kara" 花屋玉栄と「ちやあ」―伝秀吉筆『源氏物語のおこり』から (Kaoku Gyokuei and 'Chaa' in the manuscript of "The Origins of *The Tale of Genji*" attributed to Hideyoshi). *Heian bungaku no kochūshaku to juyō* (Old commentaries on Heian period literature and their reception), no. 2, pp. 130-142. Edited by Jinno Hidenori 陣野秀範, Niimi Akihiko, and Yokomizo Hiroshi 横溝博. Musashino Shoin.

Nishigaki Seiji 西垣晴次, Yamamoto Takashi 山本隆志, and Ushiki Yukio 丑木幸男 編, eds. 1997. *Gunma ken no rekishi* 群馬県の歴史 (History of Gunma Prefecture). Yamakawa Shuppansha.

Nochikagami. 1932–34. Kuroita Katsumi 黒板勝美, ed. *Nochikagami* 後鑑 (The later mirror). 4 vols. In *Shintei zōho Kokushi taikei* 新訂増補国史大系 (Newly enlarged compendium of Japanese history), vols. 34–37. Yoshikawa Kōbunkan.

Noda Hisao 野田壽雄. 1960. *Kanazōshi shū* 仮名草子集 (Collection of *kanazōshi*). Vol. 1. Asahi Shinbun-sha.

Noguchi Takehiko 野口武彦. 1985. *Genji monogatari o Edo kara yomu* 源氏物語を江戸から読む (Reading *The Tale of Genji* in the Edo period). Kōdansha.

Noma Kōshin 野間光辰, ed. 1961. *(Kanpon) Shikidō ōkagami* 完本色道大鏡 (The complete *Shikidō ōkagami*). Kyoto: Tomoyama Bunko.

Nomura Noboru 野村豊 and Yui Yoshitarō 由井喜太郎, eds. 1955. *Kōchiya Kasei kyūki: Kinsei shomin shiryō* 河内屋可正旧記: 近世庶民史料 (The records of Kōchiya Kasei: Materials on early modern period commoners). Osaka: Seibundō.

Nonaka En 野中婉. 1891. *Oboroyo no tsuki* 朧夜の月 (Moon on a misty night). In *Nihon kyōikushi shiryō* 日本教育史資料 (Materials on the history of education in Japan), vol. 5, pp. 699–701. Monbushō.

Nonaka Kenzan kankei monjo 野中兼山関係文書 (Documents related to Nonaka Kenzan). 1965. Kōchi: Kōchiken Bunkyō Kyōkai.

Ochiai Emiko. 1999. "Modern Japan through the Eyes of an Old Midwife: From an Oral Life History to Social History." In *Gender and Japanese History*, ed. Wakita Haruko, Anne Bouchy, and Ueno Chizuko, vol. 1, pp. 235–96. Osaka: Osaka University Press.

Ōguchi Yūjirō 大口勇次郎, ed. 2001. *Rai Baishi nikki no kenkyū* 頼梅颺日記の研究 (Studies of Rai Baishi's diary). Ochanomizu Joshi Daigaku Jendaa Kenkyū Sentaa.

Ōkawa Shigeo 大川茂雄, ed. 1972. *Kokugakusha denki shūsei* 国学者伝記集成 (Collected biographies of nativist scholars). Meicho Kankōkai.

Okazaki-Ward, L. I. 1993. "Women and Their Education in the Tokugawa Period of Japan." MPhil thesis, University of Sheffield.

Ōki Motoko 大木基子. 2003. *Jiyū minken undō to josei* 自由民権運動と女性 (Women and the Freedom and Popular Rights Movement). Domesu Shuppan.

Ōkubo Tadashi, ed. 1977. "*Nonaka no shimizu* tensaku" 野中の清水添削 (Corrections to *Nonaka no shimizu*). In *Motoori Norinaga zenshū* 本居宣長全集 (Complete works of Motoori Norinaga). Bekkan vol. 2. Chikuma Shobō.

Ōmama. 1995. *Ōmama chōshi* 大間々町誌 (History of Ōmama town). Bekkan vol. 2 kinsei shiryōhen. Ōmama-chō.

Onna Daigaku. 1979. *Women and Wisdom of Japan*. In *The Way of Contentment*, trans. Ken Hoshino. Washington, D.C.: University Publications of America. Reprinted from the 1905 edition published in London by John Murray.

Ono Kannosuke 小野燗之助, ed. 1892–93. *Kōtō shōgaku: Joshi shūjichō* 高等小学女子習字帖 (Writing book for girls for use at the higher elementary schools). Vols. 1–2. Yoshikawa Hanshichi.

Ōno Mizuo 大野瑞男, ed. 2001. *Enomoto Yazaemon oboegaki: Kinsei shoki shōnin no kiroku* 榎本弥左衛門覚書: 近世初期商人の記録 (The diary of Enomoto Yazaemon: An early modern period merchant's record). Tōyō Bunko 695. Heibonsha.

Ōno Sachiku 大野酒竹. 1898. *Genroku meika kushū: Fu joryū haikushū* 元禄名家句集附女流俳句集 (Haiku by famous poets of the Genroku era with verses by women as a supplement). Hakubunkan.

Ono Susumu 小野晋. 1965. *(Kinsei shoki) Yūjo hyōbanki shū* 近世初期遊女評判記集 (Collection of courtesan critiques). Vol. 1 honbunhen, vol. 2 kenkyūhen. Koten Bunko.

Ooms, Herman. 1996. *Tokugawa Village Practice: Class, Status, Power, Law*. Berkeley, University of California Press.

————. 1975. *Charismatic Bureaucrat: A Political Biography of Matsudaira Sadanobu*. Chicago: University of Chicago Press.

Ōraimono bunrui shūsei 往来物分類集成 (Collection of popular educational textbooks). 1994. Part 2: "Joshiyō ōrai hen" 女子用往来編. Yūshōdō. Microfilm publication.

Ōta Ken'ichi 太田 健一 and Takeuchi Ryōko 竹内涼子. 2007. *Aru Meiji jogakusei nikki* 或る明治女学生日記 (The diary of a woman student in the Meiji era). Okayama: Kibito.

Ōuchi Hatsuo 大内初夫, Iinuma Matsuko 飯野松子, and Abe Tamaki 阿部王樹, eds. 1986. *Kohakuan Shokyūni zenshū* 湖白庵諸九尼全集 (The complete works of Shokyūni). Rev. ed. Osaka: Izumi Shoin.

Parker, Deborah. 1996. "Women in the Book Trade in Italy, 1475–1620." *Renaissance Quarterly* 49.3: 509–41.

Patessio, Mara. Forthcoming. *Women and Public Life in Early Meiji Japan*. Michigan Monograph Series in Japanese Studies. Ann Arbor: Center for Japanese Studies, University of Michigan.

————. 2006. "The Creation of Public Spaces by Women in the Early Meiji Period and the Tōkyō Fujin Kyōfūkai." *International Journal of Asian Studies* 3.2: 155–82.

————. 2004. "Women's Participation in the Popular Rights Movement (*Jiyū Minken Undō*) during the Early Meiji Period." *U.S.-Japan Women's Journal* 27.1: 3–26.

Pearson, Jacqueline. 1999. *Women's Reading in Britain, 1750–1835: A Dangerous Recreation*. Cambridge: Cambridge University Press.

Pflugfelder, Gregory M. 2000. *Cartographies of Desire: Male-Male Sexuality in Japanese Discourse, 1600–1950*. Berkeley: University of California Press.

Pitelka, Morgan. 2005. *Handmade Culture: Raku Potters, Patrons, and Tea Practitioners in Japan*. Honolulu: University of Hawai`i Press.

Plebani, Tiziana. 2001. *Il "genere" dei libri. Storie e rappresentazioni della lettura al femminile e al maschile tra medioevo e età moderna*. Milan: FrancoAngeli.

Ragsdale, Kathryn. 1998. "Marriage, the Newspaper Business, and the Nation-State: Ideology in the Late Meiji Serialized *Katei shosetsu*." *Journal of Japanese Studies* 24.2: 229–55.

Rai Seiichi 頼成一. 1941. *Baishi kabunshō* 梅颸歌文鈔 (Selected writings of Baishi). Fujokaisha.

Rai Tsutomu 賴惟勤. 2003. *Nihon kangaku ronshū: Reishōryo sōroku* 日本漢学論集―嶺松廬叢録 (Essays on Japanese sinology). Kyūko Shoin.

Reinhard, Wolfgang. 1996. *Augsburger Eliten des 16. Jahrhunderts. Prosopographie wirtschaftlicher und politischer Führungsgruppen, 1500–1620*. Berlin: Akademie.

Rieger, Angelica, and Jean-François Tonard, eds. 1999. *Lesende Frauen/la lecture au feminine: La lectrice dans la littérature française du Moyen Age au XXᵉ siècle*. Darmstadt: Wissenschaftliche Buchgesellschaft.

Robertson, Jennifer. 1991. "The Shingaku Woman: Straight from the Heart." In *Recreating Japanese Women, 1600–1945*, ed. Gail Lee Bernstein, pp. 88–107. Berkeley: University of California Press.

Rodd, Laurel Rasplica. 1984. *Kokinshū: A Collection of Poems Ancient and Modern*. Princeton: Princeton University Press.

Roorda, D. J. 1984. "Prosopografie, een onmogelijke mogelijkheid?" In *Rond prins en patriciaat. Verspreide opstellen*, ed. D.J. Roorda and A.J.C.M. Gabriels, pp. 42–52. Weesp: Fibula-Van Dishoeck.

Ropp, Paul. S. 1997. "Ambiguous Images of Courtesan Culture in Late Imperial China." In *Writing Women in Late Imperial China*, ed. Ellen Widmer and Kang-i Sun Chang, pp. 17–45. Stanford: Stanford University Press.

———. 1993. "Love, Literacy, and Laments: Themes of Women Writers in Late Imperial China." *Women's History Review* 2.1: 107–41.

Roppyakuban uta-awase. 1998. Kubota Jun 久保田淳 and Yamaguchi Akiho 山口明穂, eds. *Roppyakuban uta-awase* 六百番歌合 (Poetry contest in six hundred rounds). *SNKBT* 38. Iwanami Shoten.

Rowley, G. G. [Gei Rōrii]. 2008. "'Okuretekita himegimi' no keifu: Keifukuin Kaoku Gyokuei no baai" 「遅れてきた姫君」の系譜―慶福院花屋玉栄の場合 (A lineage of 'too-late young ladies': The case of Keifukuin Kaoku Gyokuei). In *Heian bungaku no kochūshaku to juyō* 平安文学の古注釈と受容 (Old commentaries on Heian period literature and their reception), no. 1, pp. 21–25. Edited by Jinno Hidenori 陣野英則 and Yokomizo Hiroshi 横溝博. Musashino Shoin.

———. 2006. "Keifukuin Kaoku Gyokuei shōkō" 慶福院花屋玉栄小考 (On Keifukuin Kaoku Gyokuei). *Gunsho* 19.2: 11–16.

———. 2000. *Yosano Akiko and The Tale of Genji*. Michigan Monograph Series in Japanese Studies, no. 28. Ann Arbor: Center for Japanese Studies, University of Michigan.

Rubinger, Richard. 2007. *Popular Literacy in Early Modern Japan*. Honolulu: University of Hawai`i Press.

Rühl, Esther. 1997. "Frauenbildungsbücher aus der späten Edo-Zeit (1750–1868): Versuch einer Charakterisierung anhand beispielhafter Werke." *Japanstudien* 9: 287–312.

Ryūei fujo denkei 柳営婦女伝系 (Biographies and genealogies of women who worked for the shogunate). 1917. In *Ryūei fujo densō* 柳営婦女伝叢 (Collected biographies of women who worked for the shogunate), ed. Saitō Matsutarō 斎藤松太郎 and Inoue Naohiro 井上直弘, pp. 55–194. Kokusho Kankōkai.

Sadakane Manabu 定兼学. 1986. "Onna shōya O-Sen o megutte" 女庄屋「お千」をめぐって (On the woman village head O-Sen). *Okayama chihōshi kenkyū* 岡山地方史研究 52: 20–23.

Saitō Junkichi 斎藤醇吉. 1986. "Edo jidai no katei kyōiku, joshi no shitsuke ni tsuite" 江戸時代の家庭教育―女子の躾について (Home education in the Edo period and the training of women). *Nihon shigaku kyōiku kenkyūsho kiyō* 日本私学教育研究所紀要 21.1: 349–80; 22.1: 419–54.

Sakaguchi Kazuko. 2003. "Digital textbook collections." *Tsūshin* 9.2: 4–6. Available at www.fas.harvard.edu/~rijs/pdfs/tsushin/etsushin9_2.pdf. Published by the Edwin O. Reischauer Institute of Japanese Studies, Harvard University.

Sakai Shigeyuki 酒井茂幸. 2006. "Kinsei kinri no kasho shūzōshi ni okeru Konoe-ke no kakawari ni tsuite" 近世禁裏の歌書収蔵史における近衛家の関わりについて (The Konoe family and the history of the collection of poetic manuscripts in the early modern imperial palace). *Gunsho* 19.2: 6–10.

Sakaki, Atsuko. 2005. *Obsessions with the Sino-Japanese Polarity in Japanese Literature*. Honolulu: University of Hawai'i Press.

Sakurai Fukiko 桜井ふき子. 1893. *Fujin risshiden* 婦人立志伝 (Lives of prominent women). Hifumikan Shoten.

Sankō kōjitsuzu 三綱行実図. 2002. In *Kanazōshi shūsei* 仮名草子集成, vol. 32. Tōkyōdō Shuppan.

Sasaki Kiyoshi. 2000. "Amenominakanushi no Kami in late Tokugawa period Kokugaku." *Kami*, http://www2.kokugakuin.ac.jp/ijcc/wp/cpjr/kami/sasaki. html. Published by the Institute for Japanese Culture and Classics, Kokugakuin University.

Sasaki Nobutsuna 佐佐木信綱. 1890. *Nihon fujo yōbun* 日本婦女用文 (Writing manual for Japanese women). Hakubunkan.

Sato, Hiroaki. 2000. "Record of an Autumn Wind: The Travel Diary of Arii Shokyu." *MN* 55.1: 1–44.

Satō Satoru 佐藤悟. 2006. "*Hana yosooi kō*" 華よそほひ考 (On *Hana yosooi*). In Satō Satoru, *Nihon chūgoku yōroppa bungaku ni okeru eiiribon no kisoteki kenkyū oyobi gazō dēta bēsu no kōchiku* 日本・中国・ヨーロッパ文学における絵入本の基礎的研究及び画像データ・ベースの構築 (A study of illustrated books in the literatures of Japan, China, and Europe and the construction of an image database), pp. 50–108. Jissen Joshi Daigaku Bungakubu.

Sawada, Janine Anderson. 1993. *Confucian Values and Popular Zen: Sekimon Shingaku in Eighteenth-Century Japan*. Honolulu: University of Hawai`i Press.

Schneewind, Sarah. 2006. *Community Schools and the State in Ming China*. Stanford: Stanford University Press.

Schopenhauer, Arthur. 1974. *Parerga and Paralipomena: Short Philosophical Essays*. Trans. from the German by E. F. J. Payne. 2 vols. Oxford: Clarendon Press.

Scott, Joan W. 1992. "Women's History." In *New Perspectives on Historical Writing*, ed. Peter Burke, pp. 42–66. University Park: Pennsylvania State University Press.

Screech, Timon. 1999. *Sex and the Floating World: Erotic Images in Japan, 1700–1820*. Honolulu: University of Hawai`i Press.

Segawa Yoshiko 瀬川淑子. 2001. *Kōjo Shinanomiya no nichijō seikatsu:* Mujōhōin-dono gonikki *o yomu* 皇女品宮の日常生活:『无上法院殿御日記』を読む (The daily life of Princess Shinanomiya: Reading *Mujōhōin-dono gonikki*). Iwanami Shoten.

Seidensticker, Edward G., trans. 1976. *The Tale of Genji*. New York: Alfred A. Knopf.

Seigle, Cecilia Segawa. 2002. "Shinanomiya Tsuneko: Portrait of a Court Lady." In *The Human Tradition in Modern Japan*, ed. Anne Walthall, pp. 3–24. Wilmington, Del.: Scholarly Resources.

_____. 1999. "The Shogun's Consort: Konoe Hiroko and Tokugawa Ienobu." *HJAS* 59.2: 485–522.

————. 1993. *Yoshiwara: The Glittering World of the Japanese Courtesan.* Honolulu: University of Hawai`i Press.

Seki Tamiko 関民子. 1980. *Edo kōki no joseitachi* 江戸後期の女性たち (Women of the late Edo period). Aki Shobō.

Sekiguchi, Sumiko. 2008. "Gender in the Meiji Restoration: Confucian 'Lessons for Women' and the Making of Modern Japan." *Social Science Japan Journal* 11.2: 201–21.

Selden, Kyoko, trans. 2008. "Fireflies above the Stream." *Review of Japanese Culture and Society* 20: 253–64.

Shiba Keiko 柴桂子. 2005. *Kinsei no onna tabi nikki jiten* 近世の女旅日記事典 (Dictionary of early modern women's travel diaries). Tōkyōdō.

————. 2004. "Tabi nikki kara mita kinsei josei no ichikōsatsu" 旅日記から見た近世女性の一考察 (Early modern women as seen from their travel diaries). In *Tenbō Nihon rekishi* 展望日本歴史 (Survey of Japanese history), vol. 15, pp. 372–96. Tōkyōdō.

————. 1997. *Kinsei onna tabi nikki* 近世おんな旅日記 (Women's travel diaries of the Edo period). Yoshikawa Kōbunkan.

Shibata Mitsuhiko 柴田光彦 and Kanda Masayuki 神田正行, eds. 2002. *Bakin shokan shūsei* 馬琴書翰集成 (Bakin's collected letters). Vol. 1. Yagi Shoten.

Shibu Shōhei 志部昭平. 1992. "Sensoji kaiyaku no *Sankō kōjitsu* ni tsuite: Omo ni Jinshin no ran zen kohon ni tsuite" 宣祖時改訳の三綱行実について―主に壬辰之乱前古本について (On the new translation of *Sankō kōjitsu*, especially old texts from before the Jinshin rebellion). *Chōsen gakuhō* 朝鮮学報 145: 85–132.

Shidō Bunko. 1962–64. *(Edo jidai) Shorin shuppan shoseki mokuroku shūsei* 江戸時代書林出版書籍目録 (Collected booksellers' catalogs of the Edo period). 4 vols. Inoue Shobō.

Shiga Tadashi 志賀匡. 1977. *Nihon joshi kyōikushi* 日本女子教育史 (History of women's education in Japan). Biwa Shobō.

Shinpan Nihonshi jiten. 1996. Asao Naohiro 朝尾直弘, Uno Shun'ichi 宇野俊一, and Tanaka Migaku 田中琢, eds. *Shinpan Nihonshi jiten* 新版日本史辞典 (New historical dictionary of Japan). Kadokawa Shoten.

Shirane, Haruo, ed. 2009. *Ekkyō suru Nihon bungaku kenkyū: Kanon keisei, jendaa, media* 越境する日本文学研究―カノン形成・ジェンダー・メディア (New horizons in Japanese literary studies: Canon formation, gender, and media). Bensei Shuppan.

————. 2008. *Envisioning* The Tale of Genji: *Media, Gender, and Cultural Production.* New York: Columbia University Press.

————. 2002. *Early Modern Japanese Literature: An Anthology, 1600–1900.* New York: Columbia University Press.

Sievers, Sharon L. 1983. *Flowers in Salt: The Beginnings of Feminist Consciousness in Modern Japan.* Stanford: Stanford University Press.

Smith, George 1861. *Ten Weeks in Japan.* London: Longman, Green, Longman and Roberts.

Smith, Lesley, and Jane H. M. Taylor, eds. 1996. *Women and the Book: Assessing the Visual Evidence.* London: British Library.

Smythe, Dion C. 2000. "Putting Technology to Work: The CD-Rom Version of the Prosopography of the Byzantine Empire I (641–867)." *History and Computing* 12.1: 85–97.

Snook, Edith. 2005. *Women, Reading, and the Cultural Politics of Early Modern England*. Aldershot: Ashgate.

Sōma Kokkō 相馬黒光. 1985. *Meiji shoki no sanjosei* 明治初期の三女性 (Three women in the early Meiji period). Fuji Shuppan. Facsimile of the 1940 edition.

Sorimachi Shigeo. 1978. *Catalogue of Japanese Illustrated Books and Manuscripts in the Spencer Collection of the New York Public Library*. Rev. ed. Tokyo: Kōbunsō.

St. Clair, William, and Irmgard Maassen, eds. 2000–2006. *Conduct Literature for women*. Five multivolume sets. London: Pickering and Chatto.

Stevenson, Jane. 2005. *Women Latin Poets: Language, Gender, and Authority, from Antiquity to the Eighteenth Century*. Oxford: Oxford University Press.

Stone, Lawrence. 1971. "Prosopography." *Daedalus* 100.1: 46–79.

Strauss, Walter L., and Carol Bronze, eds. 1979. *Japanese Woodcut Book Illustrations*. Vol. 2: *The Tale of Genji*. New York: Abaris Books.

Sugano Noriko 菅野則子. 2006. "*Onna daigaku kō*" 女大学考 (On *Onna daigaku*). In *Onna daigaku shiryō shūsei* 女大学資料集成 (Collected materials on *Onna daigaku*, supplementary volume), bekkan, pp. 78–95. Ōzorasha.

———. 1998. "Terakoya to onnakyōshi" 寺子屋と女師匠 (Elementary schools and women teachers). In *Nihon joseishi ronshū* 日本女性史論集 (Essays on Japanese women's history). Vol. 8: *Kyōiku to shisō* 教育と思想 (Education and thought), ed. Sōgō Joseishi Kenkyūkai, pp. 140–58. Yoshikawa Kōbunkan.

———. 1997. "Edo jidai ni okeru 'jukyō' no nihonteki tenkai" 江戸時代における「儒教」の日本的展開 (The development of Japanese Confucianism in the Edo period). In *Ajia joseishi: Hikakushi no kokoromi* アジア女性史―比較史の試み (Asian women's history: An attempt at comparative history), ed. Hayashi Reiko 林玲子 and Yanagita Setsuko 柳田節子, pp. 228–40. Akashi Shoten.

Sugimoto, Etsu Inagaki. 1990. *A Daughter of the Samurai*. Tokyo: Charles E. Tuttle of Tokyo. Reprint of the 1925 edition.

Suzuki Ken'ichi 鈴木絹一, ed. 1901. *Joshi Tōkyō yūgaku annai* 女子東京遊学案内 (Guide for girls wanting to study in Tokyo). Sekibundō.

Suzuki Toshiyuki 鈴木俊幸. 2007. *Edo no dokushonetsu: Jigaku suru dokusha to shoseki ryūtsū* 江戸の読書熱―自学する読者と書籍流通 (The enthusiasm for reading in the Edo period: Readers' self-study and the circulation of books). Heibonsha.

Suzuki Yoshitaka 鈴木義隆. 1981. "Terakoya onna kyōshi no kenkyū" 寺子屋女教師の研究 (A study of women teachers in elementary schools). *Hakuō joshi tandai ronshū* 白鴎女子短大論集 70.1: 34–51.

Suzuki Yūko 鈴木裕子. 1986. *Kishida Toshiko kenkyū bunken mokuroku* 岸田敏子研究文献目録 (Bibliography of studies on Kishida Toshiko). Fuji Shuppan.

———. 1985. *Kishida Toshiko hyōronshū* 岸田敏子評論集 (Collection of Kishida Toshiko's critical essays). Fuji Shuppan.

Suzuki Yuriko 鈴木ゆり子. 1993. "Buke josei no seikatsu" 武家女性の生活 (The life of samurai women). In *Josei no kinsei* 女性の近世 (The early modern period for women), ed. Hayashi Reiko 林玲子, vol. 15 of *Nihon no kinsei* 日本の近世 (Early modern Japan), pp. 129–66. Chūō Kōronsha.

Szentiványi, Helga. 2008. *Frauen in der Bürgerkultur der Edo-Zeit: Anhand von Beispielen aus der haikai-Dichtung under besonderer Berücksichtung von Kaga no Chiyo*. Munich: Iudicium.

Tachi Kaoru 舘かおる. 1984. "Ryōsai Kenbo" 良妻賢母 (Good wives and wise mothers). In *Kōza Joseigaku* 講座女性学 (Lectures on women's studies), ed. Joseigaku Kenkyūkai, vol. 1: *Onna no Imeeji* 女のイメージ (Images of women), pp. 184–209. Keisō Shobō.

Takahashi Shōsuke 高橋勝介. 1989. *Atomi Kakei joshiden* 跡見花蹊女史伝 (The life of Atomi Kakei). Ōzorasha. Facsimile of the 1932 edition published by Tōkyō Shuppan.

Takai Hiroshi 高井浩. 1991. *Tenpōki shōnen shōjo no kyōyō keisei katei no kenkyū* 天保期少年少女の教養形成過程の研究 (The educational formation of boys and girls in the Tenpō era). Kawade Shobō.

Takasaki Shishi Hensan Iinkai. 2004. *Shinpen Takasaki shishi* 新編高崎市史 (History of Takasaki city). Tsūshihen vol. 3 kinsei. Takasaki-shi.

———. 2002. *Shinpen Takasaki shishi* 新編高崎市史 (History of Takasaki city). Shiryōhen vol. 8 kinsei 4. Takasaki-shi.

Takeuchi, Melinda. 1992. *Taiga's True Views: The Language of Landscape Painting in Eighteenth-Century Japan*. Stanford: Stanford University Press.

Tamenaga Shunsui 為永春水. 1971. *Harutsugedori* 春告鳥. *NKBZ* 47. Shōgakukan.

Tamura Takashi 田村隆. 2003. "Shōhitsu ron: *Genji monogatari* no johō" 省筆論—源氏物語の叙法 (Narration in *The Tale of Genji*: An essay on narrative ellipsis). *Bungaku* 文学 4.6: 176–92.

Tanabe Katsuya 田邊勝哉, ed. 1921. *Inoue Yorikuni ō shōden*. 井上頼圀翁小伝 (The life of Inoue Yorikuni). Tanabe Katsuya.

Tanaka, Yukiko. 2000. *Women Writers of Meiji and Taishō Japan: Their Lives, Works, and Critical Reception, 1868–1926*. London: McFarland.

Thomas, Roger K. 1991. "Plebian Travelers on the Way of Shikishima: *Waka* Theory and Practice during the Late Tokugawa Period." PhD diss., Indiana University.

Thompson, Sarah E. 1984. "A *Hakubyō Genji monogatari emaki* in the Spencer Collection." MA thesis, Columbia University.

Tocco, Martha C. 2003. "Norms and Texts for Women's Education in Tokugawa Japan." In *Women and Confucian Cultures in Premodern China, Korea, and Japan*, ed. Dorothy Ko, Jahyun Kim Haboush, and Joan R. Piggott, pp. 193–218. Berkeley: University of California Press.

Tōkyō-to, ed. 1961. *Tōkyō no joshi kyōiku* 東京の女子教育 (Education for girls in Tokyo). Tōkyō-to.

Tomoishi Takayuki 友石孝之. 1955. *Murakami Butsuzan: Aru ijin no shōgai* 村上佛山:ある偉人の生涯 (The life of a great man: Murakami Butsuzan). Yukuhashi: Miyako Bunka Konwakai.

Tondabayashi. 1998. *Tondabayashi shishi* 富田林市史 (History of Tondabayashi city). Vol. 2. Tondabayashi-shi.

Tone Keizaburō 利根啓三郎. 1989. "Terakoya to joshi kyōiku no jisshōteki kenkyū" 寺子屋と女子教育の実証的研究 (An empirical study of elementary schools and girls' education). *Tōkyō kasei gakuin daigaku kiyō* 東京家政学院大学紀要 29: 229–39.

Tonomura Nobuko 外村展子. 1996. "Nyōbō bungaku no yukue" 女房文学のゆくえ (What happened to women's writing?). In *Jūgo, jūroku seiki no bungaku* 15・16 世紀の文学 (Literature of the fifteenth and sixteenth centuries), vol. 6 of *Iwanami kōza Nihon bungakushi* 岩波講座日本文学史 (Iwanami lectures on the history of Japanese literature), pp. 177–98. Iwanami Shoten.

Tottori Kenritsu Hakubutsukan 鳥取県立博物館. 2006. *Onna narade wa yo wa akenu: Edo Tottori no joseitachi—zuroku* 女ならでは世は明けぬ―江戸鳥取の女性たち―図録 (Women in Tottori during the Edo period: A pictorial record). Tottori: Tottori Kenritsu Hakubutsukan Shiryō Kankōkai.

Tōyama Takeshige 遠山竹茂. 1896. *Shinsen joshi yōbunshō* 新選女子用文章 (New writing primer for girls). Osaka: Hayakawa Kumajirō.

Tōyō jokun sōsho 東洋女訓叢書 (Oriental conduct books for women). 1900–1901. 4 vols. Tōyōsha.

Toyoda Fuyuko 豊田芙雄子. 1901. *Joshi katei kun* 女子家庭訓 (Home lessons for girls). Yoshikawa Hanshichi.

Trede, Melanie. 2003. *Image, Text, and Audience: The* Taishokan *Narrative in Visual Representations of the Early Modern Period in Japan*. Frankfurt: Peter Lang.

Tsuji Michiko 辻ミチ子. 2003. *Onnatachi no bakumatsu Kyōto* 女たちの幕末京都 (Women in Kyoto before the fall of the shogunate). Chūō Kōron Shinsha.

Tsurumi, Patricia. 1998. "Visions of Women and the New Society in Conflict: Yamakawa Kikue versus Takamure Itsue." In *Japan's Competing Modernities: Issues in Culture and Democracy, 1900–1930*, ed. Sharon Minichiello, pp. 335–57. Honolulu: University of Hawai`i Press.

Tsutsumi Yasuo 堤康夫. 1988. "*Genji monogatari* chūshakushijō no jidai kubun ni tsuite (ge): Kochū sekai e no hangyaku to sono tassei" 『源氏物語』注釈史上の時代区分について（下）古注世界への反逆とその達成 (On the periodization of commentaries on *The Tale of Genji*, part 2: What the revolt against the world of old commentaries achieved). *Kokugakuin zasshi* 國學院雑誌 89.8: 36–52.

Tyler, Royall, trans. 2001. *The Tale of Genji*. 2 vols. New York: Viking.

Ueno Sachiko 上野さち子, ed. 2000. *Tagami Kikusha zenshū* 田上菊舎全集 (The complete works of Tagami Kikusha). 2 vols. Osaka: Izumi Shoin.

Ueno Yōzō 上野洋三, ed. 2004. *Matsukage nikki* 松蔭日記 (In the shelter of the pine). Iwanami Bunko.

Umihara Tōru 海原徹. 1988. *Kinsei no gakkō to kyōiku* 近世の学校と教育 (Schools and education in the early modern period). Kyoto: Shibunkaku.

Ushiyama Yukio 牛山之雄. 1985. *Ueda Akinari no bannen* 上田秋成の晩年 (The last years of Ueda Akinari). Shinbisha.

Walthall, Anne. 1998. *The Weak Body of a Useless Woman: Matsuo Taseko and the Meiji Restoration*. Chicago: University of Chicago Press.

————. 1997. "The Cult of Sensibility in Rural Tokugawa Japan: Love Poetry by Matsuo Taseko." *Journal of the American Oriental Society* 117.1: 70–86.

————. 1990. "The Family Ideology of the Rural Entrepreneurs in Nineteenth-Century Japan." *Journal of Social History* 23.3: 463–83.

————. 1986. "Introduction." In Suzuki Bokushi, *Snow Country Tales: Life in the Other Japan,* trans. Jeffrey Hunter and Rose Lesser. New York and Tokyo: Weatherhill.

Watanabe Kinzō 渡邊金造. 1942. *Hirata Atsutane kenkyū* 平田篤胤研究 (A study of Hirata Atsutane). Rokkō Shobō.

Wender, Melissa. 2005. *Lamentations as History: Narratives by Koreans in Japan, 1965–2000.* Stanford: Stanford University Press.

Wheeler, Carolyn Miyuki. 2008. "*Fleeting Is Life:* Kengozen and Her Early Kamakura Court Diary, *Tamakiwaru.*" PhD diss., University of California, Berkeley.

Williams, Duncan Ryūken. 2004. *The Other Side of Zen: A Social History of Sōtō Zen Buddhism in Tokugawa Japan.* Princeton: Princeton University Press.

Yabuta Yutaka 薮田貫. 2006. "Josei to chiiki shakai" 女性と地域社会 (Women and local society). In Yabuta Yutaka and Okumura Hiroshi 奥村弘, eds., *Chiikishi no shiten* 地域史の視点 (The view from local history). Kinsei chiikishi foramu 近世地域史フォーラム (Early modern local history forum), vol. 2. Yoshikawa Kōbunkan.

————. 1998. *Otoko to onna no kinseishi* 男と女の近世史 (Men and women in early modern history). Aoki Shoten.

————. 1995. "Moji to josei" 文字と女性 (Women and writing). In *Iwanami kōza Nihon tsūshi* 岩波講座日本通史, ed. Asao Naohiro 朝尾直弘, Amino Yoshihiko 網野善彦, Ishii Susumu 石井進, Kano Masanao 鹿野政直, Hayakawa Shōhachi 早川庄八, and Yasumaru Yoshio 安丸良夫, vol. 15, pp. 227–52. Iwanami Shoten.

Yamada Yūsaku 山田有策. 1983. "*Iratsume*" *kaidai, sōmokuji, sakuin* 「以良都女」解題・総目次・索引 (*Iratsume*: Introduction, table of contents, index). Fuji Shuppan.

Yamaga Sokō zenshū, shisōhen 山鹿素行全集—思想篇 (The complete works of Yamaga Sokō: intellectual contributions). 1940–42. 15 vols. Iwanami Shoten.

Yamaguchi Keizaburō 山口桂三郎, ed. 1982. *Nikuhitsu ukiyoe* 肉筆浮世絵 (Ukiyoe paintings). Vol. 4: *Shunshō* 春章. Shūeisha.

Yamakawa Kikue. 1992. *Women of the Mito Domain: Recollections of Samurai Family Life.* Trans. Kate Wildman Nakai. Tokyo: University of Tokyo Press.

Yanai Shigeshi 柳井滋. 1993. "Ōshima-bon *Genji monogatari* no shosha to denrai" 大島本『源氏物語』の書写と伝来 (The copying and transmission of the Ōshima text of *The Tale of Genji*). In *Genji monogatari* I, ed. Yanai Shigeshi, Murofushi Shinsuke 室伏信助, Ōasa Yūji 大朝雄二, Suzuki Hideo 鈴木日出男, Fujii Sadakazu 藤井貞和, and Imai Yūichirō 今西祐一郎., pp. 468–82. *SNKBT* 19. Iwanami Shoten.

Yokota Fuyuhiko 横田冬彦. 1999. "Imagining Working Women in Early Modern Japan." In *Women and Class in Japanese History,* ed. Hitomi Tonomura, Anne Walthall and Wakita Haruko, pp. 153–67. Michigan Monograph Series in Japanese Studies, no. 25. Ann Arbor: Center for Japanese Studies, University of Michigan.

———. 1995. "*Onna daigaku* saikō: Nihon kinsei ni okeru josei rōdō" 女大学再考—日本近世における女性労働 (*Onna daigaku* reconsidered: Women's labor in early modern Japan). In *Jendaa no nihonshi: Shutai to hyōgen, shigoto to seikatsu* ジェンダーの日本史—主体と表現、仕事と生活 (Gender and Japanese history: The self and expression/work and life, ed. Wakita Haruko 脇田晴子 and S. B. Hanley, vol. 2, pp. 363–87. Tōkyō Daigaku Shuppankai.

Yokoyama Toshio. 2000. "In Quest of Civility: Conspicuous Uses of Household Encyclopedias in Nineteenth-Century Japan." *Zinbun* 34.1: 197–222.

Yosano Akiko 与謝野晶子, ed. 1915. *Tokugawa jidai joryū bungaku Reijo shōsetsu shū* 徳川時代女流文学麗女小説集 (Collected literature by women in the Tokugawa period: The novels of Arakida Rei). Fuzanbō.

Yoshida Yuriko 吉田ゆり子. 2001. "Edo jidai ni okeru buke josei no seikatsu" 江戸時代における武家女性の生活 (The lives of samurai women in the Edo period). In *Rai Baishi nikki no kenkyū* 頼梅颸日記の研究 (A study of the diary of Rai Baishi), ed. Ōguchi Yūjirō, pp. 33–39. Ochanomizu Joshi Daigaku Jendaa Kenkyū Sentaa.

Yoshida Yutaka 吉田豊. 2004. *Terakoyashiki komonjo nyohitsu nyūmon* 寺子屋式古文書女筆入門 (Introduction to reading manuscripts written by women). Kashiwa Shobō.

Yoshii Isamu 吉井勇 and Takehisa Yumeji 竹久夢二. 1917. *Shin'yaku e-iri Ise monogatari* 新訳絵入伊勢物語 (*Tales of Ise* newly translated with illustrations). Oranda Shuppan.

Yoshikawa. 1996. *Yoshikawa chōshi* 吉川町史 (The history of Yoshikawa town). Vol. 1. Yoshikawa-chō.

Yoshioka Yayoi 吉岡弥生. 1998. *Yoshioka Yayoi Den* 吉岡弥生伝 (The life of Yoshioka Yayoi). Nihon Tosho Sentaa. [Reprinted from the 1941 edition published in Tokyo by Tōkyō Rengō Fujinkai Shuppanbu.]

Young, Blake Morgan. 1982. *Ueda Akinari*. Vancouver: University of British Columbia Press.

Yūjo hyōbankishū 遊女評判記集 (Collected courtesan critiques). 1978–79. 3 vols. Kinsei bungaku shiryō ruijū, Kanazōshihen 近世文学資料類従、仮名草子編 (Collection of materials on early modern literature – Kanazōshi section), vols. 34–36. Benseisha.

Yūrin. 1979. Imai Gen'e 今井源衛, ed. *Yūrin: Hikaru Genji ichibu uta* 祐倫: 光源氏一部歌 (Yūrin's complete poems of the shining Genji). Vol. 3 of *Genji monogatari kochū shūsei* 源氏物語古注集成 (Collected old commentaries on *The Tale of Genji*). Ōfūsha.

Zwicker, Jonathan. 2006. *Practices of the Sentimental Imagination*. Cambridge: Harvard University Press.

Contributors

✤

Anna Beerens is a publisher and independent scholar. She obtained her PhD from Leiden University in 2006 with a thesis entitled "Friends, Acquaintances, Pupils and Patrons: Japanese Intellectual Life in the Late Eighteenth Century, a Prosopographical Approach." She is currently working on a series of annotated translations from *Kyūji shimonroku*, a set of interviews with former Bakufu officials conducted in 1891–92. The latest installment of the series (an interview with two ladies from the Ōoku) appeared in *Monumenta Nipponica* in the autumn of 2008.

Bettina Gramlich-Oka is Assistant Professor at Sophia University, Tokyo. She has worked and published on the history of thought, women's history, epidemics, and economic history with a specialization in the Tokugawa period. Her main publication is *Thinking Like a Man: Tadano Makuzu* (Leiden, 2006), and recent articles include "Early Modern Japanese Women and Spacing the Self," in *Räume des Selbst: Tanskulturelle Perspektiven der Selbstzeugnisforschung/ Spacing the Self*, ed. Andreas Bähr et al. (Cologne, 2007), and "Shogunal Administration of Copper in the Mid-Tokugawa Period (1670–1720)," in *Metals, Monies, and Markets in Early Modern Societies: East Asian and Global Perspectives*, ed. Thomas Hirzel and Nanny Kim (Berlin, 2008).

Itasaka Noriko is Professor at Senshū University in Tokyo. Her most recent work concerns readers of fiction in the late Edo period, "Kusazōshi no dokusha – hyōshō to shite no dokusho suru josei," in *Kokugo to kokubungaku* 83 (May 2006), 1–13. She has also worked for many years as a member of

Kinsei Bungaku Dokushokai, which has produced a six-volume catalog of works of Edo fiction in the Library of the University of Tokyo, *Tōkyō Daigaku shozō kusazōshi mokuroku* (Tokyo, 1993–2006).

P. F. Kornicki is Deputy Warden of Robinson College and Professor of East Asian Studies at the University of Cambridge. His recent publications include "Ikeda Kikan and the Textual Tradition of the *Tosa nikki*: European Influences on Japanese Textual Scholarship," *Revue d'histoire des textes* 8 (2008), 263–82; and "The *Lesser Learning for Women* and Other Texts for Vietnamese Women: A Bibliographical Study" (with Nguyen Thi Oanh), *International Journal of Asian studies* 6 (2009), 147–69.

Joshua S. Mostow is Professor of Asian Studies at the University of British Columbia, Vancouver. His publications include *Pictures of the Heart: The Hyakunin Isshu in Word and Image* (Honolulu, 1996); *The Columbia Companion to Modern East Asian Literature* (New York, 2003); and *Gender and Power in the Japanese Visual Field* (Honolulu, 2003).

Mara Patessio is Lecturer in Japanese history at the University of Manchester. Her first monograph, *Women and Public Life in Early Meiji Japan: The Development of the Feminist Movement*, will be published by the Center for Japanese Studies at The University of Michigan. She is currently working on two separate projects. One deals with late Meiji women's writings and public activities, and the other one concentrates on the novelist, editor, and playwright Hasegawa Shigure's participation in Japanese cultural life during the late Meiji and Taisho periods.

G. G. Rowley is Professor at Waseda University in Tokyo where she teaches English and Japanese literature. She is the author of *Yosano Akiko and The Tale of Genji* (Ann Arbor, 2000) and the translator of *Autobiography of a Geisha* (New York, 2003). Currently she is writing a biography of the imperial concubine Nakanoin Nakako, who was exiled from court for her part in the sex scandal known as the Dragon Scale (*gekirin*) Incident of 1609.

Atsuko Sakaki is Professor in the Department of East Asian Studies at the University of Toronto. Her current research interests include corporeality and spatiality in modern Japanese literature and the photographic rhetoric in modern/contemporary Japanese fiction. A translator of Kurahashi Yumiko, her recent publications include *Obsessions with the Sino-Japanese Polarity in Japanese Literature* (Honolulu, 2006); "'There Is No Such Place as Home': Gotō Meisei, or Identity as Alterity," in *Representing the Other in Modern Japanese*

Literature: A Critical Approach, ed. Mark Williams and Rachael Hutchinson (London, 2007); and "Kaisetsu: Yume no hon to soine shite," in Kanai Mieko, *Kishibe no nai umi* (Tokyo, 2009).

Sugano Noriko is Professor Emerita at Teikyō University in Tokyo. She has published much on women in the Edo period over many years, including a study of women in village life, *Mura to kaikaku: Kinsei sonrakushi josei kenkyū* (Tokyo, 1992); and a study of people rewarded for their filial piety, *Edo jidai no kōkōsha* (Tokyo, 1999).

Anne Walthall is Professor of History at the University of California, Irvine. She is the author of *The Weak Body of a Useless Woman: Matsuo Taseko and the Meiji Restoration* (Chicago, 1998); and the editor of *Servants of the Dynasty: Palace Women in World History* (Berkeley and Los Angeles, 2008). Recent articles include "Masturbation and Discourse on Female Sexual Practices in Early Modern Japan" in *Gender & History*, 21.1 (April 2009): 1–18. She currently continues work on the shogun's inner quarters (*ōoku*) and has begun a project tentatively titled "Practicing Faith: The Hirata Family Saga."

Yabuta Yutaka is Professor of History at Kansai University. He is the author of *Otoko to onna no kinseishi* (Tokyo, 1998) and of *Rediscovering Women in Tokugawa Japan* (Harvard University Press, 2000). He has contributed an essay on rural women in the Edo period to a study of provincial life, *Chiikishi no shiten* (Tokyo, 2006), which he edited with Okumura Hiroshi. He is currently working on archives in the Osaka area that reveal the lives of women in the Edo period, as his contribution to this volume shows.

Index